Henri Cartier-Bresson
A Biography

PIERRE ASSOULINE

Henri Cartier-Bresson
A Biography

with 25 illustrations

Thames & Hudson

Translated from the French by David Wilson

English-language translation and layout © 2005 Thames & Hudson Ltd, London
© 2005 Pierre Assouline
© 1999 Pierre Assouline and Plon
Original edition *Henri Cartier-Bresson: L'oeil du siècle* © 1999 Plon, Paris
German edition *Henri Cartier-Bresson: Das Auge des Jahrhunderts* © 2003 Steidl Verlag, Göttingen

This edition published in 2005 in hardcover in the United States of America by Thames & Hudson Inc., 500 Fifth Avenue, New York, New York 10110

thamesandhudsonusa.com

Library of Congress Catalog Card Number 2004118015

ISBN-13: 978-0-500-51223-4
ISBN-10: 0-500-51223-X

Printed and bound in Germany

CONTENTS

INTRODUCTION: HERO AND FRIEND

I first met Henri Cartier-Bresson in 1994. I was wearing my journalist's rather than my author's hat when I knocked at his studio door near the place des Victoires in Paris, where he liked to hide away when he was drawing. He had at last agreed to be interviewed, on one condition: that it shouldn't be an interview. Having already taken on board his taste for paradox, I had decided to approach the meeting in terms of a conversation. But if he had simply offered me a cup of tea, I would still have been unable to resist, so great was my admiration and so deep-rooted my fascination for the man and for his work.

It was an unforgettable first meeting. We spent more than five hours chatting, wandering through his memories with no particular guidelines other than instinct and random association. Nothing could have created a clearer historical perspective than this journey through time, and when I left I felt overwhelmed by the images of the chaotic era he had experienced day by day, living through history.

We had evoked all aspects of the twentieth century – among them the men who had fashioned it and the places that symbolized it. But it was not so much events that we conjured up as moments along the way, as if the destination were somehow less important than the road to it. He gave no dates, above all, summoning up only impressions and shapes drawn with extraordinary vividness, but just when I least expected it he would describe something with absolute precision.

As the day drew to a close the light grew weaker and weaker, though it never occurred to him to turn on the lamp. It didn't matter. While he was preparing tea, I looked around. His furniture was simple and sparse, though his library was bursting with art books and exhibition catalogues, the bindings worn with too much fingering. On the wall, under glass but unframed, were drawings by his father, gouaches by his uncle, and two photographs, not his: one by the Hungarian Martin Munkacsi, taken in about 1929, of three black boys, seen from the rear against the light, diving into the waters of Lake Tanganyika; the other by the Mexican Agustín Casasola showing a comrade-in-arms of Pancho Villa and Emiliano Zapata in 1917, his back to the wall, facing a firing squad with his hands in his pockets and a cigarette dangling from his lips, his defiant smile showing an insolent disregard for the imminence of death. The first of these photos expressed a *joie de vivre* at its most spontaneous and intense; the second captured the moment of total liberty at the actual point when death is inevitable.

There were no other pictures – most strikingly, none of his own.

The conversation resumed with renewed intensity, though this time it was on condition that I gave him something in return for what he'd given me. That meant that I had to answer his questions. Suddenly, just as I was lifting my cup, he silenced me, looking straight at me for a moment. Then he half-smiled:

'A moment ago you asked me if I still took photographs.'

'Indeed.'

'Well, I've just taken one of you, but without a camera – it's just as good. The top of your glasses is exactly parallel with the top of the frame behind you – quite striking. I couldn't miss the chance of such perfect symmetry... there, it's done! Now, what were we talking about? Ah yes, Gandhi... did you know Lord Mountbatten?'

We returned to the topic of India at the time of independence, and naturally this led us to China and its liberation from the Kuomintang by the communists, and then straight on to Soviet Russia; from there we moved on to Louis Aragon and to Cartier-Bresson's diary at the time of the Popular Front, as a result of which we discussed Jean Renoir and of course the influence of painting, and so on and so forth, an unending range of topics. Through his profession this man had had the privilege of mixing with the outstanding people who had shaped the century from beginning to end.

At the end of the day, I had collected a wealth of precious material, and I had been charmed. If we had left it at that, the afternoon's only consequence would have been a profile of him in my newspaper. But as it happened, at the moment of our parting I was moved by something difficult to describe; I felt frustrated by his reticence when it came to discussing the war. At the risk of offending his modesty, I questioned him again about his years of captivity in Germany, the overcrowded conditions, the failed escapes. He seemed lost in thought for a while, his gaze focused somewhere distant, and then he began to talk again. The further he went on the more convinced I became that intimate confidences are most easily addressed to complete strangers. He himself told me that one day in a Parisian taxi he had unveiled to the driver secrets that he had never confided in anyone before, so certain was he that he would never see this man again.

When he recalled the names of the comrades who had been denounced, tortured and shot, his voice choked. And when he murmured their first names, he turned his head away, unable to keep back the tears.

When I finally left Henri Cartier-Bresson, I knew that one day I would devote not an article but a book to him. I would devote it to every aspect of him: the greatest photographer of his time who had resurrected his artistic career; the long-distance reporter and quiet adventurer, who had survived from a different era; a man with a permanent longing to escape, and an obsession with geometry; the restless Buddhist, the puritanical anarchist, the unrepentant surrealist, the symbol of a century of images, the listening eye. Above all I would write about the man behind all these myriad facets, a Frenchman of his century.

Ten years elapsed between that first meeting and his death in 2004. During those years we saw, talked, listened, observed one another on countless occasions. Once you get used to each other, such an ongoing conversation can survive long gaps, for you simply take it up again as if you'd parted only yesterday. And you can resume it at any time by telephone, letter or fax, until in due course it becomes something totally natural that ends only when one of the interlocutors finally departs.

For a long time Henri Cartier-Bresson would not hear of a biography. The very word appalled him. In fact, he never read biographies, as his library attested. To devote a whole book to him would be like taking his portrait – even worse, dazzling him with a flash, which he hated. Faced with such an inquisition he could explode, brandishing his knife and threatening the intruder, whom he saw as an adversary. He was never able to stand the idea that someone might do to him what he did to others. In the same way that he viewed retrospectives of his work as a somewhat premature obituary, the prospect of a biography was like the prospect of a gravestone. Living for the moment was his only valid philosophy, for life is the pulsating here and now, while actuality is already part of the past – such is what he learnt from his Leica.

This was no false pretext to enable him to indulge in the selectivity of autobiography. He never wanted to write his own memoirs, and he had nothing to hide. He would take refuge behind great authors and their books to justify his hostility to the idea of a biography. Proust of course could distinguish between the artist and his work, for his great novel was the product of a self different from the one paraded in society, evoked in letters, betrayed by conventions or confidences. Degas in his old age was forever moaning about men of letters, whom he denounced as story-tellers. To Cartier-Bresson, what went on underneath was nobody's business, and the works had to retain their mystery – though only up to a certain point, for, terrible though the prospect might have been of one day submitting to a biography, that would never have changed the way he lived his life.

His attitude always seemed to me to be totally acceptable. And yet the deeper I plunged into his contradictions, the more I found a conflict between the quest for harmony and the tyranny of chaos. It was on the outcome of this conflict that his peace of mind depended. I did not feel that I had any right to disturb this last phase of his life, until I came to realize that his whole existence developed out of his philosophy of disobedience. So I followed the master's own example, and disobeyed him.

It is strange to be writing about someone you knew. The advantages of this can easily become a handicap. The writer, steering between two extremes, has to maintain his fascination with the subject while retaining his critical faculty, and find a balance between satisfying curiosity and seizing on indiscretions. This is a *sine qua non* if the portrait is to be fair without becoming a tabloid intrusion. But how does one enter the soul of a man who is alive when the portrait is being assembled?

On the one hand, there is a subtle pleasure in extracting even the most inconsequential item of information, but on the other you have the uncomfortable feeling that your subject is looking over your shoulder as you write. How would so eminent a writer as André Maurois have reacted if Benjamin Disraeli had scrutinized each page of the manuscript that followed every step of his career? In my case, I can honestly say that I embarked on a wonderful new adventure: my hero became my friend.

It's an odd feeling to be tapping on the shoulder of a legend, exploring an institution or even setting the record straight about a national treasure. But he would shrug his shoulders or wave away this non-problem, and as for such grand descriptions, he regarded them as so much hot air. Even the unexceptionable term 'artist' was anathema to him, because he saw it as a bourgeois concept inherited from the nineteenth century.

Fair enough. How, though, was I to go back over the extraordinary life of a man who allowed me to use the familiar *tu* to him, despite a gap in age of half a century, and was willing to exchange confidences once the ice was broken? Of course, he had many friends, he never used *vous* to his peers, and he wore his heart on his sleeve. But does the biographer have the right to make use of all that he has learnt? At what point should the truth give way to discretion?

To people who know a bit about everything, he was Cartier-Bresson. To those in the profession, HCB was enough. His intimate circle preferred the sur-realist wink of his '*En rit Ca-Bré*', while others referred to Henri as if there were only one. All of them have their own ideas as to who he was. Each of these helps to illuminate the tinge of madness, the genius, the darker side. All of us con-tribute our own truth, since all who knew him have captured a part of the man who was our friend. My view is a mosaic of all these ideas. Biographers and por-trait artists, however, are go-betweens, forced to mediate inadequately between the subject and the rest of the world in order to assuage everyone's understand-able curiosity.

This legendary character, regarded by some people as impossible, never indulged in self-promotion. He was hardly ever seen on television, or heard on the radio, or featured in the press. He was perfectly happy to stay away from the nasty trappings that inevitably accompany fame, making no effort to correct the impression held by most people that he had died long ago.

He was the personification of impatience, but was also full of curiosity, indignation, enthusiasm and bad temper. He was a frenetic thinker who could not keep still or control his own temperament – to him life was inseparable from movement. His unquietness was a source of difficulty, but he was one of those who give eccentricity a good name. Nothing afforded him greater private pleasure than deliberately to indulge in the aristocratic delight of annoying people. But it is dizzying to think of all the sights that he saw in his long life, all the experiences he had.

In short, despite his objections to the word, he was an artist. To retrace his life and revisit his work is to tell the story of one man's vision.

A life is like a city – in order to get to know it, you must lose yourself in it. That is how I proceeded. I explored Cartier-Bresson's inner world in no particular order, spending days and nights reading everything written by and about him. I immersed myself in the archives, hoping, in a sense, never to emerge, and I questioned his friends – occasionally remembering the words of the poet Max

Jacob: 'One always smiles when one is speaking of the "great man" one knows, because there is a marked contrast between the reputation and the dressing-gown.' I gazed again and again at his photographs as if discovering each of them for the first time, and again and again I stared at the people in them and marvelled at how they seemed not to show the passage of time. And I listened to all the tales major and minor that emerged from the welter of his memories.

We do not know what the past preserves for us. There are some things that only the man himself knew about his life, and there are certain truths that will forever lie beyond the scope of documents and accounts. That is a good thing, because if everything could be reduced to its logical end there would be no mystery left. Facts that are strung together like pearls are made to fit a rigid pattern at the expense of all poetry, and therefore give a false picture. What is the use of knowing everything if you exclude the unknowable? It often happens that in our understanding of a work of art, it is the indescribable that lifts it beyond the scope of the most convincing analysis. Thus the effect comes from what the image does not reveal, the unseen world implicit in the photograph. Such is the vision of an observer like Cartier-Bresson, who was interested less in the pearls than in the string holding them together. The truth is found not in a comprehensive assortment of facts, but in the spaces in between.

There is no point in listing the countries he visited, since he visited nearly all of them. Nor is there any purpose in listing the great people he portrayed, since he fixed an image of nearly all of them in the mind of the public – indeed, it would be far quicker to itemize those who escaped his lens. But you do not expect a man of poetic vision to provide a complete census of the world, especially when you discover that the only observers of humanity whose work he kept at his bedside were Proust and Cézanne. His real references were not photographic but cultural.

If you want to understand Henri Cartier-Bresson, you will have to turn away from the conventional concept of time and replace it with another, sometimes anachronistic, in which the calendar of facts does not necessarily correspond to that of the emotions. You must imagine that clock time is not human time, that everyone has his own inner music, and that to relate the events of someone's life independently of his personal logic would be as futile as trying to experience an opera by reading its libretto. Proust put his finger on all this and more besides: 'There are hilly, difficult days that one takes an infinite amount of time to climb, and there are downward-sloping days that one can race down singing.'

This is how Cartier-Bresson lived his life, not merely travelling, but living abroad without thinking about when he would return home. This is not a quibble, for it is a different way of approaching the world. His work is full of it. There is an echo too of the sculptor Rodin, who says: 'What you make with time, time respects.' That is why a straightforward inventory of events in such a man's life will always yield far less than an attempt to explore the shadows cast by some of them on his memory as well as on ours.

One evening, when I asked him what he thought of Nicolas de Staël's view of the world, he jumped up and stood on tiptoe, looking down at me from on high, and boomed in cavernous tones:

'Staaal, Staaaal...'

I thought I knew practically everything about this painter, but I didn't know what Cartier-Bresson had just recalled – that he was huge and that his deep voice impressed all who met him. Timbre is important: an old recording can transmit its colour and recreate its tones, but it can never capture the person's soul. You can grasp as much about someone from the firmness of a handshake – the clasping of palms that allows you to register the texture of the skin, which will imprint itself on your memory. A certain intonation, a certain pressure can sometimes tell you more about someone than his or her confessions. Cartier-Bresson had a powerful handshake, with a vigour that reflected his whole character, and he had his own way of pronouncing words delicately from the tip of the tongue, which said more about his upbringing than he would have wished.

If there are advantages to being famous, he would also have liked the advantages of mystery. He wanted fame, on condition that he remained unknown. He manifestly intended to die young – but as late as possible. How can you pin down someone who, when stopped and asked if he is Henri Cartier-Bresson, replies: 'Maybe'?

The history of his world view is that of a man who, all through his life, asked himself the same question: 'What's it all about?' – and who never found the answer, because there isn't one.

Pierre Assouline
Paris, December 2004

1 FAMILY THREADS 1908–27

'Where does the money come from?' When you entered the room of the 11-year-old Henri, you couldn't avoid seeing an article thus entitled, cut out of *L'Echo de Paris* and stuck defiantly on the gilded wooden mirror. The home of the Cartier-Bressons just after the Great War was in a Haussmann apartment at 31 rue de Lisbonne, on the edge of the Parc Monceau, between the 8th and the posh part of the 17th *arrondissement* in Paris.

'Where does the money come from?' It was a question that would haunt Henri for the rest of his life. He felt that there was something intrinsically dirty, impure, immoral about money. A luxury limousine in the street, an expensively bejewelled woman at a reception, a VIP noisily summoning his staff, were all it took to torment him with the need to know the origin of this power. Wealth did not have to be spectacular to disturb him; even discreet wealth still bothered him, because, when all's said and done, money is an unpleasant subject.

Listening to his parents constantly complaining about the high cost of living, exhorting him to watch every penny and to be ever frugal in his eating habits, young Henri was convinced that they were on the verge of ruin. There were to be no excesses in their way of life, no pocket money, no presents except at Christmas and on birthdays, no holidays apart from when the grandparents came to visit. Anything that might be construed as ostentatious was banished from this society, where children were brought up to appreciate the value of things. At the family château they were always careful to draw the curtains so that nothing could be seen from the main road. The boy had no idea how wealthy his family was. Among dyed-in-the-wool republicans, considered as left-wing Catholics, such things were *infra dig*. Because the family were so deeply ashamed of their riches, the son would long harbour a guilt complex towards the less fortunate classes, which a whole lifetime would not assuage.

Cartier-Bresson had a Cartier side and a Bresson side. A double-barrelled name is a good way to convey the dual origins of every family, though in France it was authorized by the state only in 1901.

The first Cartier relevant to our story was a farmer from Silly-le-Long in the Oise. He came of a very old family from Noyers-sur-Serein, near Avallon in Burgundy, and his great opportunity came when he was asked to supply hay for the horses of some Parisian shopkeepers named Bresson.

Antoine, the first Bresson to figure in our story, was selling spun and twisted cotton in Paris during the Revolution. It is through him that we are able literally to follow the thread of the story. He settled in St-Germain; eventually his haberdashery business was established and flourished in rue St-Denis.

The Cartiers and the Bressons really came together when the town-dwellers sent their children to be wet-nursed by the country-folk. In the mid-nineteenth century father Cartier apprenticed his two sons to the Bresson haberdashery, at a point when it was launching its reels of sewing thread on to the market. The two sons married the boss's daughters, and with this new status soon rose to the rank of partners. The *paterfamilias* himself, Claude-Marie Bresson, joined in the spirit of the enterprise, for when his wife died prematurely he immediately married his young sister-in-law. All these events combined to bring great joy to the patriarch, who watched his family of shopkeepers evolve into a dynasty of industrialists. The shop expanded into manufacture with the acquisition of steam-driven machines to make the thread – and the Second Empire was still barely halfway through its course.

The factory was in Pantin, a town specially chosen because of its good network of communications; there were branches in the east. The factory stretched along the rue du Chemin-Vert, which by the turn of the century had become rue Cartier-Bresson, since the little empire covered 23,000 square metres, with an average of 450 employees. The firm made thread for sewing, embroidery, darning, knitting and lacemaking; it was not a mill, but encompassed laundry, dry-cleaning, twisting and spooling.

Although they rapidly became captains of industry, the directors of the Pantin factory nevertheless preserved a paternalistic spirit. They looked after their staff, and spared no expense when it came to charitable work. They built a crèche, a school, a dispensary and a church, believing that it was the least good Christian employers could do to help keep together families destabilized by the effects of the Industrial Revolution.

In France at the beginning of the twentieth century Cartier-Bresson was an illustrious name, associated with a famous make. There was scarcely a home without hanks and skeins of thread crowned with the Cartier-Bresson label. On it were a mother and daughter hard at work sewing, under the legend 'Cartier-Bresson threads and cottons "at the cross", fast colours'. In the centre were the letters C and B in stylized script, set in an oval ribbon and separated by a cross. More than just a logo, this was the coat-of-arms of the upper middle classes.

Although he was baptized with the name of his paternal grandfather, Henri was very much his mother's son. He was said to take after her in good looks, sensitivity and character. He was clearly the son of a Norman. Marthe, née Le Verdier, came from an old Rouen family that owned a large estate in the valley above Dieppe. She was a woman of supreme elegance, whose portraits by Boissonnas and Tapenier, taken in their studio on the rue de la Paix, reveal her natural grace and charm. She was, however, of a nervous disposition, for ever racked by uncertainty, and could spend entire days absorbed in reading, which she would abandon only in order to go and sit at the piano.

She was proud of her ancestors, the most illustrious of whom were the sister of the dramatist Pierre Corneille; the Revolutionary Charlotte Corday, who stabbed Marat to death in his bath, and was subsequently guillotined; and a French peer, mayor of Rouen, treasurer of its Philharmonic Society. These were the memories among which young Henri grew up.

Cartier-Bresson's Normandy – a wall of chalky cliffs and the Caux plateau of clay and flint and fertile loess – inculcated in him a sense of history as much as of geography. His childhood in Seine-Inférieure, the world of his maternal grandparents, was haunted rather than cradled by the enigmatic atmosphere of the port of Rouen, where mysterious figures waited on the quays, ships arrived from the ends of the earth, sailors balanced on the sterns of Liberian freighters, and the smoke-filled taverns created their own myths.

Of the Cartier-Bresson parents, Marthe was the intellectual, the musician and the thinker. André, her husband, was quite different, both in his nature and through circumstance. A severe man, upright to the point of rigidity, he was above all a man of duty, moulded at an early age by the death of his father. Too preoccupied by his responsibilities to open himself up to the world of ideas, he had chosen to study commerce so that he could take over the general direction of the company as soon as possible. He was nonetheless a man of taste, who channelled all his artistic talents into drawing, painting and furniture. He brought back three sketchbooks of drawings from a world tour undertaken in order to study the evolution of the cotton industry. But when his son tried to get him to talk about the rest of the world, he would invariably respond with a simple statement: 'Here at Fontenelle the sunsets are far more beautiful.'

Seeing his father spend nearly all his time locked away in his office, even when he was at home, young Henri grew to hate the business world. His father might just as well have been abroad. To create some kind of connection between them, Henri found he had to concoct an artistic pretext, such as selecting colours or patterns.

Henri was the eldest of five children and a Norman, despite his cheeky determination to pass for a Sicilian because he was conceived in Palermo, where his parents spent their honeymoon. There was something touching, if slightly calculating, about the way he kept in with them both: he would accompany his mother on the flute as she played the piano, but he would go hunting with his father in the forest. While there was an equal division of work and leisure between the parents, as an adolescent he naturally tended to be closer to his mother. In the great families of the bourgeoisie, it was the mother who played the major role in a child's upbringing, and in this case there were many subtle affinities and clear similarities that bound them together. Her influence on him was decisive.

Even at a very early age, Henri showed one trait of character that he would never succeed in conquering, no matter how hard he tried: his temper. When someone annoyed him, or when events refused to bend to his will, he simply could not control himself. He would even roll on the ground or bang his head against the wall, though, curiously, not actually hurting himself. His grandfather, who regarded this as a profound lack of self-control, was convinced that the boy would become the black sheep of the family.

His mother frequently took Henri to concerts, partly because he loved chamber music, and partly to prevent him from murdering his younger sisters Denise and Jacqueline. The music and the sisters represented either end of his emotional range. He would be overcome by intoxication on hearing a piece by Debussy, and César Franck's sonatas could make him cry. It was his mother who took him to the Louvre in search of wonders they could not encounter elsewhere. She gave him an enduring love of poetry, sometimes entrusting him – as lovingly as if it were some kind of private message – with one of the slim volumes of poems that she always kept in her bag. And it was she who gave him the Song of Songs at Mass, in the hope of bringing him into the spiritual fold, since she could not tie him to her own religious convictions. She would often lament: 'My poor darling! If you had a good Dominican confessor, you would not be in such a state.' But she did not appear to give up completely, for she gave him the pre-Socratic philosophers to read.

It was all in vain. This nonconformist soul would never embrace any faith. He was totally convinced that man invented God, not the other way round, and he would never budge. Right from the start he was attracted to paganism and Greek mythology. He felt stifled by the certainties of his background, which weighed him down because he could believe only in universal doubt.

His childhood began in Chanteloup, a village near Marne-la-Vallée, now on the eastern outskirts of Paris, where he was born in the family château on 22 August 1908. Later he would go back there only to spend the summer holidays with his grandparents. He would also spend holidays with his mother's parents in Rouen and the region around it, but whether in Seine-Supérieure or Seine-et-Marne, in Saint-Saëns where the Le Verdiers lived or in Fontenelle near Lagny where the Cartier-Bressons lived, his childhood was spent in family châteaux. Finally there was Paris, his true home.

Despite their great wealth, the Cartier-Bressons were not the owners but the tenants of the huge apartment at 31 rue de Lisbonne. They would have regarded it as wasteful to tie up capital outside the business. The upper middle classes were not particularly interested in property investments, and their sense of grandeur was tailored to the economic demands of the new century.

The boy's life was spent between a bewhiskered butler, who called him 'Monsieur Henri', and nannies who came from London or Ireland and taught him to speak English from an early age. The street was as 'des. res.' as a street can be. Behind the massively impressive house façades it boasted as residents the Martells, Baron Empain and Albert Guillaume, caricaturist of high society. But other images of this quarter were etched on Henri's memory.

There was the great bridge of iron girders that spanned the rails of the Gare St-Lazare, transfigured by Gustave Caillebotte's paintings with such power that the onlooker at the original scene no longer knew if he was seeing a simple iron bridge on the place de l'Europe or bumping up against an invisible frontier between the world of the rich and the world of the poor, between the social whirl and urban isolation. Then there was Ruhlmann's, a furniture shop in rue de Lisbonne itself, where the marquetry-work was as unforgettable as the *galuchat*, the dyed sharkskin encasing some of the wooden panels. And there used to be a very old man whose weary figure would appear every Friday evening in a doorway opposite the Cartier-Bresson residence; he had something to do with the regular dinners that the Rouarts gave for artists and writers in their extraordinary house, whose walls were covered with Impressionist paintings. When the great collector Henri Rouart died, this venerable white-bearded gentleman continued to haunt the place, visiting the sons in homage to the father, to whom he was a faithful friend. More than once, Henri would hear his own father come home and call out to no one in particular: 'I've just seen Degas, the painter.'

If he'd said that he'd just left President Poincaré, the effect could not have been more electrifying. For young Henri painting was everything. One of his father's younger brothers was the living embodiment of it: not Uncle Pierre, director of the Pantin factory, where he lived in the family home with his wife and children, but Uncle Louis, who had refused to follow the path laid down for him but chose to devote himself entirely to his passion for art. It was Uncle Louis – one-time resident at the Villa Médicis, many times laureate of the Institut, winner of the Prix de Rome in 1910 – who introduced him to the world of art as something not merely for contemplation but for internalization.

Henri first met him on Christmas Eve 1913, when he was just five years old, and was allowed to follow him into his studio – the holiest of holies. He was to go there more and more frequently, even if initially it was only to smell the paints. There is something everlasting about such a delicious sensation, and for the rest of his life it would bring back the world of his childhood, a kind of Paradise Lost, with all the nostalgia evoked by Proust's narrator as he dips his madeleine into his tea.

The Great War took its toll on all families, rich or poor. The Cartier-Bressons were not spared: two brothers were killed at the front, Uncle Louis first, in 1915. Henri had never really known him well, but there had been a genuine bond between them and he remained faithful to the lessons he had learned – in itself a kind of memorial to his uncle. Henri regarded him as his 'mythical father', to use his own words, and the myth was embellished by Louis' heroic death at the age of 33, which somehow finally drew the curtain on the nineteenth century. His end coincided with the end of a world.

Henri was ten years old on Armistice Day. He would never forget the joy in France on that day. But in his memory it was intercut with a family tragedy: the funeral of his Uncle Pierre, who had survived Verdun badly injured, but finally died from his wounds. The Cartier-Bressons followed the cortège on foot from the factory in Pantin to the cemetery in Montmartre, crossing a city that was dancing with happiness in stark contrast to their own sadness. When you walk behind a coffin, no one asks where the money comes from.

Art in all its forms was the only sphere to which the boy applied himself with complete discipline and devotion. It was as if he knew that this was his only true and worthwhile inheritance. It was not the business that mattered but art, because everyone had always drawn in his family – not just his uncle and his father, who had brought him up to adore the Quattrocentro, but also his grandfather and his great-grandfather. All of them had filled sketchbooks from nature or with copies of the great masters, and this too had been their business in a way. Armed with this philosophy, Henri set out on a lifelong quest not for the whole picture but for the details of which it is made up.

Apart from music – he had his own flute teacher – he spent his time painting. When he tackled a theme, it was never purely by chance. How could he avoid thoughts of Proust when at the age of 16 he painted *L'Eglise de Guermantes*, in oil on cardboard, in warm shades of green and brown? On the other hand, he had to wait until the end of the twentieth century to learn from the writings of John Rewald, the eminent historian of Impressionism, that his *Rue des Saules à Montmartre* had been painted from exactly the same viewpoint in about 1867 by an artist named Cézanne. To this revelation, Cartier-Bresson gave a typical response: 'What a surprise and what a comfort, to be aware that the subjects are always the same, and that everything has already been said at all times. What counts is what you do with your ingredients.'

When he was not painting, Henri was drawing. On Thursdays and Sundays Jean Cottenet, a friend of his uncle's and a pupil of the famous Cormon, director of the popular studio at the Ecole des Beaux-Arts, took charge of his artistic education, replacing the 'mythical father'. He made Henri take lessons to familiarize himself with the technique of painting in oils.

Another teacher had just as much if not more influence, but in a different way – simply by his presence and his example rather than by anything he taught. The 63-year-old Jacques-Emile Blanche, who for six months of the year retired to his manoir du Tôt in Offranville, near Dieppe, one day magnanimously invited the 16-year-old Henri and his cousin Louis Le Breton to come and paint in the park of his seventeenth-century brick mansion, and then to join him in the studio, there, in silent admiration, to watch him at work. Descended from an ancient Rouen family, and a friend and neighbour of the Cartier-Bressons, he had not perhaps forgotten that 40 years earlier he had himself been invited to Edouard Manet's studio on the recommendation of his father, a close friend of the painter's. It was now his turn to help others, as if the baton – or in this case the palette – had to be passed on from one generation to the next.

He was a protean artist, more of a draughtsman than a painter, who enjoyed writing. He wanted above all to be a portrait artist, but was too much of a dilettante, too superficial to capture the soul behind the face. The arts columns of *L'Intransigeant* regularly made fun of him, calling him 'the modern painter *à la mode*'. All his life he was lucky enough to have independent means, but he was not the easiest of men. History does not paint a kindly picture of him. He is said to have been pessimistic, melancholic, vain, snobbish and cruel. He was anti-Dreyfus – a prejudice fed by his daily reading of *L'Action française* – and obsessed with the thought of suicide. It didn't matter. The two schoolboys saw none of this. For them he was more of a bridge between a bygone age and their own time, who had breathed the atmosphere of the salon and recreated it in his own way. They saw in him not simply the artist in thrall to the business of painting, but a man who had been intimately acquainted with Manet and Proust.

This passion for art was all-absorbing for the youngster, to the exclusion of every other activity whether mental or physical. He had very little interest in sport, apart from the occasional game of real tennis or pelota, played under the supervision of an abbot whose suicide – a scandal that was hushed up by the school – had a profound effect on Henri. The boy was tall and thin, well-proportioned, but with no taste at all for competitive activities. While many children enjoy school for the sense of fraternity it engenders, he could see only the glorification of rivalry, the challenge to out-perform – moral values that were completely alien to him. Only scouting, organized by the parish of Saint-Honoré-d'Eylau, gave him any taste for the outdoor life. For a long time he kept a souvenir of this in his pocket – not quite like Citizen Kane's Rosebud, but a large knife with a retractable blade. He would pull it out several times a day. His father also had one, and his grandfather – clearly it was a male accessory, both a weapon and a tool. Once a scout, always a scout. He was known, aptly, as 'Slippery Eel' because he was always trying to run away.

He was mediocre at his studies, not because he lacked the intellectual capacity but because he simply wasn't suited to the discipline of a Catholic education. There is a sense of how ill at ease he must have been at the Ecole Fénelon, no matter how good or bad his teachers – abbé Berthier, abbé Aubier, abbé Pessin (known as Pet-sec – 'dry fart'). The traditional form photographs show a youth who is partly aloof, looking anywhere but at the camera, and partly rebellious, his arms defiantly folded. The one bright spot was getting to know a man who was secretly as out of place as himself there: the chief supervisor. A layman in a Catholic establishment, and a lover of the symbolist poets, one day he caught the youngster reading Rimbaud – not a poet that most Catholic establishments would recommend. He was impressed by the sight of a boy going off the rails in contrast to most of the others, who were perfect little bourgeois, but nevertheless he bawled him out in public: 'No messing about in study time!' Immediately afterwards, however, he took him on one side, addressing him as *tu*: 'You can go and read in my office.'

It was a small thing, but a small thing can make a big difference. Those few words were to revolutionize Henri's daily life at school, and his inner life afterwards. Thanks to this secret conspiracy, he spent most of his time devouring books in the chief supervisor's den. The titles were not explicitly banned, but the authorities advised against them so strongly that they might as well have been. He read everything, though some things went over his head: Proust, Dostoyevsky, Mallarmé, and many other novels that were not part of his studies at the Lycée Condorcet, including Manzoni's *I Promessi Sposi* and James Joyce's *Ulysses*. He knew that he would return to these books later in life. Some were like bibles to him; Rimbaud's poetry gave him answers to everything. 'Too offhand, Henri? One is not serious when one is 17. Too bad-tempered, Henri? O seasons, o castles, what soul is without defect?' Then there was the Baudelaire of 'My heart laid bare'. Baudelaire alone was enough to nourish Henri's rebellion, with his description of the French as farmyard animals so domesticated that in art, as in literature, they did not dare to jump over the fence.

He became a compulsive reader, living somewhere between supervised liberty and clandestine indulgence, a state in which literature took on the delicious flavour of forbidden fruit. After adolescence, reading became the only activity he could never stop. It became for him one of the fine arts, fuelling the sort of conversation considered to be part of a true gentleman's way of life, and made him suspicious of claiming ideas as his own. This lesson in humility might be summed up in four words: one never invents anything. It is the perfect illustration of Friedrich Hölderlin's elliptical phrase 'the intercourse that we are'. With this strikingly concise description, the poet tells us that even when stagnating in the depths of our solitude, we cannot control our thoughts. They are the fruits of our exchanges with others, the friction between their intelligence and ours, the subconscious workings of everything we have read, seen and heard.

The freedom allowed by his chief supervisor saved the boy's spirit from the despair that would otherwise have engulfed him. From then on, the lifeblood of these formative years was provided by prose and poetry, and he was to go on imbibing it for the rest of his life. It was a development that confirmed the failure of his teachers, for he embraced literature as he turned from religion to painting. Nevertheless, in old age he looked back on his schooldays as one of the most painful periods of his early life.

As well as reading, he was drawn to the cinema and to exhibitions. His unconscious mind seemed to be assembling all the forces that would train his eye and sharpen his vision. But photography had still not entered the equation. Perhaps he followed the example of the young Jacques-Henri Lartigue and caught images in an 'eye-trap': this consisted of opening the eyes, closing them, opening them again and spinning round once. For the moment, however, like many youngsters, he was content to use a modest Box Brownie to capture a few holiday souvenirs and nothing more.

While he scarcely looked at photos, he saw a lot of films. They were silent, of course, since the first talkie was not made until he was 20 years old. In the film archive of his imagination were several works that seemed to epitomize the historic meeting between technology and magic: *The Perils of Pauline*, with the unforgettable Pearl White in the role of the rich heiress risking her life as she confronts a gang of lawless ruffians; the D. W. Griffith masterpieces, from *Birth of a Nation* to *Intolerance* and *Broken Blossoms*, which impressed him not only with their epic sweep and their dramatic power but also with their technical audacity, seen at the time as revolutionary – the care in composition, the movements of the camera, the repetition of close-ups. Then there was Buster Keaton, whom he preferred to Charlie Chaplin, although he liked Chaplin's silent films much more than *Limelight*, which he found sickeningly sentimental. A little later came *Greed*, Erich von Stroheim's flawed masterpiece about people disintegrating; *Battleship Potemkin*, in which Eisenstein's stroke of genius was to give the crowd the leading role; and above all *The Passion of Joan of Arc*. He was as impressed by the authenticity and the stylistic attention to detail as he was by the actors, who included the stunning Renée Falconetti – rendered all the more fascinating by the use of large close-ups revealing the very pores of her skin – and the remarkable Antonin Artaud in the role of the monk Massieu.

All these wordless images with their musical accompaniment were jumbled together in his mind, along with those that he had seen in the museums and art galleries. There were plenty of these, even within his own part of

Paris. Chez Devambez on the boulevard Malesherbes held the first posthumous exhibition of his 'mythical father' Uncle Louis' paintings and studies, in 1924. He discovered Bonnard's first drawings in a window on the avenue Matignon. There was the Simon gallery in the rue d'Astorg, where Daniel-Henry Kahnweiler reigned supreme, the Percier gallery, and Barbazanges, where he would stand for hours admiring Seurat's *Les Poseuses*, still for sale at that period. Most of all, he was drawn almost inexorably to the Louvre.

Reading, painting, looking – those were the things that mattered to Henri, and he had no intention of changing.

Every Fénelon child aspired to go to the Lycée Condorcet, and from there to university. In principle, most young people of good family followed the path trodden by generations before them. At the age of 19, Henri Cartier-Bresson was a man of principle – but not the same principles as everyone else's.

Trying to comply with his own, he took the baccalaureate three times, and three times he failed. On the first occasion he failed by three marks, on the second by 13, and on the third by 30. Even in French his spelling was merely approximate, he couldn't come to terms with punctuation or accents, and he preferred contemporary authors to those on the syllabus. His literature teachers, Messrs Chambry and Arbelet, willingly acknowledged that one can be passionately devoted to literature without entertaining the slightest academic ambition or being transmogrified into a bookworm or a swot.

Henri's persistent pursuit of failure, demonstrated by the alarming decline in his results, finally destroyed his father's ambitions for the boy's future. He had fondly imagined his eldest child going to the HEC (Hautes Etudes Commerciales) – the most prestigious of all business schools – and subsequently rising rapidly through the ranks of the Pantin company before eventually taking over as general director. That was the great plan. But Henri's manifest lack of interest in any subject that might lead him to the cherished goal soon made it apparent that for once a Cartier-Bresson had failed to cotton on.

It was a family tradition to present the successful exam candidate with his first hunting rifle. Henri's Le Verdier grandfather had been looking forward eagerly to this moment. Great, then, was his disappointment – though, it will be recalled, he had somewhat prematurely considered Henri to be a potential black sheep. Although there were bonds of respect and admiration between the two of them, they often clashed. The grandfather was a strict and solid Norman, a man of conviction, Catholic and pro-Dreyfus at a time when such an attitude was far from the norm. Once, having caught his grandson absorbed in Gide's *La Porte étroite*, he solemnly lectured him in his office: 'We all know this André Gide. His wife Madeleine, who is a Rondeaux, is our cousin. He may be a good writer, but let me tell you that he is a bad man.'

It was all in vain, for nothing could keep young Henri from his reading. Family mealtimes were often tense. His father would repeatedly tell him that he must learn to control his impulsive nature, but such reprimands fell on deaf ears. Henri's instinct always got the better of him, and this was taken for insolence. One day at table he could not contain himself, and drily responded to his grandfather's criticism by quoting Hippolyte Taine: 'One doesn't ripen, one merely rots away in places.'

The white moustache of the patriarch quivered with rage, but his only reply was to summon the bewhiskered butler: 'Would you please take Monsieur Henri out of here.'

His father resigned himself to the fact that the boy would not be what they wanted him to be. So what was to be done? He well knew that a lifetime could be spent drawing without making a career of it. The important thing was to find him a vocation that would eventually lead somewhere. But nothing suitable came to mind. Henri had a pretty good idea of what he wanted to do (art), and an absolute certainty as to what he didn't want to do (go into the family business). On the one hand, he was all joy and impetuous enthusiasm, on the other, all pride and passionate fury. His mercurial temperament despised money, even the mention of which roused feelings of guilt.

Having complained that he was being stifled by his surroundings, he then had to bear the consequences. His father informed him: 'You can do whatever you want to do, but you will not be your father's son. You will have the revenue from your allowance to finance the studies you choose. Whatever you decide on, do it well.'

At the time, Henri saw himself as a Baudelairian spirit. 'Useful' people seemed anathema to him, but how could he explain this to his family when they could see a 'useless' life only as an affront to society? You can't explain it, you don't even try, you simply have to leave. And so he left.

2 DECISIVE MOMENTS 1927–31

Are people more serious at the age of 19? Who can say? Henri wanted to become a painter, and so he had to learn to be one. No matter how talented, no one is born an artist – you become an artist. For his family, there was no argument about this.

Cartier-Bresson therefore set out to acquire a technique. The advice given by his friend Max Jacob to another friend – the spirit of which he always remembered, if not the letter – summed up his quest perfectly:

> Look for the means; a work of art is a collection of means assembled to make the effort. Artists are not penitents flaunting their sins but makers heading for a goal; they have a profession, and a novel is made just like a coat, with cuts and patterns. What you pour into it of yourself is all very fine, but you must learn how it is put together, what is a situation, how to create it, how to end it. Who is speaking? Why is he speaking? Where is he? Where is he going? Why?

For a picture, in the same way as for a novel, you must know precisely how its inner mechanics work. There was no shortage of Paris studios willing to dispense knowledge. Many great artists had taken that route before branching out, and it was not *infra dig.* to follow their example. Private academies holding courses on the fringes of the Ecole des Beaux-Arts had been part of the Parisian scene since the middle of the nineteenth century. Students could sketch nudes to their hearts' content, learn all about the practicalities of art, study theory with their tutor, or do a combination of all three. The institution was chosen according to its reputation, the prestige of the painters working there, the talents of the teachers, the agreeableness of the area, the quality of preparation for the Prix de Rome and the selection of available models. Among the academies were the Julian, Ronson, de la Grande Chaumière, Frochot, de la Palette and Moderne.

Bonnard taught at one, Jacques-Emile Blanche at another, but Cartier-Bresson chose the Lhote, one of the most recently established, which boasted such renowned teachers as Kisling and Metzinger. Along with the Julian, the Lhote had the greatest influence on the colony of foreign artists exiled, more or less temporarily, in Montparnasse. It had premises in the heart of the district, in both the rue du Départ and the rue d'Odessa. It was in the second of these that the courses took place, sandwiched between a wooden staircase and walls hung with reproductions of Cranach.

André Lhote was the owner of the premises, the master of painting, the master of drawing, in short, The Master. His image – a mass of frizzy hair, a thin moustache, the gentlest of expressions, a beatific smile – gazed out from the 1927 portrait by Kertész. Born 23 years before Cartier-Bresson, he had grown up and learnt to paint under the influence of Gauguin 'in the extraordinary solitude of Bordeaux'. He was one of the great characters of the intellectual and artistic world in Paris. An actor who had observed the cubist saga, not its golden age but its second period of 'synthetic cubism', he had opened his academy in 1922, while continuing to review art for the *Nouvelle Revue française*. He was often referred to as one of the masters of neoclassicism, but he would have preferred to be considered as the inventor of a modern visual language.

His painting never achieved the heights of his social success or of his teaching; his life and work were proof of the fact that an artist can be a major teacher and a minor painter. It is rare to find a teacher who is also a genius. Lhote had a heavy hand and an acute eye leavened with a twinkle. While he had a certain personal charisma, he drew his authority from his teaching. Despite his position, he liked to think of himself as rebellious and regularly denied all accusations of didacticism. He liked to speak his mind and had a taste for polemics, which was not out of place. To the great delight of his students, he never missed a chance to denounce the sordid practices of the old Prix de Rome winners in the provinces, where they still reigned supreme; he would dismiss as the pinnacle of vulgarity an excess of reality, and – with proofs at the ready – condemn repetition as the worst enemy of the visual artist; as for thinning and impasto, they were the running sores of painting.

Under him the students learned about the art of the portrait, engraving, sketching, and above all composition. In the eyes of Cartier-Bresson and many of his fellow students and friends, such as Dora Maar, he was not only a marvellous teacher, but also the living embodiment of the cubist phenomenon. He saw himself as the trustee of a tradition, an artistic missionary. 'Cézanne is our present-day director of conscience,' he would often tell them, for he was Cézanne's most ardent supporter. He could not go to enough trouble to restore the lustre of an artist treated with disdain by too many painters – if they acknowledged him at all – even though it was to him that they owed their liberty. For Lhote, anyone who dared to express the tiniest reservation about his hero's genius was condemned never to understand painting. Cézanne was the heir to Greece and the Middle Ages, the twin peaks of Art: he soared high above the madding crowd, he was patron and originator of painting's modern *Angst*, he had opened new windows on to the infinite. He was the humble genius who had accomplished in the visual arts what Rimbaud had achieved in poetry, capturing in his depictions of Mont Sainte-Victoire the truth of the senses, which displaced all other truths.

Lhote's passion for composition, which he felt his contemporaries had sadly neglected in favour of detail, led him to look back longingly to the Middle Ages and the Renaissance, when illuminators and fresco painters succeeded in superimposing different elements. Mastery of this art required rhythm, perspective, draughtsmanship and colour. No composition, no salvation – this was the message that he hammered into his students. Composition was everything, and everything was in the composition. Contrary to the generally accepted view, composition expressed the temperament of the artist just as much as bravura displays. And Cézanne had understood that better than anybody.

Lhote pulled his students in two directions, each distinct but also complementary: technique was one, the ineffable the other. He believed in the virtues of theory as the only possible basis for practice, and his lessons were an unceasing plea for visual intelligence. He was forever exhorting his students to look for the invariables in the works of the past – the absolute values that had become the laws of composition. Painting, as he presented it in the course of his lectures on method, was an exercise of the mind. All that mattered at the start was patterns, principles, ideas, a system. And so it was, under the glass roof of the great studio in the rue d'Odessa, that Henri Cartier-Bresson was surprised to find himself going back a few years to the worst period of his schooldays – because in order to examine the divine proportions of Leonardo, it is first necessary to explore Pythagorean theories of number and geometry.

Cartier-Bresson caught the virus of geometry from Lhote, who was positively riddled with it. For him, the only way to find order was through a structure imposed on the world. In his analysis of cubist landscapes, this former member of the group of painters known as the *Section d'or* constantly emphasized that the geometrical treatment of the different elements in no way detracted from their atmospheric qualities; it simply endowed them with a degree of flexibility. Even when he lavished praise on Seurat's *Un dimanche à Porte-en-Bessin*, it was to extol his capacity to make use of the principles of geometry, which placed him among the immortals.

In Lhote's studio Cartier-Bresson heard for the first time a precept that was to become his creed: 'No one enters here but geometricians.' Since this came to him from a man steeped in humanism, he remained convinced that it originated in the Renaissance – he even believed that the source was Raphael. In fact, these words had appeared on the façade of the Academy that Plato had founded just outside Athens; there he had taught what is eternal, and what is integral to the personality, but not what comes into being and therefore has inevitably to disappear.

Cartier-Bresson's personal gospel might have begun with the words 'In the beginning was geometry'. There could have been no better summing-up of his inner torment, his quest to delve beneath appearance and find the order hidden in universal chaos, to untangle the one from the other and combine visual emotion with the best way to express it. The painter that he aspired to become could not imagine that an artist could fail to recognize the existing order. It would be as absurd as an orchestral conductor without a sense of rhythm.

Lhote's ideas were a never-ending inspiration for Cartier-Bresson. He had only to hear him or read him to be convinced. The great teacher's discourse was packed with allusions to the rhythm of the rhomboid, matters of scale, the power of the line, the value of intervals, the purity of the pictorial language, and the interior rhythms of the painting. With his lessons on structure, he could indeed have been taken for a geometry teacher, if only geometry covered aesthetics. He preached with the elegance of a mathematician, adopting the same attitude of equating mathematical theories with the absolute truth. His commentary on Cézanne's *Le Pont*, for instance, overwhelmed his students with its rhetorical power.

Great teachers are driven by a passion, and this one communicated both his passionate likes and his passionate dislikes. He could not conceal his scorn for Caravaggio, whose genius was ruined by his lack of visual intelligence, his defective soul and his technical blunders (composition without rhythm, *trompe-l'oeil* perspective and so on).

Where Braque wanted emotions to be governed by rules, Lhote wanted imagination to be restrained by discipline, serendipity to be governed by geometry. The secret, he thought, of a harmony rediscovered lay precisely in the balance between prose and poetry.

Lhote himself, however, was not the kind of man to 'correct' things. To his students he knew just how to deliver his message through discreet little comments, precisely aimed. It was all a question of tone. Some of these remarks were destined for general consumption, though: 'If you have an instinct, you have the right to work', or, rather more poetically, 'There is no brighter smile than that rising from the bosom of discipline'. Such remarks, often repeated, became maxims, and when on occasion they were directed at an individual they would rarely be forgotten. When, one day, he leaned over the work of Henri Cartier-Bresson, instead of telling him off for being too much under the influence of Max Ernst, he murmured: 'Ah, pretty colours, little surrealist, carry on...'.

Instead of bringing out the painter, however, Lhote was actually moulding the subconscious mind of the future photographer. Cartier-Bresson may have been no good at mathematics, but he knew exactly where to find the golden section. It was ingrained in him, this universal principle of harmony, key to an absolute concept of beauty. He could now instinctively reconstruct the universe according to the laws that governed it. But he could do so naturally, as a complete artist, without having to stand before a canvas and work things out before painting. The young man had come a long way since discovering the effects of the purity of the air; for Stendhal's 'magic of distances' he now substituted the notion of aerial perspective. This was less an evolution than a revolution.

He loved Paolo Uccello and Piero della Francesca because they were the painters of divine proportions – one critic had described *The Death of Adam* on the Arezzo frescos as 'a symphony in angles of 135° with chords of 1100°'. What the early art historian Vasari criticized in them was precisely what our budding painter loved most: Uccello's love of perspective, the strain on his graceful genius in trying to solve problems of engineering, while Piero could have passed for the greatest geometrician of his time. Cartier-Bresson was so immersed in their works that his mind filled with protractors and plumb lines. Like them, he dreamed of diagonals and proportions, and became obsessed with the mystique of measurements, as if the world was simply the product of numerical combinations.

From then on his eye had a built-in compass, thanks to André Lhote. To him he owed his taste for form, his passion for composition moulded with effectiveness and authenticity, his clarity of thinking and his vigour of expression. All these things were assimilated at once; what may have required premeditation in others became natural to him. By inculcating in Cartier-Bresson his own vision of the world, Lhote did not take him out of one straitjacket only to put him in another; on the contrary, he liberated him from all his inhibitions.

He did, however, encourage Cartier-Bresson to submit to a certain number of rules, without which he would achieve nothing but messy sentimentality. He taught him not to be afraid to commit errors of proportion, to 'read' works of art for himself, to look at them with a formal eye instead of merely identifying them, to seek out the subliminal intentions of the great masters, to discern Cézanne's invisible mountain in the architecture of Picasso's *Demoiselles d'Avignon*. And he taught him to keep the visual constants strictly in line with the Greco-Latin tradition, so that with this basis of discipline his instincts could fly free.

Thanks to this great teacher, Cartier-Bresson developed the eye of an artist. This does not mean that every time he admired a beautiful landscape he saw a signature in the bottom right-hand corner. It was simply that at all times he adopted a visual approach. If he was to paint with his soul, all he had to do was to shut down his surveyor's cast of mind and forget everything that Lhote had drummed into him, so that he could allow it all to burst forth spontaneously.

He now knew what he wanted to achieve – a state of grace that would combine order, balance, harmony, proportion and all the other classical virtues, also considered French virtues *par excellence*.

The most important thing Lhote taught him was that there is no liberty without discipline. Passion can only blossom within a fixed frame; there is no flesh without a skeleton. 'When my plan is ready, my work is ready' – very Racinian. What painters and dramatists have in common is the soul of an architect; the art lies in making people forget the geometry. The true backbone of art is the perception of time, an indefinable awareness that we are living through a moment touched with grace.

Even the best academy is a prison, and a prison is a place to escape from. Although now infected with the viruses of composition and geometry, Cartier-Bresson nevertheless could not abide the mind-set of the system. He admired his teacher, but the theoretical Lhote began to irritate and even exasperate him. He had to get away in order not to become a sub-Lhote. He wanted to be himself – to paint, which meant to change the world. In any case, he knew that Lhote – who once thought of writing an *Aesthetics of Infidelity* – encouraged his pupils to embrace rules and theories so that they could be unfaithful to them, forcing them to build a carapace of logic so that they could have the pleasure of break-ing out of it.

Cartier-Bresson spent two years at the Lhote Academy. Hergé, creator of Tin-Tin, spent two hours at the Académie Saint-Luc before walking out and slamming the door behind him. It could be argued, however, that Henri Cartier-Bresson learned photography by studying painting.

There are some people whose souls are constantly restless, who feel exiled spiritually and dream of escape. Cartier-Bresson was one of these.

It may have been Jacques-Emile Blanche who transmitted another virus to Cartier-Bresson – Anglophilia. Henri decided to accompany his cousin and friend Louis Le Breton to Great Britain in order to study. At least, Le Breton intended to study, for Henri would as usual live his own life. The two young men duly found themselves at Magdalene College, Cambridge, in 1928. Henri stayed there for eight months, during which he sometimes attended courses in English literature.

College society was a clannish collection of privileged people with their own long-established customs and rituals, ripe for anthropological research. Some considered the quest for pleasure to be an end in itself, while others saw themselves as part of the generation that had been crushed by the weight of the glorious dead in the war and yearned to throw it off. And there were those who thought the only way to make any headway in such surroundings was to be accepted into one of the famous inner circles of the elite, homosexuals, the decadent, the intelligent, the skilful, the rebellious, the hypocritical, not to men-tion the most notorious of the lot, the Apostles, who liked to think of themselves as immoralists (and who included a few of the above categories).

As an outsider, Cartier-Bresson was in no position to make choices. A liber-tarian by nature, he preferred to nourish his spirit by immersing himself in L'Evolution, la révolution et l'idéal anarchiste by the geographer Elisée Reclus, and the militant articles written by the latter's nephew, the art historian Elie Faure. He felt more in common with the aesthetes than with the athletes, but the distinction was purely academic, since he scarcely concerned himself with any of this student gamesmanship. That did not mean, however, that he shut him-self off completely, for he formed a close friendship with John Davenport, while his cousin became inseparable from a budding actor named Michael Redgrave. But generally, in this tiny closed world, such dilettantes were classed as mere tourists, and he spent most of his time painting.

One of his pictures, *The Couple*, shows the people with whom he had lodgings. An oil on canvas measuring 55 x 40 cm, it is one of the rare works of his youth, together with a *Nude*, painted in the same year, that his mother managed to rescue after he had destroyed most of his work. Another, entitled *Composition*, was clearly influenced by Miró at the time when the latter was pulling away from surrealism. It was reproduced in *Experiment*, a prestigious student magazine published alongside *Venture*, an artistic and literary review launched in the same year by Anthony Blunt to denounce the laxity of free verse and surrealism.

When he left Cambridge, Cartier-Bresson took with him a few happy memories. It had been a reasonably enjoyable way of prolonging adolescence in the company of dandies and aristocrats, while devoting himself to painting and postponing entry into the real world. But for this natural outsider the most important memory of his English interlude was an unexpected treat: a conversation at home with the great philosopher and ethnologist Sir James Frazer, while Lady Frazer – who had translated into French *The Golden Bough*, his enormous masterpiece on the history of primitive religions and their rituals – served tea.

One of the pleasures of returning to Paris was seeing his friends again. Two were especially close to him: Henri Tracol and André Pieyre de Mandiargues. He had met Henri at the academy, and had been introduced to his uncle, the art historian Elie Faure, a man of dazzling brilliance (and as it happens the nephew of Cartier-Bresson's favourite geographer, Reclus). As for André, they had known each other since they were children, when they used to spend holidays together in Seine-Maritime. Their families had been close for many years, although it was only on Cartier-Bresson's return from Cambridge that the friendship really blossomed. They had a great deal in common – background, origins and sensitivity.

André lived in the 17th *arrondissement*, close to the Parc Monceau, first on the avenue de Villiers and then in the rue Murillo. Like Cartier-Bresson he was a Norman on his mother's side, and a dreamer, with the same independent nature and sense of irony that some people took for indifference; he had also failed the baccalaureate several times at the Lycée Carnot. Unlike his friend, he had received a Protestant education, and he was an intensely private and solitary person. When he was just seven years old, he had lost his father in the war. He finally passed his baccalaureate and entered the HEC, only to go on to the Sorbonne to study the humanities. At the age of 23 this stuttering, shy young man had reached the same point as Cartier-Bresson, not knowing what he wanted but absolutely certain about what he did not want. Having inherited some money from his grandfather he had just left the family home, not through any disagreement but simply in order to live somewhere else.

The two of them longed to escape from middle-class mediocrity and so find the path to liberation. Cartier-Bresson was one year older, though this had no bearing on the fact that in their partnership he always led the way. This was a matter of temperament. According to André, he was pretty authoritarian and never hesitated to moan at him, especially because of André's broadmindedness. André was shy to the point of neurosis, and he did not dare to start writing until 1933; even then it was in secret, and he did not venture to publish until 1946, whereas Cartier-Bresson never hung back from anything. Together, in their discussions and their wanderings, they exposed themselves to everything that was new in poetry, literature and painting. But Henri was always one step ahead of André, and according to the latter was more 'civilized'. In reading, listening and looking, he set the pace – sometimes tyrannically so.

Mandiargues never did catch up, even if he never stopped hoping he would. He attributed this partly to Cartier-Bresson's intellectual curiosity, extreme flexibility and inexhaustible dynamism, but also to his self-confidence. Although Cartier-Bresson was still young, he had already made contacts. He was no more a social lion than his friend was a hermit, but he had a personality that moved quite easily from one circle to another without effort, without forcing himself on people or knocking on doors. Effortlessly, spontaneously, he soon got to know the men behind the cultural output of the day, and to take the pulse of living art.

Jacques-Emile Blanche was the first vital contact. He had known Cartier-Bresson as a youth, and now that the boy had grown into a young man, he virtually adopted him. In 1928 he presented him with the last volume of his series *Propos de peintre*, which had just been published by Emile-Paul, dedicating it in affectionate terms that referred to their 'conversations in Offranville between recordings of black music'. He took it upon himself to introduce his protégé to all the important art circles and salons.

The first sortie was not, however, very successful. Blanche took him to 27 rue de Fleurus to meet Gertrude Stein. Very much a writer's writer, she had so far published only a collection of short stories (*Three Lives*), an interminable novel (*The Making of Americans*) and some poetry (*Tender Buttons*), but these had already marked her out as a sort of literary cubist who had had the effron-tery to deconstruct form, strangle syntax and murder punctuation. The extraordinary salon of this patron of the arts lacked nothing except social graces. Countless young poets, novelists and artists of all types crossed her threshold in order to seek advice, a helping hand, an introduction, or even an informal imprimatur. The more naïve among them hoped to take advantage of her intellectual prestige and reputation for good taste, which were equally well established in the best circles on both sides of the Atlantic. Few of them realized that these qualities could mask a cynicism amounting almost to cruelty, trig-gered by the slightest provocation. If the budding painter Henri Cartier-Bresson was hoping that she would encourage him to persevere along the diffi-cult path of creation, he was in for a rude awakening. In the driest of tones that brooked no response, she merely said: 'Young man, you'd do better to go into your family's business!'

More than one would-be genius has been comprehensively crushed by such a pronouncement. People of influence, looked up to and admired, are not always aware of the impact of such authoritative statements, or indeed of the responsibility that comes with power.

The young man was mortified. Blanche himself was deeply offended, for this was not at all what he had envisaged. To make up for it, he introduced Cartier-Bresson to Marie-Louise Bousquet, with much happier results. Once he had been accepted into her famous salon in the rue Boissière – frequented by Gide, Derain, Giraudoux and Colette among others – Henri greatly enjoyed his frequent visits, even if he was only a silent observer of this brilliant society, too intimidated by their great minds to risk joining in the conversation.

His mentor did not stop there. He arranged a meeting that was to prove decisive, introducing Cartier-Bresson to René Crevel. He had no idea that Crevel would in turn lead him into a veritable hotbed of activity, the ideas from which would influence him for the rest of his life.

Eight years his senior, Crevel might have been the elder brother that Cartier-Bresson never had. In addition to the elegance with which they both dressed, in clothes that seemed to float on the body, they had the same angelic faces, magnificent blue eyes, fine features, wide mouths, and youthful looks accentuated by the hairlessness of their cheeks and chin. But Cartier-Bresson's eyes revealed an unquenchable desire for action, whereas Crevel's were dark with fear and melancholy. These sons of the middle class detested middle-class morality, perhaps because one had a strict father who was the successful head of a famous company, while the other had been confronted by his father's suicide, his body hanging on the end of a rope. The unconscious mind has its own way of registering such things.

Cartier-Bresson loved life too much to embrace Crevel's nihilism, but that in no way diminished his admiration for his friend. He was too fascinated by such original, eccentric outsiders to stay away from this unhappy and insecure man. Crevel was 28 at the time, but for several years had been frequenting the places 'where things happen'. These were not only the most exclusive salons and the shadiest brothels, but also the cafés where life was buzzing. He had already published magazine articles and books (with reputable publishers) including, in that year, his latest work, under the programmatic title *L'Esprit contre la raison*. He was a dandy who was fascinated by nightlife, and once left a ball given by the comte de Beaumont – the acme of social refinement – in order to be with his black lover Eugene MacCown, a jazz pianist at the Boeuf sur le Toit. One book – *Les Caves du Vatican* ('The Vatican Cellars') – had helped him break all taboos. André Gide's farcical satire was a decisive influence on him, and he was forever haunted by the figure of Lafcadio, whose only desire is to ignore everything and avoid all challenges.

Crevel was a permanent rebel, who affected an air of detachment that some people felt was offhand in the extreme. He talked a lot, very rapidly; he burned the candle at both ends, never held back from anything risqué, flaunted his homosexuality, avidly indulged in sensual excess, initiated his friends into spiritualism, engaged in all types of pleasure, and underwent psychoanalysis. In short, he lived life to the full, and more. He was one of those who subscribed to 'absolute surrealism'. The young Cartier-Bresson was enchanted, and what he discovered when he delved deeper was to transform his vision of the world.

Cartier-Bresson met Crevel four years after the first *Surrealist Manifesto* had been published by Sagittaire. It seemed to have been tailor-made for a whole generation whose imagination had been checked by reality, showing them how to channel their burning desire for liberty. Dreams, wonders, Gothic horror were invoked as catalysts to change their lives. For Breton, the invasion of daily life by poetry was the basis of the whole revolution, along the lines of the following definition:

> Surrealism, masculine noun: pure automatism by which one proposes to express either verbally, in writing or in any other fashion the real functioning of thought. Dictation of thought in the absence of all control exercised by reason, and beyond all considerations aesthetic or moral.

René Crevel had followed this path all his life. It was he who revealed to André Breton, Tristan Tzara and the rest of them the technique of hypnotic sleep, from which they tried to create a sphere of illumination and poetic effusion. He found himself torn between the rival factions of the movement before finally siding with André Breton, its founder and ultimately its pope.

Cartier-Bresson devoured *La Révolution surréaliste*, the official mouthpiece of the movement. There he discovered what he had been vaguely seeking for years without ever managing to put a name or a form to it. It was not a political party, nor a philosophical system, but an attitude of mind, a way of living life. He hated positivism, and now almost spontaneously he found himself in the surrealist world. The pages of this journal gave off a whiff of perdition. They contained a permanent justification for all forms of rebellion – against war, against obsolete values, against anything that posed a threat to liberty. The journal spoke of dreams, suicide, social insubordination, Communism – and also of painting, automatic drawing, photography and the beauty of dead bodies. It celebrated life, the whole of life, like an explorer discovering the globe.

When he was admitted into the back-room of the Dame Blanche in Montmartre, and then into the Cyrano near the place Blanche – the hallowed meeting-places of the surrealists in Paris – Cartier-Bresson felt that he had entered the true inner sanctum. These were not mere cafés, they were the salons of the élite. Here were the very people who had written in the magazine that had become his bible. They were no more than ten years older than him, but they had all made their mark, each of them distinguished by their scars of battle – a public scandal, a libel, a slap in the face, a spit in the eye.

Thoroughly intimidated by the sheer quality of this gathering, the young would-be star eagerly attended meetings as its members planned developments and pooled ideas. But this was hardly a route to self-confidence. He would always sit at the end of the table in order not to be a nuisance and draw attention to himself. This left him too far away from Breton to catch anything but vague snatches of his comments, but nothing in the world could have induced him to elbow his way close to the 'Sun King'. From time to time he would latch on to the great man's utterances, spoken with such solemn authority that they precluded all objections – such gems as 'It is inadmissible for a man to leave any trace of his time on Earth.'

It mattered little that Breton sometimes out-pontificated the pontiff, so long as the sum of his virtues exceeded the sum of his faults. Cartier-Bresson considered him to be a man of dignity and integrity, polite, honest, and as timid as he was intimidating. In his eyes the leader was the incarnation of rebellion, the epitome of the power of instinct and intuition. Breton basked in the glory of the books that he had already published, but the one that he brought out that year, 1928, quadrupled his prestige and his power over Cartier-Bresson, who was utterly fascinated by it, but not just because it was lavishly illustrated with about 50 photographs from different sources in the pure spirit of the *Manifesto*, which proscribed all literary description.

Nadja is the account of an adventure – in the surrealist sense of the word – between the narrator and a woman who is as seductive as she is mysterious. It describes their meetings in great detail, day by day, following the very precise timetable of their movements through Paris. At the end, the reader realizes that the mystery of Nadja is a pretext to reveal the poet's quest for his own identity. *Nadja* invites the reader in fact to take a step to the side in order to gain a new view of reality. This is how Cartier-Bresson would henceforth always contemplate the world, people and life – from an angle rather than full-frontally.

When he visited Breton's studio for the first time, Cartier-Bresson was struck by how closely the place reflected its occupant. It was filled with odds and ends, every one of which had its proper place. Breton was surrealism personified.

Cartier-Bresson did not dare to intervene in the quarrels that broke out within the group during the next major crisis. Breton was then 32 years old; he had been a member of the French Communist Party for two years; he was in the throes of a divorce and embroiled in an emotional tangle of personal relationships, so he was not best placed to resolve the tensions. He sometimes tied himself in knots trying to reconcile his own intransigence and over-hastiness to throw people out with his genuine desire for collective cooperation. On this occasion, however, the rupture led to the departure of Michel Leiris, Jacques Baron and Jacques Prévert. Tucked away at the end of the table, the junior member of the club observed the tumult without joining in, being far too impressed to break his own silence. Perhaps this was a relic of his Catholic education – the novice has no say at chapter meetings.

He was there, and that was all that mattered. There was a kind of religious aura about such meetings, and his very presence over a glass of grenadine meant that he was part of the ritual. It expressed his allegiance to the chief, an explicit endorsement of the new head of state.

For the surrealists, the café was the point at which all passions intersected. Cartier-Bresson was indeed there, but he was there in his own way. In the café, as in the brothel, to which he would accompany his friends Mandiargues and Josse, he would spend hours observing the convolutions of those who gave and those who took, taking in their conversations as he sipped his drink. He was there, but he was not involved. He was the permanent looker-on. Governed by a natural instinct that remained with him all his life, he would automatically steer clear of anything that might compromise his free will and independence, or his own judgment. And so from the very start he was unable to accept surrealism in total. He rejected its paintings, for example, whereas he defended passionately those great artists of the past who had inspired him, most notably Uccello. He was irritated by the anecdotal character of surrealist art. 'It is literary painting,' he would often complain. 'Magritte is full of clever tricks, but you are caught up in solving a literary puzzle, not in art. Good for advertising!'

He respected Man Ray and his portraits; he had a great affection for Max Ernst and his collages; but he liked these artists more than their art, whereas he had nothing but praise for the violence and derision expressed in *L'Age d'or*, Luis Buñuel's second surrealist film. And so, even in his chosen field, young Cartier-Bresson remained an outsider, refusing to play the game because he refused to be committed to anything. He could never be excluded, because he had never been a member in the first place.

Nevertheless, his debt to surrealism was immense. He would always acknowledge this, even though his allegiance was to its ethics rather than to its aesthetics. Unable to choose between Rimbaud's exhortation to change one's life and the Marxist injunction to change the world, he took the better option advocated by Breton. He would always retain a predilection for questioning all things at all times, and for allowing the power of the imagination to come first.

His cult of coincidence was derived from surrealism, for, after all, this whole adventure had begun through a chain of chance events. Thanks to Jacques-Emile Blanche he had one day found himself in the café de la Dame Blanche, and from there he had been admitted to the café on place Blanche. Other even more significant coincidences were to punctuate his life, fostering a talent for interpreting the signs. A spiritual acrobat, he remained faithful to surrealism all his life, but it was a Norman kind of fidelity which sought to distance itself from the dogma without actually betraying it. He was a professional dreamer, much as it used to be said of great reporters that they were salaried idlers.

In addition to Jacques-Emile Blanche and René Crevel, there was a third enabler who helped Cartier-Bresson to gain easy access to a world which had previously been closed to him. The least that one can say about Harry Crosby is that he turned up in the most unlikely manner.

During these years that were so fruitful for Cartier-Bresson's intellectual and artistic development, he found time to fulfil his military obligations. It could even be said that he sacrificed himself, since such activities were totally contrary to his nature in terms of the mental discipline and the physical demands required, and even respect for the national flag. Anyway, he thought of becoming a pilot, although the prospect was certainly viewed more from a romantic than from a technical angle. He enlisted in the air force, and was stationed at Le Bourget, near Paris, with a Lebel rifle over his right shoulder and a copy of the 1928 NRF edition of *Ulysses* tucked under his left arm. This was not merely for his image. He genuinely needed the pleasures of Joyce to compensate for the regimented atmosphere of the barracks.

One day, when he was filling in one of the endless forms so beloved of the military, he hesitated over the question of how he would assess his military service. He could not stop himself from writing: 'Do not rock so hard – the sky belongs to everyone.'

He was immediately summoned to the office of Colonel Poli-Marchetti.

'What exactly do you mean?'

'It's not me, it's Cocteau.'

'Cocteau what?'

The officer started to yell at him and threatened to send him to the Bataillon d'Afrique – a punishment battalion stationed in Africa – for repeated insolence. It was inevitable that the rebellious Cartier-Bresson should constantly be singled out for disciplinary proceedings, though he was never sent to Africa. This was, first, because his crimes were not particularly serious, secondly because it became obvious that he would not be able to fulfil his aeronautical ambitions, and finally because everyone knew who he was. Le Bourget and Pantin are both in Seine-Saint Denis, a north-eastern suburb of Paris; everyone had heard of the Cartier-Bresson factory. He was therefore put on cleaning duties, and, when that didn't do the trick, close arrest and the guardroom.

With variations, the scene was repeated many times. One day the young man once more found himself standing to attention in the presence of his commanding officer, but on this occasion there was a visitor, an American who was taking flying lessons with one of the instructors at the base and who was on good terms with all the officers there. He had served in France during the war as an ambulance driver. Now chance willed that he should be there on the umpteenth occasion when the young rebel had been had up for insolence, and that he should recognize him as someone he had once met at André Lhote's studio. Finding the whole business more amusing than disconcerting, and intrigued by the young man's personality, he sprang to his defence: 'General, it's not such a big deal. For once let him serve three days' detention doing something more positive. Let him spend them with me, and I'll take the responsibility. You know where I live, and my prisoner will not escape.'

The commanding officer, moved by a spirit that was more sociable than military, gave way to the whim of this local VIP, and Cartier-Bresson left the airport in his new protector's car. They headed for the forest of Ermenonville where the American lived, at the Moulin du Soleil, rented from his friend Armand de La Rochefoucauld.

The detainee's punishment was not restricted to these three days. He was invited regularly for weekends, and soon became a friend and companion. It was as if he had been adopted, although in his wildest dreams he could never have hoped for such a patron.

Harry Crosby was the local eccentric, but he was much more than that. He came from Boston's high society and was the nephew of the mega-rich banker J. P. Morgan. After finishing his studies at Harvard he had come to the Old World, where he lived in Paris in a large apartment on the rue de Lille with his wife Caresse (her real name was Mary, but she wanted to have a first name that sounded cuddly and began with a C). Everything that surrounded them, everything they wore was white, and life was a ball, filled with the avant-garde, alcohol, sexual freedom, eccentricity – at least, that was how their families back in New England saw it. They were not far off the mark. The couple themselves boasted of their crazy, extravagant life, but this was not the whole story.

The Crosbys were mad about poetry and literature. Not content with writing verse of their own – Harry's in particular was very dark, and revealed a character deeply preoccupied with self-destruction and haunted by the spectre of the war dead – in 1925 they founded the Black Sun Press in order to publish things that they liked, in a suitably luxurious, handcrafted, élitist style. The typography, the quality of the paper, the layout, the choice of illustrations, even the number of copies printed – everything was designed to give each of their books the unmistakable seal of rarity. They began, of course, by publishing their own work. Three years and five books later, while continuing to issue their own words under their own imprint, they began to publish writings by Oscar

Wilde, Edgar Allan Poe, D. H. Lawrence, Choderlos de Laclos, Ezra Pound, even Laurence Sterne and Omar Khayyam, as well as fragments of work in progress by James Joyce. Some titles simply demanded to be published, for Harry Crosby had inherited an extraordinary library from his cousin Walter Berry. It contained not only some very rare first editions and incunabula, but also original correspondence with Henry James, Paul Valéry, Ralph Waldo Emerson, and even an exchange of letters with Marcel Proust, who had kindly dedicated *Pastiches et Mélanges* to him.

Black Sun Press published only what pleased its founders, and they could not conceive of doing it differently. 'Cartier', as the Crosbys called him, had a close-up view of how they worked. He spent every weekend at their mill, where he watched a parade of writers, poets, painters and musicians from all over the world. It was a cultural cauldron. Each week a whole section of Paris society would make its way to party in Ermenonville. Once more, Cartier-Bresson was the young outsider, but this time he soon became friends with Max Ernst and many others, for the surrealists were far from being a minority group. Among them was another man who was to play an influential role in the early part of Cartier-Bresson's career.

Had it not been for his American accent, Julien Levy could easily have passed for a Central European, so steeped was he in the culture and history of the region. The son of a New York property tycoon who was not averse to investing in paintings, he studied art history at Harvard before going to France at the instigation of Marcel Duchamp. He was known as a talent-spotter with an insatiable curiosity, always on the look-out for beautiful women and budding geniuses. During one of his many trips to Paris, he was introduced by Man Ray to Atget, from whom he immediately bought a large number of photographs. He thought of opening a bookshop, but in due course set up a gallery in New York, considered a bit of a fringe establishment since it exhibited photographs.

In 1927 he married the daughter of the poetess Mina Loy, and, unsurprisingly for such a keen Francophile, he chose the town hall of the 14th *arrondissement* – Montparnasse – for the wedding. Constantin Brancusi and James Joyce were to be his witnesses. The former arrived late, panting and clutching *Le Nouveau-Né*, a little bronze sculpture that he had made as a wedding present. Joyce never turned up.

Apart from Max Ernst and Julien Levy, young 'Cartier' made friends with other regulars at the Ermenonville mill. An American couple, almost as eccentric as the Crosbys, Gretchen and Peter Powel, were particular friends of theirs, and equally determined to escape from the puritanism of their origins – they liked to travel. This too was an acquaintanceship that was soon to affect Cartier-Bresson's future.

Gretchen was a Texan blonde with brown eyes and a finely sculptured face framed in a pageboy hairstyle held by a large ribbon. She was taking Bourdelle's courses in sculpture at the Académie de la Grande Chaumière, together with her friend Caresse. Peter, a Rhode Islander, was an amateur photographer who could pass for a professional. It was he who introduced Harry Crosby to the art of photography – a revelation which induced Crosby not just to take but to look at photographs. It was therefore not by chance that very soon the Black Sun Press was publishing *The Bridge*, a poem by Walter Crane, accompanied by three photographs of Brooklyn Bridge taken by Walker Evans. When in due course the Powels entrusted publication of their collection of photos to the Black Sun Press, the result was *New York 1929*, the most sophisticated, exclusive and expensive work in the history of the new publishing house.

The Powels adopted Cartier-Bresson too. Peter showed him what could be done with a camera, what can come out of it and what must be put into it. Gretchen meanwhile shared her passion for jazz with him, along with passion of another sort. She was ten years older than him, married to a man whom she greatly respected but who was hardly ever there, and she and Cartier-Bresson enjoyed an intense affair that could lead nowhere.

As 1929 came to an end, the glory of Sundays at Ermenonville began to fade. Harry Crosby had finished writing his book of dreams before going off to New York. His diary and poems revealed that a mystical faith in a sun-worshipping cult had failed to vanquish his inner torment, the phantoms of the Great War emerging as mud-covered skeletons from the trenches under a soot-black sky. He took a room on the 27th floor of the Savoy Plaza, and one day informed his wife that he was leaving to meet someone at sunset – which she thought rather strange. He was found in his studio, entwined in the arms of one of his mistresses; each of them had committed suicide with a bullet in the temple. It was two weeks before Christmas.

Henri Cartier-Bresson did not even contemplate so radical a solution to his problems. He was too young to have internalized the horrors of the war, and so he was not tortured, as Harry was. He was undoubtedly a romantic, but without the dark and tragic despair that sometimes went with the romantic soul. Reading Crosby's posthumous book *Aphrodite in Flight* did not help very much: it was a little treatise on the aerodynamics of love, in which the poet set out a fantastic inventory of the disturbing similarities between aviation and seduction.

Cartier-Bresson's affair with Gretchen Powel was a mixture of pleasure and pain, but eventually the pain outweighed the pleasure and he realized he had to do something about it. The idealist side of him recognized his own spirit as that of an adventurer. He came of a generation prepared to experience endings and find new beginnings; he felt stifled under the restrictions of the Old World, where the air suddenly seemed polluted and the atmosphere deadened; above all Gretchen's image was driving him crazy. Once again he had to break free.

The world is a big place for those who want to forget, but no matter how far you may travel, you will always have to face your demons. Murnau said it all in a cartoon about *Nosferatu le vampire*: 'And when he had crossed the bridge, the phantoms came to meet him...'. Perhaps Cartier-Bresson was himself vaguely aware that at this point in his life he was crossing a bridge.

Paul Morand, who had just published *Magie noire* and *Paris-Tombouctou*, suggested that he would find it cleansing to go and watch the storms in Patagonia. But this was the approach of a man who had already done a good deal of travelling. Cartier-Bresson's only travelling had been through books. Rimbaud's Abyssinian sojourn had stimulated more and better dreams than anyone else. He was thinking of Rimbaud when he went to Rouen and, with the help of his grandfather, got himself a berth on a wine tanker heading for Douala. From Cameroon he went to the Ivory Coast, his Abyssinia.

By now he had read too much and too widely to allow himself to be guided by a single reference. The novelists of the new, troubled spirit of the times, as well as those of more classical bent, were all in one way or another fixed on the decline of the West, exhorting their readers to quit the easy lethargy of European nights and their simplistic luxury. It was difficult to resist the siren calls of the French intellectuals who for years had been citing the journey to Africa as a true baptism. A few years earlier, André Gide had caused a sensation with his *Voyage au Congo* and *Retour du Tchad*, in which he had expressed vehement indignation at the abuses suffered by the natives, though his stance was more poetical than political, since he did not question the legitimacy of colonization. Even when similar revelations were made by a journalist rather than an author, the foundations of the French Empire were in no danger of crumbling. Like Gide, Albert Londres had no intention of starting a revolution when he travelled to Africa in 1928; he campaigned only for radical reform. As with Gide's writings, the series of articles that he published at that time in *Le Petit Parisien* resulted in questions being asked in Parliament, a hate campaign in the press by the colonial lobby, and a major rumpus. But there were no significant changes either in the situation or in people's attitudes.

Along with his tickets, Cartier-Bresson had 1000 francs in his pocket and several books in his baggage: Rimbaud's poetry, of course, Blaise Cendrars' *Anthologie nègre* – a collection of oral African tales – and the comte de Lautréamont's *Les Chants de Maldoror*, a prose epic celebrating man's rebellion against God, in the edition published by Au Sans Pareil, a bookshop-cum-publisher on the avenue Kléber, where Cartier-Bresson regularly went to buy his books. He also carried a thick volume which he had thinned down a little prior to his departure: the long preface by Philippe Soupault – the co-signatory, with Breton, of the *Surrealist Manifesto* – had not been to his liking, and with one violent and definitive gesture he had torn it out. During a stopover in Sierra Leone, he made a collage out of it by sticking pages on to postcards with the sap from a rubber tree. The book itself, *Pour l'amour et contre le travail industriel*, set out not only to denounce specialization, but to sing the praises of amateurism in all things.

The country that he discovered was one of France's eight colonies in West Africa, regarded as nothing but a vast forest punctuated by lagoons. It did have a coastline, but the French administrator was only interested in what could be made out of rubber, palm, mahogany and cacao trees. Even though a railway line had been built from Abidjan to Ferkessédougou and the forests had been thoroughly exploited, it seemed as if nothing much happened here because it was too remote and there were too many obstacles to overcome. The motherland was indifferent to its colony, just as nobody cared that the Dark Continent had been decimated by the inhuman practice of porterage. At worst, people thought of the Ivory Coast as a country of fetishists and witch doctors, rife with animism; at best, a bit of France with sunshine, where people ritually awaited the catalogues from the department stores.

At the beginning of the 1930s, there were reckoned to be some ten million natives living in the wild, outside the villages. They had fled from the white men's recruitment drives for soldiers, road-builders and, above all, woodcutters. In truth, this was slavery, and those who organized it were no better than slave traders. The forests were majestic, but they stank of decay and death – the deaths of the black woodcutters cowering under the blows of the site foreman, who knew that the forest either made you rich or killed you. Cartier-Bresson's long letters to his family – regular and affectionate – were full of such references.

Initially he took any job, no matter how small. After trying all kinds of things he considered working for a wood merchant, but thought better of it when he realized that the man had been under the African sun too long and was clearly going out of his mind. He worked for a planter, and then a store-keeper, until he met up with an Austrian hunter who introduced him to some of the local customs as they went up the River Cavally.

From then on, he hunted for a living. The African bush is not the forest of Rambouillet. His father and grandfather had taught him to use a rifle, and he had accompanied them enough times to know how to sniff out an animal in the woods, but that was nothing compared to the nocturnal hunts on which he now embarked. He would set out in search of his unknown prey, an acetylene lamp fixed to his forehead like a miner so that he could identify the beast by the colour of its eyes. Then he would dry the meat and take it to the villages to sell. But it was the tracking he enjoyed, not the killing. When eventually he returned to France, he never went hunting again. At the time, though, he found it exhila-rating – so much so that his sister wrote and asked him if, now that his gun had brought him into such close contact with hippos and crocodiles, he would ever again deign to chase rabbits in Normandy or pheasants in Brie.

When he was not hunting, Cartier-Bresson took his first photographs, using a camera he had bought before leaving for Africa – a second-hand Krauss with its lens cap acting as a shutter. There were very few landscapes but plenty of people – in action by the riverside, on quays and in ports. Ships provided thick lines of rigging and thin lines of cables to reflect his preoccupation with geometry. It was as if he had already developed his own aesthetic grammar and his own pictorial language, albeit unconsciously and unsystematically, and these fitted in quite naturally with a vision of the world from which he would never deviate.

One photograph is particularly striking. Taken from the stern of a dugout, it shows the rear view of three half-naked black men paddling; each of them is wielding his paddle with a different movement – either in the air or in the water – and the image captures the unusual sight of motion perfectly divided into three rhythms within a single bar.

These views of Africa are in no way journalistic. They are simply diverse images – all the more scattered since Cartier-Bresson kept only a small selec-tion of the negatives. The unreliability of the technology affected his choice, since the camera had been eaten away by mildew, resulting in double exposures and fernlike patterns appearing during development.

One day he was horrified to see that his urine had turned black – extremely black. It got worse – he imagined that perhaps he had inadvertently eaten an army of black ants, or the brain of a rabid monkey. He became feverish, then convulsive, and several times he actually blacked out. At last came the diagnosis – the parasitical disease bilharzia. His condition worsened during the next few weeks. He had plenty of time to contemplate the conclusion of Albert Londres' report on the Ebony Coast: 'If I were Governor General, I would stretch a huge banner over this accursed coast, and on it I would paint these words: "The White Man who makes a futile effort will immediately be punished by Nature".'

He was almost certain that this would be his fate, and resigned himself to dying. The locals made no bones about it: most people who caught the disease died of it. Bilharzia was the most prolific killer in the region. Unable to obtain the only medicines that might save him, Cartier-Bresson decided to try medicinal herbs. Doua, his hunting companion, was an expert in these arts, but he had once refused to pass on his knowledge to save a white woman who was desperately ill (it must be said that she had been extremely arrogant).

There was only one chance in a hundred that such remedies might help, and in any case Cartier-Bresson had no faith in them, believing that Pascal may have been right in thinking that man's problems arose from his inability to stay quietly at home. He gathered his last remaining strength to write as legibly as possible on the back of a postcard to his grandfather. It was a kind of testament, in which he warned of his imminent demise and set out his last wishes: his body was to be sent back to France and buried in the Varenne Valley among the beech trees of his beloved Eawy Forest, to the strains of a Debussy string quartet. He did not have long to wait for his family's reply, but it was somewhat less romantic: 'Your grandfather thinks that will be too expensive. It would be better if you came home.'

Even when he was on his deathbed, Henri's family never took him seriously. Fortunately, Doua did, and proceeded to save his life.

Cartier-Bresson never forgot his time in the African bush, and he celebrated it to the end of his days. Had it not been for his illness and near-death, he would have remained in Africa. Instead, Africa remained in him. He always kept a beautiful fetish near him – a wooden sculpture of a woman, given to him by a young Ivorian girl who did not tell him that it was possessed of magic powers.

The Ivory Coast crystallized his concept of travel: if you want to be integrated, the only acceptable way of travelling is to stay for months or even years in one spot and lead the everyday life of the people who live there. Travel means coping with transitions between countries, and even if integration may be illusory, you can at least have a go at it by earning your living in the same way as the natives. And it doesn't really matter if you fail, so long as you are not taken in by your own illusions.

He spent a year in Africa – very little in relation to a long life, but unforgettable because it was as magnificent as it was tragic. No one could ever say to him afterwards that he had not seen the darker side of life. Twelve months were scarcely long enough for him to start missing the ancient fortresses of Europe and Rimbaud's *Le Bateau Ivre*. If circumstances had been different, he would probably have given up hunting and taken more note of the many fascinating characters whom he had merely met instead of getting to know them. He would not have missed out the culture of the natives in this country of some 60 ethnic groups, all intriguing: the Appolonia and the Bete, the Yacuba and the Baule, the Malinke and the Senufo. And during a long interlude at the Liberian frontier, in the little port of Tabou near Cape Palmas, where he stayed with M. Ginestière at Bereby, perhaps he would have delved more deeply into the lives of the white settlers who typified the most destructive elements of the colonial spirit.

He returned home aboard the *Saint-Firmin*, a cargo ship belonging to the Naval Society of the West. It was on this return journey that he discovered *Heart of Darkness* and *Journey to the End of the Night* – two brilliant novels telling the sort of story that he himself had lived through, explaining the people he had just left, and confronting him again with scenes that he had witnessed. Here were his own experiences both to the letter and in spirit. Already fascinated by the mythical Rimbaud version of Africa, he found fiction and reality face to face. Thanks to the genius of Joseph Conrad and Louis-Ferdinand Céline, he identified with their characters – Marlow going upriver in pursuit of the deepest origins of the world, Bardamu, delirious as he flees the colony of Bambola-Bragamance, where he had come in order to forget the madness of the West. Cartier-Bresson no longer wondered if it was life that resembled literature or literature that followed life. Now he knew.

A geometrical vision of the world, the shock of the revelation of surrealism, the near-death experience – these were all decisive moments in the life of the young Cartier-Bresson. He owed as much to the people he met as to the books he read – one had led to the other and vice versa. Ingratitude was not in his make-up, and his life was one long, discreet homage to Lhote, Breton and

Doua. The studio in the rue d'Odessa, the café de la Dame Blanche, and the Ivory forest remained among the most honoured places in his memory.

By 1931 all the essentials were in place – personality, temperament, character, culture, eye, vision of the world. He was ready for life. Everything that was to come would serve to develop, strengthen and perfect these features without basically changing them, for now he, who had taught himself so much, was fully formed.

What was special about him was a surprising wisdom in so wild a man, for he already knew something that many others take years to discover: that one must have an idea and pursue it to the end. One idea alone is enough to fill an existence. He might have adopted for himself the motto of the House of Orange: 'I will stand firm'.

Henri Cartier-Bresson was 23, and all that remained was for him to live through the century and go on to the next one.

ole Fénelon,
ris 1918–19:
nri Cartier-
esson in the
nt row, to the
ht of the teacher

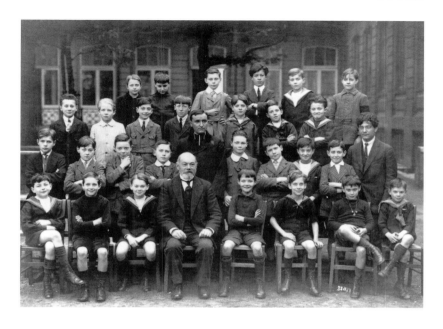

Henri, in the foreground, with his camera

New York, 1935; photo Beaumont Newhall, All rights reserved

New York, 1935; photo George
Hoyningen-Huene, All rights
reserved

Manuel Alvarez Bravo and Henri Cartier-Bresson, Mexico; 1935,

With Ratna Mohini, New York, 1946; photo Edward Steichen, taken with Henri Cartier-Bresson's camera, All rights reserved

Chim and Cartier-Bresson, reporters on Ce Soir, ironically indulging in the little courtesies, Paris 1938, during a very 'popular front' 14 July celebration; photo David Seymour, Magnum

China in 1948–49, Cartier-Bresson was one of the few reporters to span the last
months of the old regime and the first months of the new communist government;
to Jim Burke

*Whether he was in a street in Havana (above) or anywhere else,
the choreography was always the same; photo Ara Güler, Magnum*

Cuba, 1963; photo René Burri, Magnum

Henri Cartier-Bresson,
New York, 1959; photo
René Burri, Magnum

Cartier-Bresson expounding his views on the future of the agency during a Magnum meeting in New York
in 1959. He is talking to Marc Riboud, Michel Chevalier and Sam Holms; photo René Burri, Magnum

3 THE ARTIST IN SEARCH OF HIS MEDIUM 1932–35

What was he to do now? He was certainly not going to toe any conventional lines and sacrifice his life for the sake of making a living. That would have been stupid – life is too short to waste on such mundane matters. He therefore returned to the mill at Ermenonville and resumed his friendship with the surrealists, among them Max Ernst. But the suicide of their master of ceremonies had changed the atmosphere, despite the dynamism and competence of Caresse Crosby. In Montparnasse, Cartier-Bresson rediscovered friends, cafés and habits from the past. Indeed, it was now essential for him to get over his longing for the African forests and to put behind him the unique intoxication of that time. Africa had revealed him to himself, and in so doing had changed him for ever.

From now on, he would follow nothing and no one but his own instincts. There was absolutely no question of his entering the family business, to which he had already amply demonstrated his aversion. As it happened, there had been a change here too. While he had been hunting in the bush, the Société Cartier-Bresson had merged with Thiriez, another big family company dealing in cotton, based in Loos (in the north), and the result was the TCB Group (Thiriez Cartier-Bresson).

And so, what next? The answer was photography.

When he informed his father of his intentions, he made sure that he was accompanied by Max Ernst, 17 years his senior, since he deemed that some back-up might be necessary to convince the head of the family. His father was not too surprised by his son's eccentric choice, although he didn't consider photography to be a proper career – merely a distraction, a hobby, a pastime. Henri pleaded and explained, justifying his choice: he was giving up painting for photography because it was the best way for him to live life to the full. He did not have the patience or the will to work for ever on copying nature; any rigid discipline would make him run a mile; it was a question of character, of temperament, of personality; he was still devoted to the visual, still passionate about composition, but nonetheless he remained a man of instinct and above all of movement; it was essential for him to move about and see everything, and only photography could satisfy all these aspirations. Henri's father took so little pride in his son's chosen path that he did not even tell his friends – not that it mattered, since they would hear about it soon enough.

When he renounced painting for photography, Cartier-Bresson underwent an exorcizing ritual, a rite of passage: he destroyed nearly all his canvases. It was as if they had to disappear for the new medium to take over. It was a romantic gesture – a distant, unconscious echo of a chapter in Victor Hugo's *Notre-Dame de Paris* entitled 'This Will Kill That', in which the writer evoked the age-old myth that a new means of expression has to supplant its predecessor. Similarly, it was said that photography would kill painting, and later it was claimed that the cinema would kill photography. But no matter how the argument may develop, nagging questions remain: are the newcomers really artists? Should they be allowed to enter the exclusive club? How can they be so presumptuous?

Numberless photographers have turned their backs on painting, starting with the great Louis Daguerre himself, and continuing with many of the pioneers of the medium. Cartier-Bresson, now more than ever under the influence of his hero Baudelaire, was deeply aware of the poet's contribution to the discussion that had gone on raging since the mid-nineteenth century (and indeed is still raging, since it is still questioned whether photography does or does not constitute an art). Having left Lhote's academy not so very long ago, Cartier-Bresson could not forget Baudelaire's remark that the photographic industry was the refuge of failed painters who were 'too talentless or too lazy to finish their studies'. Baudelaire had denounced the foolishness of those who worshipped this golden calf, this universal craze, above all the pretensions of the newcomer. It was, absurdly, as if printing had set out to replace literature. Baudelaire assigned the humblest of positions to photography – that of a 'servant to painting'. At the time the latter was in fear of the former. About 20 painters, including Ingres and Pierre Puvis de Chavannes, signed a manifesto demanding state protection and aid in their struggle against the distorted efforts to treat photography as art. On the other hand, Emile Zola – admittedly many years younger than they – seemed to be light-years away from this artistic protectionism, for not only did he make constant use of photographs for his own pleasure and for the locations of his novels, but he argued that you could never truly see an object so long as you had not photographed it.

When Cartier-Bresson entered the world of photography, it had achieved a double breakthrough: for professionals it was a medium of information, and for amateurs it had become more and more of a hobby. The debate as to its status was still going on, and all that had been said and written on the subject for a good half-century had done little to settle the issue. Brassaï, a 33-year-old Hungarian refugee who had begun to photograph graffiti with a Voigtländer, had just published his first album, *Paris de Nuit*. The article he wrote in *L'Intransigeant* on 15 November 1932 is worth quoting:

> There is a fundamental difference between photography and painting. The one observes, the other creates. The one is a document and remains a document, even if it is devoid of all general interest. The other is based entirely on personality, and everything crumbles into a mess of fine materials if the latter is defective. How can one talk of rivalry between the two? Only photographic painting and pictorial photography are rivals. They should devour each other, so that they may disappear for ever! Photography is the very conscience of painting. It constantly reminds the latter of what it must not do. So let painting take its responsibilities.... After admiring all that the sensitive photographic plate can reveal to us, we must search for a new sensitivity – namely, that of the photographer. What attracts the photographer is precisely the chance to penetrate inside phenomena, to uncover forms. That impersonal presence! That permanent incognito! The humblest of servants, the dislocated being *par excellence*, lives only in latent images. He pursues them into their last refuges and surprises them at their most positive, their most material and true. As for knowing whether he should be distinguished with so controversial a name as 'artist', in truth it is of absolutely no importance whatsoever.

Many famous photographers never forgot their debt to their training in drawing, painting and sculpture. As for Cartier-Bresson, one of his private maxims was: 'One paints while one is taking a photograph.'

During the early 1930s in Paris, this 'pastime', art or craft, was booming. People flocked to regular exhibitions, once the bolder gallery-owners had dared to put snapshots on show. Man Ray was regarded as an art photographer, Kertész as the master photojournalist; Hungary was the first country to export photographers, so talented were its exiles in this field. Some critics divulged their method of distinguishing documentary photography from artistic: the one was clear, the other blurred. Photo booths were to be found all over Paris, in such disparate locations as department stores (the Galeries Lafayette), newspaper premises (the entrance hall of the *Petit Journal*) and the zoo. When they were installed in Prague, Franz Kafka christened them the 'mistake-yourself' booths, so certain was he that photography camouflaged the true, hidden nature of things.

Cartier-Bresson had seen his first 'photographers' photos' at the home of his American friends the Powels. Proofs of Eugène Atget's work had made a big impression on him, as had others by André Kertész, whom he always regarded as a poetic inspiration.

Atget had died in poverty some years earlier. Had it not been for the perceptive flair of Berenice Abbott, Man Ray's young assistant (who herself acknowledged her debt to her artistic training), most of his prints and negatives would have been destroyed or scattered. His Parisian streets are strangely deserted, because they were photographed at dawn, when the freshness of the day has a kind of innocence. The surrealists interpreted this as the imaginary veering away from the real rather than, in blandly and academically convenient terms, from realism.

Kertész had been a bank clerk who left his native Hungary for Montparnasse, and there survived thanks to his photographs. He swiftly discovered his own individual style, above all his own way of looking at things – a mixture of art and reportage, the avant-garde and the instant snapshot.

Apart from the work of these two men, there were others whose images had impressed Cartier-Bresson. Some made their mark through expressive force, such as the very recent one of President Doumer, secretly photographed on the steps of the Hotel Berryer moments after he had been assassinated, when the crowds were still unaware of what had happened. Others were inspiring through the emotions they aroused. But there was one that stood out from all the rest, both at the time and long afterwards, because there was a before and after. This unique photograph came as a shock in the noblest sense of the word, and it overwhelmed him with its matchless visual beauty.

It was taken in 1929 or 1930, and published in 1931 in the magazine *Photographies* under the name of Martin Munkacsi, a former sports photographer who became a reporter and summed up his philosophy in the following words: 'To see in a thousandth of a second what indifferent people come close to without noticing – that is the principle of photographic reportage. And in the thousandth of a second that follows, to take the photo of what one has seen – that is the practical side of reportage.'

The photograph showed three naked black youths, seen from the rear, plunging into the waves of Lake Tanganyika. It had all the elements that moved Henri Cartier-Bresson, for it corresponded to all the things he loved: Africa, which continued to haunt his dreams; the waters out of which the surrealists had created an abyss that could split the unconscious; the sense of composition in the interplay between the figures, the masses of sand, and the lines formed by the foam; and then the movement, youth, energy and speed of the boys. It was life, nothing else but life, and it accompanied him throughout his own life. Even at the end of his days he struggled to find the words to express his debt to this image:

> I suddenly understood that photography can fix eternity in a moment. It is the only photo that influenced me. There is such intensity in this image, such spontaneity, such *joie de vivre*, such miraculousness, that even today it still bowls me over. The perfection of form, the sense of life, a thrill you can't match... I said to myself: Good Lord, one can do that with a camera... I felt it like a kick up the backside: go on, have a go!

And so, without ever knowing it, one photographer paved the way for another, and one work changed a life. What Cartier-Bresson said of this photograph, his friend Walker Evans would say of Paul Strand's *Blind Woman*, and many great photographers would later say of Henri Cartier-Bresson's own pictures. Even if you may wish to avoid it, your example is always bound to influence the destiny of other people.

This was not a photograph taken by a camera fixed on a tripod – a procedure already regarded as outmoded – but an image of motion captured by a portable camera. By being mobile, such a camera enabled the photographer to go where he would never have gone, and to bring back images never before imagined because they had hitherto been inaccessible. Resembling little more than a toy, the pocket camera has changed our vision of the world.

A new version of it had just appeared on the market and facilitated precisely this flexibility: the Leica. Henri Cartier-Bresson became a photographer on the day in 1932 when he bought one in Marseilles. This was his true baptism: the artist had found his instrument.

The Leica would become a mythological object. It was Cartier-Bresson's constant companion both inside and out – in the street, at home, at other people's houses, everywhere and at all times. This was more like the behaviour of a bounty hunter than an artist – always lying in wait, on the lookout, ready to shoot. But the attachment was also sentimental – it is rare to find such perfect understanding between a man and a machine. Like lovers, each complemented the other. By extending his vision in the most natural manner possible, the camera was indeed a part of him. His new awareness, engendered by the impact of Munkacsi's photograph, had changed everything, and from now on Cartier-Bresson and his Leica were inseparable.

This miracle of quality, precision, discretion and speed was the work of Oscar Barnak, an engineer who developed the idea of a miniature camera in 1913 on behalf of Leitz, a firm of optical instrument-makers in Wetzlar, Germany. Once the design had been perfected, his invention no longer used plates but the ordinary 35 mm films previously confined to the cinema; progress was rapid, and the new process allowed photographs to be taken in reduced light and at an instant's notice. Nothing could be more efficient.

The 6 x 6 plate camera is a state of mind, but the 24 x 36 pocket version is something else. To Robert Doisneau the Rolleiflex was the epitome of courtesy, respect and humility on the part of the photographer. You bowed down in front of people, and you didn't challenge them by looking them straight in the eye. Cartier-Bresson saw in the Leica the art of hunting executed by different, more aggressive methods. The first time that the two men met, Doisneau, a devoted admirer of Cartier-Bresson, dared to show him his first reportages, and was told: 'If the good Lord had wanted us to take photographs with a 6 x 6, he would have put our eyes in our belly. It's embarrassing to look at people's navels. And when you prostrate yourself, the only thing left is to bring on the prie-dieu.'

The body of the Leica fitted perfectly into Cartier-Bresson's hand. It was no bigger than that. It had no telemeter to measure distances, and no cell to gauge the light. Its viewfinder was rectangular, creating proportions that were ideal for his pursuit of a concept that had always been of paramount importance: the golden section. The single 50 mm lens with a 3.5 mm aperture could not be unscrewed. In any case, Cartier-Bresson would not have wanted another, because this one was ideal for capturing his vision of humanity, whereas a longer or wider lens would have distorted it. With this camera and this lens, he felt that he had found perfect harmony – the only natural way to reconcile the verticality of man and the horizontality of the world. This was drawing with a different technique.

The Leica was to become his travelling companion, like an artist's sketch-book – an indispensable notebook without which the images would have remained buried in unreliable memory. From the very start, Cartier-Bresson considered his Leica less as a piece of apparatus that could record beautiful images than as a Geiger counter to register the secrets beneath the surface of life. It gave him the feeling that he was never disturbing the natural order of things, for it always picked out the silent moments. It was the ideal instrument for surprising life *in flagrante delicto*, anticipating a scene and then recording it for ever in a snapshot. Later, when he looked at the work of others, he would himself move into reportage. For the time being, however, he did not think of telling stories but only of snapping individual moments, though he knew that the Leica, a breaker of barriers, could do just about anything. 'It can be like a passionate kiss,' he said, 'but also like a gunshot or a psychoanalyst's couch.'

Henri Cartier-Bresson enriched a club that already embraced other Leica experts: Ilse Bing was using it for her reports in *Das illustrierte Blatt*; André Kertész, Lucien Aigner and others were attracted by its flexibility, even though some magazines were not so enamoured of it because the reduced format of the negative made touching up more difficult. Its rapid rise to success was linked to two other factors: the establishment of professional laboratories and the development of the illustrated press.

Photojournalism was not born at that moment – it in fact went back to the mid-nineteenth century, when Queen Victoria authorized Roger Fenton to pho-tograph the Crimean War. He and Matthew Brady were not content merely to report on one event, but told a complete story through a series of photographs. Initially these were given long captions, but subsequently they were accom-panied by an article so substantial that there was no longer any question of which complemented the other. The First World War, however, gave the medium a massive boost. The abundance of new illustrated journals brought it to new heights. At the end of the 1920s Paris witnessed the birth of the weekly *Match*, conceived as the sporting version of *L'Intransigeant*, and simultaneously the creation of the Dephot Agency, the first to provide complete photographic records to the press.

In ridding themselves of static encumbrances, photographers had given themselves freedom. And if some of their colleagues – conservative to the point of archaism – looked down on this new apparatus as a mere toy, that was their loss. Even in the specialized field of fashion photography, the new development found an immediate echo at the beginning of the 1930s in the permanent war between *Vogue* and *Harper's Bazaar*. Although *Vogue* prided itself on publishing the first cover in colour, thanks to the talents of Edward Steichen and various technicians, the demand for utter clarity that was imposed by its owner Condé Nast meant using a heavy, restrictive 20 x 25 chamber. At the same time, its rival produced more ethereal covers with its famous 'portable cameras'.

Not everyone used a Leica – far from it. As well as the devotees of the Rolleiflex, there were those who swore by the Ermanox, a small, light camera that was able to take interior shots without a flash. The German Erich Salomon was a virtuoso on the Ermanox, and even managed to use it secretly during a trial; his candid camera shots offered readers a variety of angles, atmospheres and expressions which soon became his trademark, most notably during major international conferences.

In France, one particularly enterprising gentleman followed the same trend by founding *Vu* ('Seen') in 1928 – a magazine whose title made its intentions obvious. Lucien Vogel was not an inventor, but he showed that even by reinventing something one can evince great talent, if not genius. His publication was a French version of the German style of photojournalism that was particularly successful in the *Berliner illustrierte Zeitung*. It was Vogel who pioneered the use of the photograph as an autonomous means of information as opposed to being merely an illustration to complement an article.

Lucien Vogel, a failed architect originally from Alsace, rapidly became a force to be reckoned with. He was a charismatic figure, a giant with the elegance of an English dandy and a face that was permanently flushed. He was obsessed with current affairs – political, social, legal – and he covered the major events in all the different fields. By nature more of an experienced press baron than a reporter, he nevertheless attached great importance to form, and even if short-term profit was probably the main objective of the Swiss bankers who backed him, it was not his, or at least not his only one. Before discovering his vocation as managing director at the age of 42, Vogel had been the brilliant artistic director of several fashion and design magazines, among them *Vogue* and *Jardin des Modes*, and he had regularly commissioned work from the most avant-garde photographers and designers of the period. Since he also ran *Arts et Métiers graphiques*, it is clear that he was devoted to the intensive and effective use of photography. *Vu* took on a style that distinguished it even from the predecessors that had inspired it. Typography, layout, choice of material, informative nature of the illustrations, variety of photographs – everything combined to make this magazine special.

It is scarcely surprising, then, that Henri Cartier-Bresson was immediately seduced by *Vu*, the most modern, most original and most left-wing current affairs weekly on the market. He had numerous links and affinities with its founder. Vogel's father was the painter Hermann Vogel, his daughter Marie-Claude was married to the journalist and politically active communist Paul Vaillant-Couturier, his artistic director Alexandre Libermann was a former student at the Lhote Academy, and his chief editor Louis Martin-Chauffier was a friend of Henri's mother.

If Vogel had had to specify his profession in his passport, he would probably have written 'café-crème drinker'. He was a permanent fixture at the Café du Dôme, an elegant place made all the more Germanic by the company he kept. There was a billiard table at the back, a noticeboard that served as a *poste restante*, a large stove that heated the terrace in winter, a continual hubbub punctuated by orders given to the waiters, the Babel-like chatter of a thousand and one different conversations, people drawing or writing at or on the tables – this was the world of the 'Dômians'. It was like a railway platform heaving with people who never bothered to catch any of the trains.

Cartier-Bresson preferred the Dôme to the Select, which opened at night but was too select for his liking, or the Rotonde, famous especially for its foreign newspapers; la Coupole he simply didn't like. He was one of those Montparnasse natives for whom café culture had been invented. There were those you went to, and those you didn't go to, and whichever you chose entailed entering a particular society. The Lhote studio was just a few doors away, there were bookshops all around, and the jazzy Rosebud, a bar-restaurant of almost mythical status, was just behind.

During the 1930s, even more than at the beginning of the century, this meeting-place was a refuge of intellectual and artistic bohemia. It was so cosmopolitan that sometimes only the waiters could be heard speaking the local dialect. It was a melting pot of cultures and sensibilities, 'a kind of Vatican of the Imagination where sirens whistled'.

For Cartier-Bresson and most of his friends these cafés functioned as an office, social centre and second home. Some even considered them to be their first home. The Dôme, at the corner of the boulevards Raspail and Montparnasse, was where he met writers, poets and painters, where works of art circulated that would one day adorn the walls of great museums, where poems were read that would be quoted by generations of scholars. Here, too, the first refugees from Nazi Germany warned of the barbarism that would threaten all democracies if they did not take action against it. It was here that the last heated exchanges between Jacques-Emile Blanche and André Lhote were chronicled as they settled accounts; here people had the illusion that they were taking the pulse of Parisian intellectual life.

Some of the regulars remained friends. One of them in particular stood out because of his personality and the subtle influence he had for many years over Cartier-Bresson – not the photographer but the painter and draughtsman behind the photographer. This man was, quite simply, Henri Cartier-Bresson's mentor.

Efstratios Eleftheriades, known as Tériade, was of average height, with a slight Greek accent, always immaculately dressed, well informed, fascinated by the world of *haute couture*, naturally drawn to the avant-garde, a reticent, temperate person. He was 11 years older than Cartier-Bresson, but his influence had nothing to do with the generation gap. He came from the Francophile middle class of Mytilene, and his father – who ran a soap factory – had allowed him to come to Paris on condition that he studied law, even though he himself had no doubt that he would never finish his studies. Just like Cartier-Bresson, he had no intention of entering the family business. He too was obsessed with art, and had tried his hand at painting but had had the good sense to move on to something else. He never turned his back on art, but simply chose to comment on it rather than practise it. It must be said that he was one of the few people able to talk well about art, with measured good taste, for his analytical abilities rested on a strong cultural basis. He regarded his constant visits to the Louvre as an indispensable means of honing his critical faculty, and they gave him a taste for the classical spirit that is supposed to be typically French.

Tériade was an amateur in the noblest sense of the term – a 'lover' of art who had a unique gift for evoking the 'skin of the painting', with a poet's ability to find the right words to make visible the invisible. Cartier-Bresson admired the mixture of sharpness, subtlety, fervour, vivacity and flair.

For four years Tériade had been writing reviews in the arts section of *L'Intransigeant*, which he co-authored with Maurice Raynal under the ironic pseudonym 'The Two Blind Men'. After collaborating on the *Cahiers d'Art*, run by his exiled fellow-countryman Christian Zervos, he was appointed artistic director of *Minotaure* by its publisher Albert Skira. Such a strong personality, however, gifted with so clear and trenchant a vision of what art should be, could never truly express itself until he had his own magazine.

No matter what the subject, Tériade always seemed to have given it a great deal of thought before voicing his opinion. And so Cartier-Bresson listened attentively when his new friend announced that he should take the subject of money seriously, because people would only take his photographs seriously if they made money. Cartier-Bresson listened, understood, and followed his advice. The two of them were on the same wavelength, as was confirmed when by chance he happened to read one of Tériade's first articles in the *Cahiers d'Art*, reviewing an exhibition by the students of André Lhote. The last lines of this were music to his ears, and resolved any lingering doubts that he might have had: 'And if, as he says himself, he helps each of them to find themselves, we shall believe that he is a man beloved of his pupils. As most of them are young and gifted, we invite them to be disobedient.'

Disobeying others in order to obey oneself – that was the message Cartier-Bresson heard from all around and absorbed from all that he had read up to now. In that year, 1932, his friend René Crevel's *Le Clavecin de Diderot* ('Diderot's Harpsichord') was published by Editions Surréalistes, a series of satires both incisive and excessive – but the excess was Baudelairian – and this had a lasting impact on Cartier-Bresson. Nothing escaped the whiplash of Crevel's pen – no lie, no institution. He was as unfair as the society that he was attacking, but the attack was fluent, well-meaning if somewhat chaotic. According to Diderot, being a harpsichord meant responding correctly to the correct melodies. Crevel never ceased to listen to his own music, which meant that he was intoxicated with himself – this might have been surrealist, but was certainly suicidal.

Neither the African adventure nor the revelation of geometry nor the discovery of the Leica had drawn Cartier-Bresson away from surrealism. This did not prevent him from exploring elsewhere, especially when he came into contact with exceptional characters. Max Jacob was a poet, a bald little man with big lively eyes, who divided his life between his devotions, his work, and the world. A dazzling conversationalist, raconteur and mimic, he painted 'gouacheries' in order to live, did drawings in order to keep living, regarded pain as the health of the soul, and knew from experience that genius was a matter of unending patience. An irresistible charmer, he seemed to have all the talents, including that for giving. In the Dôme people said 'Max' as if there had only ever been one Max. In 1932, however, he was feeling alone, exploited and persecuted. To help him, two young men from his immediate circle, Christian Dior and Pierre Colle, hung some of his works in their gallery on the rue Cambacérès.

It was at Max Jacob's – where he would go on the slightest pretext – that Cartier-Bresson met Pierre Colle. The two of them became firm friends, and one day Henri asked Pierre to take him to see his mother. Mme Colle was reputed to have a 'gift': she could see what other people, including poets, could not. Cartier-Bresson wanted to know the future, but not merely out of 'hatred of memory' as Breton suggested. Even though the path of his life seemed predestined, there was a secret thrill, an irrepressible urge to know the unknown in advance without necessarily submitting to fate – a deep-down desire to live in anticipation.

The character of the clairvoyant has a special place in surrealist mythology. Cartier-Bresson had been as impressed by the accounts of Crevel, the insider, as by the memory of Mme Sacco, one of the characters portrayed in *Nadja*. Mme Sacco had needed just the date and place of birth and a few words from the lips of the client. Mme Colle, however, used tarot cards. She spread them out on the table. What did they tell her about Cartier-Bresson? Things that she could not have made up.

'I would like to go to sea, and to go to the Orient....'

'No, no, maybe later... before that someone close to you is soon going to die, which will cause you enormous grief... you will marry a woman from the East, not someone from China or the Indies, but not white either, and it will be a difficult marriage... you will make a name for yourself in your profession... you will remarry – someone much younger... then you will become a father.'

Before he left, she spoke to him about death – his own. He had wanted to know everything, and now he knew.

More often than not, Cartier-Bresson went out – especially at night, the best time for true conversation. With his friends, the surrealists and others, he was to be seen in Montparnasse, of course, listening to Kiki singing *Les Filles de Camaret* at the Jockey, or Fanny Cotton 'Chez Frisco', or getting carried away by the jazz at the Dingo, the American bar on the rue Delambre. He frequented the West Indian dance-hall on the rue Blomet, the Tempo, Boudon's and other nightclubs on the Pigalle, where black musicians from all over town would hold a jam session before going to bed in the early hours. All this was not mere entertainment (that would have been far too bourgeois) or deliberately slumming it (just as bourgeois), but a matter of 'researching violent emotion and breaking with the disciplines of everyday life as we know and can barely endure it – a certain dazzle and a certain heartbreak', as his childhood friend André

Pieyre de Mandiargues put it, accompanying him on his wanderings through Paris. If anyone asked what they did for a living, they would shrug their shoulders. The very prospect of a career appalled them. Together they toured not only the provincial brothels (following the example of Aragon) but the cafés and bars, discovering humanity wherever it was in action.

At the age of 24, Henri Cartier-Bresson was already in search of paradise lost. Once he found that entry was barred, he felt the urgent need to explore the world – just to find out whether there might not be some other means of access.

On the Boulevard Saint-Germain, in an apartment above a toyshop called 'A la joie pour tous', lived André Pieyre de Mandiargues and Léonor Fini, a young and clever girl, a painter, from Trieste, whom Cartier-Bresson had introduced to André. From there they set out in a second-hand Buick, in 1932 and again in 1933, to explore the Old World. There were three of them, sometimes two, sometimes just one on these voyages of discovery.

From Belgium they went to Germany, Poland, Czechoslovakia, Austria, Hungary, Romania, then on to Spain and Italy; France too. There was even a brief and tentative excursion into African territory, to Asilah in Spanish Morocco. There is nothing like this kind of trip to reveal people's true nature. Mandiargues had already experienced Cartier-Bresson's authoritarian side, and knew that he could be tyrannical. Their journey across Europe sometimes turned very sour indeed. It was not uncommon for Henri suddenly to instruct André to turn round and drive back some 50 kilometres simply because he thought he'd seen something that might possibly be worth photographing. His manner was imperious, as if he were himself obeying some urgent command, and he would not brook even the slightest delay.

More often than not, however, their differences were intellectual. The poet found the photographer far too narrow-minded, whereas the photographer found the poet too tolerant. They clashed over and over again on details, not for political but for artistic reasons. They bathed in the streams of Italy, all three of them often stark naked, but in Italy they also quarrelled. Henri and André both loved Florence, but they could not agree on Venice. André fell in love with it at first sight, whereas Henri announced straight away that it made him feel sick. And he said so loud and clear, regardless of his friend's feelings. He would not listen to any argument, any invocation of surrealism or anything else. Nothing could assuage his destructive fury. The iconoclast in him did not hesitate to describe the ceiling of the Sistine Chapel in Rome as a prophetic strip announcing the end of the world. His next offence was to proclaim his aversion to Caravaggio and Tintoretto, to the disgust of Léonor, who had had enough of such nonsense. Henri in fact took malicious pleasure in criticizing Venetian artists simply in order to irritate the young lady from Trieste.

'Henri found in it nothing but what he called ignoble,' recalled André. 'The Renaissance with its baroque connections was ignoble, the theatrical setting was ignoble, the glowing colours and their reflections in the water were ignoble.'

But when provoked, he too could be wicked. To shut Henri up he would seize the Leica and threaten to throw it into the Grand Canal. Then it would be Henri who would see red. They would separate, come together again, and make up. But all the same, a kind of distrust had developed between them, and it would take a long time to repair their friendship.

The photographs that Cartier-Bresson took during those years were among his freest – without commissions and critical scrutiny he was free from all constraint. They were the work of a carefree wanderer of whom nothing was expected and who demanded nothing himself. This detachment from normal restraints allowed his little camera to delve into the depths, the lowest regions of the subconscious mind. It was as if he was stubbornly seeking to express what the conscious mind had not yet organized – which basically is the definition of surrealism itself. He really did not see himself as a photojournalist, for he was still too much under the spell of Baudelaire and the sentiments of *Mon coeur mis à nu* ('My heart laid bare'), in which the poet denounces the tissue of horrors and crimes that the reader digests over breakfast every morning: 'I cannot understand how a pure hand can touch a newspaper without a shudder of disgust.'

It is no longer possible to reconstruct the various sequences of photographs, because Cartier-Bresson destroyed or cut up many of the negatives, and so only an incomplete record of that time can be reconstructed: we may recognize one image, but have no idea what preceded or followed it. The Cartier-Bresson spirit, however, shines through, without the need of a chronological reconstruction. All his sense and sensitivity were already firmly fixed behind his viewfinder.

His lucky streak shows triumphantly in one of his earliest masterpieces – a snapshot of a man jumping over a puddle, when he had placed his lens at a gap in a fence behind the Gare St-Lazare (which Caillebotte and Monet found so attractive to paint). If the graphic perfection of this image is due essentially to the sharpness of his eye, and if the remarkable rhythm, the richness of detail, the interplay of reflections and the alchemy of lines and curves are all owed to his instinct, how can we explain the little poster in the background, in which a female dancer seems to be mocking the jumper as he leaps over the water? Perhaps it can be attributed to unfathomable luck, which he was the first to allude to when he grew tired of looking for explanations.

The anti-traveller in him was already evident from his refusal to even talk in such terms, for he did not travel – he moved about, slowly if possible, for he was one of those people who take the time to spend their time. Time itself was of no importance. Cartier-Bresson would arrive, settle himself down, and make himself forget. A state of grace, of receptiveness, is attainable only by those who do not seek it. Cartier-Bresson was always on the lookout for surprises, but never expected them. He had an appointment with chance, and that could not be fixed in advance. He remained open to whatever might come, in the perfect state to encourage the most amazing experiences. It may seem a senseless challenge to try to stop life, to conquer time, for pressing a button can never achieve that, but sometimes it can achieve the impact of a thunderbolt.

It is obvious that such an approach to the world does not lend itself easily to companionship, even that of a dear friend. It seemed that nothing could satisfy his visual appetite. While he was in Spain he took photo after photo, totally preoccupied with seizing the essentials of a scene within a single image. A lover of liberty, the artist in him reacted to the challenges of reality by allowing the senses to roam free – his only rule. There was no concern with narrative, and even less with aesthetics. He was not indifferent to beauty, as long as it was not governed by academic precepts. Beauty was discernible in the mysterious expression, like that of a hunted wolf, on the face of the unemployed man in Madrid who is unable to stretch out his hand in order to feed the child nestling in his arms; in this indescribable misery the photographer can discover the picturesque nature of man that René Crevel spoke of. Beauty is sensed in the fantasy of the games played by the prematurely aged children of Andalusia, or in the urchins of Seville as their *joie de vivre* lights up a world of rubble and desolation. According to Henri Cartier-Bresson, beauty is as much in comedy as in tragedy, because life is made up of both.

This approach is not a method or a technique, but a way of life, improvising as you go. He spent his days walking, sniffing the air and watching like a hawk. This active spontaneity was in many ways a game. Why, for instance, did he go to Alicante and not somewhere else? Because in his pocket he had a third-class railway ticket for 300 pesetas to cover 300 kilometres, and the train happened to go via Alicante. There was no plan – he just went where chance and his money took him, slept in the cheapest hotels, ate frugally, but extracted the maximum from life's great spectacle.

Any photographer worth his salt is a kind of thief, for no matter what angle you consider it from, any photograph is a kind of theft. You must shoot without thinking, because the unforeseen will never present itself again. From the exposure of his very first films, Cartier-Bresson was immediately aware that he was committing an act of violence as soon as he incorporated human beings and not just nature or the inanimate world of objects. What would a passer-by think if the photographer pointed his Leica at him? You could be as discreet, as rapid and as charming as you liked, but this aggressive Cyclops eye would strip the subject naked in his most intimate moments.

Walking along the avenue du Maine, Cartier-Bresson happened to look through the window of an otherwise empty restaurant, and caught sight of an old man lost in thought, wrapped in his coat, with bowler hat and umbrella, sitting on his chair as if all alone in the world, gazing blankly at nothing in particular. Seizing this astonishing moment of truth, Cartier-Bresson took it upon himself to capture the man's melancholic, nostalgic daydreaming, the dark part of the spirit that is deemed inalienable. What right did he have to steal it?

His ability to be invisible now came into play. Obsessed by the image, he was also gripped by the idea of disappearing, which in some sense is just another way of appearing. Many photographers seize the slightest opportunity to indulge in the ritual of self-portraiture, but Cartier-Bresson allowed himself to do so only once. This historic incident took place in Italy. On a country roadside he stretched out on a parapet, took off his shoes, and lying flat on his back proceeded to photograph the rest of his body, with his right foot standing out against a background of trees and foliage. 'Take the route of my foot,' the blacks had told him before they went into the African forest. Perhaps this was the image he wanted to retain of himself. There is something delightfully impudent and innocently mischievous about the photograph of a toe. When he thumbed, or rather 'toed' his nose at society in this way, Cartier-Bresson was 24 years old, and this triumphant self-portrait was the first and the last. There could have been no truer reflection of his spirit.

The geometrician was evident from the first photographs that he took in

Marseilles in 1932, most notably in the lanky bourgeois figure in cape and bowler hat, striking because of the mysterious aura surrounding him; he stands, quietly majestic, at the very centre of the perfect perspective formed by two lines of bare trees whose vanishing point falls exactly at the end of the avenue du Prado.

The surrealist in him gave free rein to a kind of visual automatic writing. His urban fantasy was worthy of the best pages in *Nadja*. Sometimes it was objects held in affection by his friends at the Café de la Dame Blanche that presented themselves to his lens. Thus he photographed Léonor Fini – a woman passionate about the theatricality of life, hostile to the frozen moment of the snapshot, willing to take off her clothes because nothing is more revealing than such a pose – when she was playing in the street with tailor's dummies. Such dummies, made of wax or wood or wicker, are often to be seen in De Chirico's paintings, as well as in Breton's arsenal of symbols, and before these, in some of Atget's snapshots. These artists' decapitated mannequins, like their animal skins and their wrapped objects, demonstrate the eye's ability to make something extraordinary out of the ordinary, to exalt the strangeness inherent in the banal.

When it was not objects, it was allegories that stimulated Cartier-Bresson's surrealist streak: reflections of the busy port and the swarming crowds in the window of a sunlit Marseilles bistro; the painted mask of a solitary man resolutely turning his eyes away from a bad colour print; evoking the joys of married life in the corner of a window in Budapest; everywhere people asleep, and always this slightly unreal slant that enables one single element to lift a scene into the realms of the irrational.

The settings themselves could also bring this about. Spain, where he took some photos that would eventually become icons, is in itself surrealist. Its rich character singled it out as the chosen land for Breton and his disciples. Spanish has two words for 'to be', and for them Spain was torn apart between permanent being, *ser*, and being of the moment, *estar*, between the private personality and its representation, between its poetry and its prose. Nature, climate, traditions – everything seemed to be fascinatingly excessive, above all the Spanish preoccupation with death. These excesses are evident in the photographs that Cartier-Bresson brought back – of the ecstatic prostitutes and transvestites of Alicante, the poverty in Madrid etched into the ascetic dignity of the workers' faces, the sheer joy of the child playing in Valencia, whose exuberance enchants and disturbs us at the same time.

Another place beloved of the surrealists and found everywhere is the slaughterhouse. A few years before Cartier-Bresson, the Romanian photographer Eli Lotar had gone to the abattoirs in Vaugirard and la Villette together with the painter André Masson, where he saw the slaughtermen as sacrificing priests. From this encounter he had brought back images of a cruel beauty that were later published in *Bifur* and *Documents*.

In just a short time, Cartier-Bresson had gone from the Lhote Academy into the wide world, from the studio out into the streets, and his principles had not changed. But for all that, and for all his wanderings through Europe in the early 1930s, he was not a surrealist photographer. At most he was a young man drawn into the magnetic field of surrealism, with no better tool than a little Leica, a 50 mm lens, and Perutz or Agfa films, hunting and capturing the strange and disturbing realities of human fantasy. This very special style marks all his early work, with a photographic syntax and sign language entirely his own: a brilliant eye disciplined by the spirit of geometry, an instinct tempered by a taste for composition, poetry suffused with prose.

Back to Paris, to Montparnasse, to the Dôme: France looks different when you have been all round Europe. Cartier-Bresson returned yet again to friends old and new – the poet Charles Henry Ford, whom he had met through another American, the writer Claude McKay, during a stay in Tangier, and two emigrants from the East who were to become very important for him, in both human and professional terms.

He met the first of these two quite by chance on a bus. He was small, with receding hair and eyes hidden behind thick glasses, but with a liveliness of mind that was immediately apparent, and with the head of a chess-playing maths professor. He was studying the Leica that Cartier-Bresson held lovingly in his hand, and he ventured the sort of bold question that could only be put by a stranger to a stranger: 'What sort of camera is that?'

It was the beginning of a lifelong friendship. David Szymin was not only three years younger than Cartier-Bresson and physically his exact opposite, but he was also from a totally different background, in origin, upbringing and education. Perhaps it was simply the attraction of opposites. 'Chim', as everyone called him, was the son of a publisher who specialized in Yiddish and Hebrew books. Serious, thorough, determined, he had left Warsaw at an early age for Leipzig and then Paris in order to study the technical disciplines – from typography to lithography, including the graphic arts – that would one day enable him to take over the firm. Because of the economic crisis he had had to break off his studies and was now earning a living as a photojournalist for a small agency. He had had his work published in several magazines, notably *Vu*.

Where does the money come from? This was the question that had haunted Cartier-Bresson since his youth, and it was just as valid now, since his own private income was no longer adequate. It would not be unpleasant to live on photography, so long as this did not compromise his liberty.

He had nothing but praise for Chim's analytical mind, his psychological insight, his culture, his perspicacity, and especially his sensitivity. He was a mixture of worrier and mischief-maker, with a melancholic streak. You could not help noticing him, whether through his appearance (he loved to show off his black silk ties) or his conversation, which ranged with equal ease through the political situation in the Balkans, a knowledge of wine, or gastronomy. His career set something of an example, and so when Lucien Vogel, the proprietor of *Vu*, suggested that Cartier-Bresson too should work on current affairs, he did not hesitate to accept. He was to go, not to Germany, now under the heel of the new Chancellor Hitler, but to Spain, which he already knew. It would not be the cultural Spain, where the première of García Lorca's *Blood Wedding* had just taken place, but the political Spain of the parliamentary elections, two years after the establishment of the Republic. About ten of his photographs were published in 1933, in three successive issues, tackling political and social themes in accordance with the magazine's policy. This reportage, which did not even appear under his name, was a starting-point; it did not in any way force him to go against his own nature or predilections. It was the first commission for a man who had always refused to take orders: an unforgettable moment.

It was on the terrace of the Dôme that he met his second Central European emigrant. Pierre Gassmann was a German Jew who had left for Paris at seven o'clock one May morning in 1933, and who was constantly astounded to find that the France of René Clair which he had loved so much in *Sous les toits de Paris* and *Le Million* really existed, and was not a figment of the cinematic imagination. A penniless refugee, slightly younger than Cartier-Bresson, he said he knew no French 'more or less'. What struck him was that Henri seemed almost proud of the fact that, like all their friends, he was broke. Indeed, Henri was like the rest, except in one particular aspect: he was born French, and he would always be a Frenchman. In the photographic Dôme clan, he was pretty much unique, and even if he tried to hide behind his initials, people always managed to decode the powerful French family from the letters HCB.

Gassmann was torn between drawing, painting and the cinema. Like Chim he was small, stocky, lively, nervous, and passionate about photography – but more in the context of the laboratory than in taking pictures. At the time, Cartier-Bresson was developing his own photographs, unless the magazines did it themselves, and he had set up a makeshift laboratory under the shower in the bathroom of his studio on the rue Danielle-Casanova. He made no secret of the fact that he did this work from necessity and not from choice. He would never be interested in it. Time spent under the light of the enlarger meant less time spent in the light of the street. The darkroom really was not his world; he knew nothing about its chemistry, and he didn't want to know.

Gassmann, on the other hand, had absorbed it from childhood. His mother had been a radiologist in Berlin, and he himself had learnt very early on to develop negatives. When he saw the makeshift darkroom of his new French friend, he was appalled – not so much by the do-it-yourself nature of the installations, but by their sheer technical inadequacy. Sometimes the water from the shower was too hot, sometimes too cold, which can affect the development of a film. Even the paper that Cartier-Bresson was using for his prints was unsuitable – a 'special contrast' by Krumière, reputed to be the hardest in Europe. 'That's what the ironmonger gave me,' was the only explanation offered.

Gassmann immediately took everything in hand, and developed his friend's photographs in the basement of the hotel on the rue Jean-Jacques-Rousseau where he had been living since his arrival from Germany. This cellar turned into the antechamber of Pictorial Service, which in due course was to become the top laboratory for professional photographers.

From then on, all Cartier-Bresson's negatives and prints passed through the hands of Pierre Gassmann. The laboratory was of vital importance, and even if he was not interested in the technology he still kept an eye on it. Right from the start, he had certain inalienable principles which had to be respected, one of them being a ban – with very rare exceptions – on any cropping when enlarging a photograph. Nothing must be touched. The whole impact of a snapshot lay in its spontaneity, even if there were defects. Therefore any rearranging would not only indicate that he had got it wrong, but would also expose the emotions behind the image. There was to be no trickery. He was even more inflexible when it came to the quality of his prints, for he was aiming in two different directions: at the journals publishing his work, and at the galleries exhibiting it – a double outlet that was rare, particularly for someone so young.

He had been working for scarcely a year, but this in no way held him back from displaying his wares. In 1933 Julien Levy, whom he had got to know at the

Crosbys' mill, offered to show his work at a September exhibition in the New York gallery he had opened two years earlier on Madison Avenue, at the top of 57th Street. There could hardly be a more exciting setting for the Parisian avant-garde than in the heart of Manhattan – a collection of surrealist, European photography, though it was not an exclusive show. Levy combined Cartier-Bresson with Marcel Duchamp and Alfred Stieglitz, whose names were already legendary. He included in the catalogue a manifesto of his own, written under the pseudonym of Peter Lloyd. Perhaps it was written in order to forestall criticism, in which case his fears were well founded, since the verdict overall was mediocre, and Cartier-Bresson in particular was dismissed as pretentious, while his prints were considered defective. Seen as iconoclastic by the purists, he found himself out of kilter with the spirit of the age. His cult of the snapshot did not chime with the prevalent taste for the polished, sophisticated image, carefully staged and artistic. Levy-Lloyd's text was in fact rather surprising, not in its invocations of the art of Charlie Chaplin, but in the thesis that Cartier-Bresson was the finest representative of a trend that he called 'anti-graphic photography'. He seemed to feel that form and content were separable, that form was not content when it came to the surface, and that the natural union of the two was not the supreme harmony that Cartier-Bresson was searching for. Of course a gallery-owner cannot be expected to have the judgment of an expert or the discernment of an art historian. Apart from the laws of the marketplace, he is subject only to the demands of his own likes and dislikes, and these are purely a matter of taste. But the point of view communicated by his text seems all the more mysterious in that, unlike many of its kind, it sought to cast permanent doubt on the value of composition – so vital for Henri Cartier-Bresson himself.

Montparnasse was light years away from the Place de la Concorde, and the echoes of the bloody riots of 6 February 1934 were muffled there. At the Café du Dôme, there was talk only of Africa: of the new Black African room in the Trocadéro Museum, and of the issue of the *Minotaure* that had been devoted to it; of *L'Afrique fantôme*, an account of the ethnographical mission to Dakar and Djibouti that Michel Leiris had just published with Gallimard. But Henri, the Africa-lover, had already gone elsewhere: to Central America, to Mexico – surrealist territory, a country of fantasy.

This was his first major journey as an official photographer. Spain had been only a stepping-stone. He went to Mexico not as a traveller, and certainly not as a tourist, but as a type of pilgrim. He was part of a French geographical expedition organized by the Trocadéro Museum of Ethnography in the context of the construction of the great Pan-American highway. When the liner *San Francisco* made a stopover in Havana, the smiling members of the expedition posed on the bridge for the benefit of the Cuban press. In addition to Cartier-Bresson, this group photograph figured Alvarez de Toledo, Bernard de Colmont, the painter Antonio Salazar, someone called Tacverian, and Julio Brandan, a former diplomat and Argentine lawyer who had become an anthropologist; the Mexican government had commissioned him to do a study of the Indians, since their way of life was certain to be radically altered by the construction of the highway. Missing from the photograph was the seventh man, who would be joining them in a few days: the Cuban writer Alejo Carpentier, Paris correspondent for the magazine *Carteles*. In the meantime, Cartier-Bresson wandered round the town and managed to take one of those surrealistic snapshots so typical of this period of his life: wooden horses escaping from a merry-go-round in a vague, end-of-the-world terrain against a background of flaking walls.

Henri would sit in various cafés, reading and rereading letters from his father. The latter, always pragmatic by nature, encouraged him to pursue his chosen career, but with one proviso: he should undergo some formal technical training, which M. Cartier-Bresson considered to be the only way he could make real progress. This advice came not just from the head of a major enterprise, steeped in Cartesian logic, but from a father who was not sure that he could go on indefinitely financing his son's future. He was eager to see Henri succeed by swiftly making a name for himself, and he wanted to cast aside all doubts, in spite of misgivings caused by certain letters that he had forwarded to Henri. One of these, dated 28 June 1934, was from the *Arts et Métiers graphiques* and was written by Charles Peignot:

> I have received some interesting photos from you for my next book, but it seems to me that you could certainly have done better, and in any case the photographic quality is hopeless, if you'll forgive me for saying so. Since you took the decision several years ago, on my advice, to launch yourself into photography, I owe it to you to say what I think. Your compositions are never without significance, you always have an idea, but the photographic substance is not good. Some time I will show you documents that I have from elsewhere, and you will be astonished to see how quality of composition is combined with technical quality.

The expedition was to travel overland from Mexico to Buenos Aires, going through Guatemala, Honduras, Nicaragua, Costa Rica, Panama, Colombia, Brazil, Bolivia and Paraguay. Cartier-Bresson had an agreement with the *New York Times* that he would offer them any photographs that were not used.

Several years before Antonin Artaud (actor and theorist of the Theatre of Cruelty), André Breton and the surrealist poet Benjamin Péret successively set foot on Mexican soil, Cartier-Bresson had already wandered through a country that was one of the favourite territories of surrealism. But as soon as he disembarked at Veracruz, Mexico's biggest seaport, he was brought back to earth. The head of the expedition, who was older, more experienced, and certainly more cunning, disappeared silently one morning, taking with him all the group's funds, having first got the photographer to sign a blank cheque and then emptied his account. Overnight, Cartier-Bresson found himself thousands of miles from Paris without a penny to his name. His father was not best pleased, though he was willing to help, but his offer was declined with the pride appropriate to someone used to coping with such situations. He had nothing left besides his personal effects, his Leica, a few rolls of film, an IOU for $1200, and a mixture of uncertainty and determination about his short-term future. He had plenty of time to contemplate Mme Colle's first prediction, and her words reverberated in his memory as if she had just spoken them: 'You will go to the other side of the world, you will be robbed, but it simply won't matter to you.'

Originally the expedition was to have been financed by the Mexican government, which was concerned first and foremost with the route of the Pan-American highway. But now there was great scepticism, especially as the country was in a state of transition. Lázaro Cárdenas had succeeded Abelardo Rodriguez as president of the Republic, and the mood had now swung in favour of popular reforms; ministers had different economic and social priorities. As for the ethnographical material that the Trocadéro Museum expected in return for the money it had advanced, that was now more or less out of the question. The whole project ended before it had begun, and the various members went their separate ways, the majority going home in a state of shock and despair. But not Henri Cartier-Bresson. The clairvoyant had been right: it didn't matter. The fascinating otherness of the places he saw quickly blotted out his misfortune; indeed, it was love at first sight for a country that comprised several countries, since it was home to at least 53 different ethnic groups with their own languages and beliefs.

Hearing the sounds of Veracruz made him feel like an adopted Mexican, and he decided to stay there indefinitely. He would live on his photographs. But he would not emulate the American Edward Watson, who had opened a portrait studio in Mexico some ten years earlier; Cartier-Bresson would do things his own way. He wanted to earn his living like a native, and once more fell into the illusion of integration in a strange environment. The fact that he didn't even speak the language was a trump card. When you don't understand what people are saying, it sharpens your vision. Anyone who is beyond the reach of words will focus better on the visual. This was the philosophy of a man who would never escape the influence of the silent cinema that had enchanted him in his youth. Having once been an African hunter, he would now become a Mexican photographer.

The habitué of the Dôme took over again, following his instincts, moving from one pavement café to another, rapidly making contact with all the eminent artistic and literary expatriates. One of them, six years his senior, invited Cartier-Bresson to live with him, somewhere among the prostitutes and funeral parlours. Langston Hughes was a left-wing poet, novelist and playwright, who not only helped to bring about the renaissance of Harlem, but was one of the first black Americans to earn a living from his writing – not a good living, but a living all the same. He was bilingual (the Castilian edition of *Don Quixote* was his bedtime reading), and translated Mexican poems and short stories into English in order to find a market for them in the USA. Early in his career he was regarded as the leading light of a sort of Pan-African romanticism, and he certainly had some strange stories to tell. He said that he could feel the jungle drums beating in his blood. For some years now, he had turned to writing proletarian poetry celebrating the radical, left-wing black. But everyone who was privileged to know him was well aware that deep in his heart he was a thoroughly jazzed-up American who used language like a musical score.

Hughes was already sharing his house with Andrés Henestrosa – a native Mexican, a poet, hard at work on the first dictionary of his own Indian dialect – and the painter Ignacio Aguirre, known as Nacho. They lived in one of the most notorious districts of the capital, la Candelaría de los Patos. Prostitutes, pimps, thieves and gangsters congregated there in such numbers that the police never ventured into the area. There could scarcely have been a more sordid place than this rancid underworld. It was here that, three years previously, Sergei Eisenstein's producer had suddenly withdrawn his funding and so stopped him filming *Que Viva Mexico!* – his masterpiece on the country's history and civilization.

The danger, the overcrowding, the lack of money – none of these mattered; the days and nights in this louche quarter remained etched in his memory as a time of rare happiness. An important factor in this happiness was Guadalupe Cervantes, his barefoot fiancée from Juchitan, who sold fried corn patties in the market. 'Lupe Cartier', as she became known, spoke only Zapotec, and in her own language she found an apt and popular name for Cartier-Bresson: 'the little white man with the cheeks of a shrimp'.

He spent his days, Leica in hand, on the lookout for humanity in all its strangest manifestations, in the Merced market or at the Cuadrante de la Soledad. The expressions that he captured showed deep solitude, the disenchantment of the deprived, the apathy of people resigned to inescapable poverty. When he tore himself away from these haunting expressions, revealed in the little makeshift laboratory he had installed in his room, it was only to go out into the streets again to see the same sights. His mind was filled with people and objects, forms and emotions, the Mexican pathos that never left him in peace, though it was not in his nature anyway to close his eyes. It was impossible not to be seduced by a country whose artists had resurrected the spirit of Giotto's frescoes (but more social, more political, and clearly more pre-Columbian) on the walls of their own monuments. There was no need to go to museums to admire the works of these pioneers of the Mexican art renaissance. The muralists worked everywhere in the city – at the National Preparatory School, at the Ministry of Education, at the Ministry of Health. Cartier-Bresson, who had not ceased to be a painter even after exchanging his brushes for a camera, could not remain indifferent, either to the way they reflected their culture, or to their technique: Diego Rivera painted in tempera and wax, and David Siqueiros in pyroxene – a method that created impressive effects of very high relief.

Even the unforeseen regularly occurred. One evening, Cartier-Bresson was attending a small party at the home of a prominent local whose bachelor flat had been decorated by his friend, the painter Antonio Salazar. The tequila was flowing. Only Henri abstained, as he was suffering from amoebic dysentery. Bored, he went round the house with Tonio, and they got lost in the maze of rooms. Upstairs they heard a slight noise:

> I was very lucky. I had only to push the door open. Two lesbians were making love. It was so voluptuous, so sensual... I couldn't see their faces. It was miraculous – physical love in all its fullness. Tonio grabbed a lamp, and I took several shots... There was nothing obscene about it. I could never have got them to pose – a matter of modesty.

It was a photo bursting with life, movement, eroticism and emotion, making an accomplice of the observer; it duly found its way into the pantheon of Cartier-Bresson icons – one of Mandiargues' favourites, he called it *The Spider of Love*. The negative got separated from the original film, like all the rest taken at that time, and so it is impossible to establish the sequence. But 65 years later, in an exhibition devoted to the gallery-owner Julien Levy, an unknown print from the series miraculously turned up – the same two women, joined by a man: Tonio.

Cartier-Bresson spent his evenings at private parties with his fellow lodgers. In their more prosperous periods, when one of them had sold translations, articles or photos, they would celebrate at Butch Lewis's American restaurant, calle 5 de Mayo, or at Las Casuelas. At other times they were to be found in bars and nightclubs, steeping themselves in illicit intoxication. Cartier-Bresson was never more true to himself than when he was on the margins – in the most untrendy places, or in daily contact with creative spirits, above all the young painters and draughtsmen of the Mexican avant-garde.

He enjoyed total liberty when taking photographs, whether in the avenues of Mexico City, the slums of Juchitan, the picturesque streets of Puebla, or the rodeos of Oaxaca; he went as far as the Gulf of Tehuantepec, and from there finally managed to bring back faces and smiles that expressed some kind of *joie de vivre*. And everywhere, just as he had done in Spain and would soon do elsewhere, he took photos of people stretched out on the grass or on pavements, caught unawares, totally without aggression, because sleep had prevented them from being offended by the Cyclops eye that was observing them. You could be forgiven for thinking that Mexico was entirely populated by sleepers. But some of them did wake up. Cartier-Bresson received a severe reprimand from the mayor of a village after he had taken some completely harmless shots of a tree in front of a wall – but the wall in question was that of the ladies' baths, and so any picture at all could only be indecent. Again, it was a matter of modesty.

Cartier-Bresson sold some of his photos to local journals such as *Excelsior*, and was quite proud of having done so, since he was in competition with the locals. Others were exhibited at the Palacio de Bellas Artes, together with those of a young Mexican photographer named Manuel Alvarez Bravo, who was influenced by Picasso, cubism and pre-Hispanic art. His most famous photo, *Striking Worker Murdered*, taken that year, reflected his own personality – a mixture of social engagement, political militancy and magic realism. It revealed his imagination, that of a man who had been confronted too early with death in the Revolution and who had never recovered.

With their works hanging side by side in the palacio, Cartier-Bresson and Alvarez Bravo met and became friends. What they had in common was their intense fascination with the street, as if they were drawn to it by some hidden magnetism. And in addition, they shared a passion for the world of Eugène Atget.

The Mexican was particularly struck by his compatriots' interest in the work of the young Frenchman, since the popularity rating of photography in Mexico was practically zero. It could only have been due to something special that lay behind the images.

The exhibition, which took place in March 1935, marked the end of a stage in Cartier-Bresson's life. He had been living in Mexico for a year – as long as he had spent in the Ivory Coast – and it seems almost as if he were following a cycle. Here, as there, he had experienced and survived loneliness, illness and bad living conditions – not as a rich man diverting himself among the poor, seduced by the sordid attractions of low life, but as a traveller absorbing a foreign world. Henri now felt himself to be an honorary Mexican, and at the moment of departure he described Mexico as the country where he had been most happy, and from which he would carry memories of great joy.

He had found his way. He was not a warrior, or a reporter, but an honest wanderer with an eighteenth-century spirit supported by twentieth-century technology. In other words, he was an adventurer, not in the exotic sense of the term, but in personal development, finding a path that would allow him to live in harmony with his own artistic needs, no matter how unreasonable. A telephone call from Pierre Josse, however, suddenly brought him back to a different reality. In Paris, in the apartment on rue Nicolo, their friend René Crevel had done what he had described in his first book, *Détours*: 'A tisane on the gas stove, the window tightly closed, I turn on the gas, I forget to strike the match...'.

Crevel was convinced that he was the final link in a family curse. Suicide seemed to him like 'destiny inescapable', and he had been haunted by the spectre of it since the age of 14. His life had been a sad and continuous scandal, and his death was in keeping with his life: the Church had reclaimed him and had laid a crucifix on his breast, but his surrealist friends refused to attend the service. At the age of 35, the son of the hanged man had gone to the big sleep, leaving behind the following message: 'Please cremate me. Disgust.'

In New York, in 1935, Henri Cartier-Bresson decided to give up photography. It was the first, though not the last time. There was something odd about this recurrent desire to give up the occupation that had provided the most lasting satisfaction. The exhibitions in New York and Mexico had earned him a bit of a reputation early on in his career, but this was not binding. His decision to remain in America rather than go back across the Atlantic was because he had at the back of his mind the idea of changing his medium. No more photos; not quite the cinema but, instead, the film documentary beckoned. It seemed like a natural development for a young man of the time: from the paint-brush to the pocket camera to the film camera. The cinema and its offshoots were synonymous with speed, impatience, fame and fortune. Several photographers had already appeared to glide effortlessly from one to the other.

The moment he set foot in Manhattan, he began to look for a room where he could put up his Mexican camp bed. He had got to know enough Americans in Paris to be able to avoid hotels by staying with them. He met up again with Elena Mumm, probably the most beautiful of all the former students at the Lhote Academy, and with Charles Henry Ford, whom he had met in Tangier and again in Montparnasse. Ford had a lot of contacts, at least in his own circle, a kind of literary and artistic bohemia, largely homosexual. His partner, the painter Pavel Tchelitchev, put the word about on behalf of the penniless Frenchman, and so Cartier-Bresson finished up living on 39th Street, in the studio of a Russian immigrant who had not yet obtained American nationality. Nicolas Nabokov, first cousin of the writer Vladimir, was a composer. They had met in Paris when Nabokov was writing music for Diaghilev's Ballets Russes, before launching into a lyrical symphony, an oratorio, and a *serenata estiva* for string quartet. The two exiles swiftly established a bond, and lived amicably together in the tough world of New York, even though the Frenchman was as intransigent, straitlaced and serious as the Russian was capricious, eccentric and unstable. They shared everything, frequently made do with apple pies, hamburgers and fruit, and didn't bother to separate their living quarters with anything more than a simple screen. They would embark on lengthy discussions, often lasting till dawn, on morality and politics, but they were both progressive. Nabokov came from an upper-class Russian family, and was the nephew of a liberal member of the Duma; he found it hard to believe that Communism could really represent the future of mankind – unlike Cartier-Bresson, who because of his visceral anti-Fascism looked more indulgently on the heirs of Lenin.

In Manhattan, as in Mexico and Montparnasse, Cartier-Bresson had a supreme ability to integrate with his environment, and his contacts snowballed. At the home of the composer George Antheil, he met and befriended Paul Bowles. They had both stayed in the mythical city of Tangier, but the budding writer and the now almost tried-and-tested photographer found they had another experience in common: both had suffered a humiliating put-down when they had been to see Gertrude Stein. After having read Bowles's surrealist-inspired work in the magazine *Transition*, she had told him straight out to give up poetry.

As for Cartier-Bresson's photographic career, he was finding it difficult to move on, but this was where Julien Levy stepped in. In April 1935 he mounted a new exhibition in his Madison Avenue gallery on his favourite theme of 'antigraphic photography', presenting the works of Henri Cartier-Bresson, Walker Evans and Manuel Alvarez Bravo. In the circumstances, Henri could hardly call an abrupt halt to his career – especially since Walker Evans, his new photographic brother-in-arms, for whose work he always retained the greatest admiration, was himself deeply impressed by Cartier-Bresson's photographs: 'There is a new route there which we have scarcely begun to explore,' he confided to the art critic James Thrall Soby.

A former literature student at the Sorbonne, Walker Evans never turned away from his heroes, Baudelaire and Flaubert, but simply substituted one means of expression for another. Photography was a form of writing, and life was in the streets – that was his creed. From the very first pictures he took of New York and Boston his urban realism was brilliant. His naturalistic abilities flourished in many parts of America, thanks to an assignment he carried out for the Farm Security Administration. In this same year, 1935, Roosevelt's Democratic government launched a social programme under its New Deal to help give a kick-start to agriculture, and to increase public awareness. With a dozen other photographers, Evans criss-crossed America for several years in order to create a visual record of the ravages on the countryside resulting from the 1929 Depression; he focused mainly on living conditions, habitats, and his own passion for life in the streets.

Had he been an American citizen, Cartier-Bresson might have reined in his individualism in order to employ his sharp vision in such a cause. For the moment, though, he concentrated on being less of a Frenchman and more of a New Yorker. As always, his concern was integration, the desire to be absorbed by the new world he was in – the exact opposite of the conventional tourist.

He was such a singular character that he never failed to make a profound impression on the Americans he came into contact with – and one day their various memoirs would bear witness to this impact. He appeared to them to be a young man with an angelic face – pink, blond and clean-shaven – whose shyness was evident even before he opened his mouth. But his gaze was clear, a little cunning even, lively and mobile. He was ambitious, confident of obtaining the means to achieve his ambitions, never for an instant doubting the quality or originality of his work. 'Ambition' should be seen here solely in the context of his art and not of a career. Such self-assurance may seem puzzling in one so young, and it was all the more striking when he spoke about his photography, for then he emitted the same quiet power that was typical of the socialist leader Jean Jaurès' great political speeches. Such unshakeable confidence in his own faculties, in direct contrast to the delicate awkwardness of his appearance, convinced everyone that such a person could not possibly be motivated by any sort of self-hatred, but, as always, the reality was a good deal more complex.

It might be said that right from the start Cartier-Bresson had a particular vision of himself, of what he should do and how he should do it, and he was determined to pursue this vision to the end. But he expressed it with such seriousness and such certainty, and his indifference to material things clashed so radically with the American obsession with money, that his attitude could not even be considered presumptuous, let alone arrogant. And yet this detachment could easily be read as arrogance, in the same way that people who are secretly conscious of their upper-class origins can be arrogant. Such an impression, though, was false. The cinema director Ralph Steiner was amazed at this degree of self-assurance, but although everything that was said suggested extreme immodesty, by the end of their first conversation he was deeply impressed. The only indecision from which Cartier-Bresson suffered remained his choice of medium, but there was no doubting his own ability to use that medium to bring out the best in himself.

For the time being he went on wandering the streets of Harlem for days on end, Leica in hand, eyes everywhere. Some of his photos were published straight away in the *New Theatre*, a left-wing avant-garde magazine. Strangely, he used a pseudonym – Pierre Renne – though perhaps he was simply being cautious for fear of sharp eyes in the immigration service. At night, he went to Father Divine's and various other restaurants in the company of a black woman he was living with, as well as with Paul Bowles and other friends. In

Harlem, a place that fascinated him so much that he even lived there for a few months, there were very few nightclubs where he did not indulge his passion for jazz. Many of his friends, however, were intellectuals, artists and musicians from this area, including blacks and progressives, not to say overt communists.

The question still remained whether he should stick with photography or turn his attention to documentaries. A master might have set him on the right path, as André Lhote had done for his painting. It could have been Paul Strand – but it wasn't. There was a whole generation between them, and an equally wide artistic gap. Cartier-Bresson was not impressed by the legend that had grown up around Strand, a former member of the 291 Gallery and the pioneer of 'straight photography' – direct reproduction of reality pure and simple. Strand's work on landscapes, rocks, plants, tree roots and clouds, divorced from the academic spirit and the pictorialism of the previous century, left Cartier-Bresson completely cold. He was equally unenthusiastic about Eugene Smith, whom he considered too artificial and aesthetic. The greatest American photographer in his eyes was still Walker Evans.

Above all, though, Cartier-Bresson felt unable to respect the man behind the photographer. He found him heavy going, and felt that morally Strand would remain a Stalinist all his life. With Strand, or rather at his house, he learned the rudiments of film-making, which was a different way of pursuing his vision of humanity. But in 1935, when Cartier-Bresson was becoming a New Yorker, Strand was busy in Mexico making his own films, *Redes* ('Fishing Nets') and *The Plow that Broke the Plains*, and was doing a lot of travelling. The two men in fact saw very little of each other, and so it would be wrong to say that Cartier-Bresson was in his debt. What he learned about technique and editing he gleaned mainly from his 'Nykino' friends (a word derived from 'New York' and the Russian for 'cinema') – a little left-wing group that included Willard van Dyke and other documentary-makers under the influence of the Russian masters. Paul Strand was one of the leading lights, and it was in his apartment that the meetings took place, but he attended only sporadically to give advice, and nothing more.

Cartier-Bresson was beginning to feel that he was stagnating, and once more his restlessness took over. He had felt the same when he had gone from Africa to Europe, from Europe to Central America, and from Central to North America. He left the United States without even exploring it, having spent a year in Manhattan – as 1935 gave way to 1936, he was itching to get away. It was at the precise moment when his hero André Kertész came to New York, and it was at the precise moment when a team of journalists got together to found a new current affairs magazine, with great emphasis on photographic illustration, to be launched under the title *Life*; this would have been a golden opportunity for him, as the managing editor had already contacted him two years after his photographs had first been published in *Vu*. But it made no difference – nothing could keep him in New York, and nothing could make him keep up photography. *Harper's Bazaar*, anxious to enhance its visual appeal, commissioned him to do a series of fashion photographs, but the attempt was judged by both parties to be inconclusive, and the project was swiftly terminated. In any case, it was not what Cartier-Bresson was looking for.

He wanted to make films, not photographs, and that was it. All that remained was for him to find a position as assistant director, but he felt this would be easier in Paris, his own city, where he had heard that things were buzzing once more, politically, socially and culturally. Paris was the place to be.

4 THE END OF THE OLD WORLD
1936–39

The Café du Dôme was the same as it had always been. The moment he got back to Paris, Cartier-Bresson was back in his old haunts among his old friends. And yet something had changed imperceptibly: there was a tension in the air, discussions were more heated, people seemed less carefree. The mounting dangers in Europe seemed to have cast dark shadows over the light-heartedness of yesteryear, as if people were becoming aware that they were shifting from post-war into pre-war mode, and that one day this period would be looked back on as 'between the wars'.

At the beginning of 1936, France was counting down to the May elections. On the café terraces, all the talk was of a second government under Albert Sarraut, the military reoccupation of the Rhineland, and the dissolution of the extreme right-wing league with the founding of a new fascist party by Jacques Doriot, a former communist MP. Those who preferred to ignore the morale-undermining sound of jackboots turned their attention to the ridiculous jousting between Jacques-Emile Blanche and André Lhote. At every opportunity, each would publicly belittle the other, criticizing him for tyrannizing students with his theories, and the accused would respond with equal vehemence in the columns of the *Nouvelle Revue française*. If the nature of their teaching was not under attack, it was Cézanne-worship, with Lhote jealously guarding the great man's memory and Blanche daring to express reservations. All of this greatly entertained the galleries and cafés, though it was little help to a 30-year-old photographer who dreamed of working in films. It didn't matter now whether these were to be documentaries or feature films, so long as he could work in the cinema. His thinking was perfectly reasonable, since other photographers had followed the same path – notably Marc Allégret, Maurice Cloche, Jean Dréville and Robert Bresson. There seemed no reason why he should not do the same.

He decided to try the obvious short cut of going straight to a director and asking to be taken on as his assistant. All he needed was a bit of savoir-faire, innocence, cheek and luck.

His first attempt resulted in his first failure. He approached Luis Buñuel, who said no. He had chosen Buñuel because he knew him, and for many other reasons. Buñuel was the most surrealist of all film directors; they had a great deal in common; his first three films, *Un chien andalou*, *L'Age d'or* and *Terre sans pain*, were magnificent; and perhaps he would remember that he himself had been given his chance by Jean Epstein, who had taken him on as an assistant for *The Fall of the House of Usher*. But Buñuel said no.

The second attempt resulted in the second failure. He approached Georg Wilhelm Pabst, choosing him because he regarded him as one of the masters of silent film, because he had made the marvellous *Comrades of 1918*, *Pandora's Box* and *The Beggar's Opera*, and because he was known to edit his films on set. Paul Morand, the novelist and diplomat, had been employed by him to write the screenplay of *Don Quixote*, and it was he who advised Cartier-Bresson to knock on the director's door. It was not a good idea. Although Pabst was preparing to shoot *Spies from Salonika*, a film intended for distribution in France, he had nothing to offer the young man, and he too said no.

The third attempt was successful. After failing with a Spaniard and a German, Cartier-Bresson approached a Frenchman – one with whom he felt the closest intellectual and artistic affinity. He went to see Jean Renoir, armed with an album of photographs, hoping that the 50 or so prints of somewhat uneven quality would be impressive enough to get him the job. He must have thought that photography was some sort of qualification for the post of assistant director, whereas in fact the job was more that of a general factotum. 'I felt like a sales rep offering his catalogue,' he recalled.

To his great surprise, Renoir immediately said yes. From then on, he regarded his little album – now destined to become legendary – as a kind of talisman. He would keep it under lock and key, and to the end considered it his most precious possession.

Renoir had already made ten or so films, the latest being *Le Crime de M. Lange*. But he had yet to make his mark, for he was anything but a commercial director. At the time he was putting together a team to make a propaganda film at the behest of Louis Aragon for the Communist Party – a project that was to lead to *La vie est à nous* ('Life is Ours'). Renoir was once defined by the producer Pierre Braunberger as fundamentally a right-winger who had never recovered from his Blimpish career at the Military School in Saumur. So the reason why he accepted this proposal – or to be more precise, this commission – from the Communist Party was that he hoped he would at last find an audience. It must therefore be seen as political opportunism on the part of someone who thought of nothing but the cinema.

This was not yet the moment for Cartier-Bresson to appreciate Renoir's human qualities, to latch on to their shared admiration for the art historian Elie Faure, to take part in the processes of film-making or to work with the actors. Not only was this the wrong type of film for such matters; Renoir followed the filming only from a distance, delegating most of it to his assistant directors, working on just a few scenes himself and supervising the overall project, but not even doing the editing. Cartier-Bresson therefore found himself as one of five assistants engaged on a series of sketches under no fewer than four different directors (André Zwoboda, Jacques Becker, Jean-Paul Le Chanois and Renoir himself). The title credits made this perfectly clear: 'A film made collectively by a team of technicians, artists and workers'.

The film's thesis can be summed up in a few words: France is a rich country being pillaged by members of the most ferociously capitalist bourgeois dynasties and controlled by the militants of fascist leagues. A teacher tells his pupils how this situation has arisen, and explains why only the Communist Party can oppose it and re-establish social justice in the country. It goes without saying that such a film had little to do with art and everything to do with the forthcoming elections.

La vie est à nous was not a film of subtle nuances. The 200 'bourgeois dynasties' (Wendel, Schneider and so on) were held up to public contempt with no chance to defend themselves. Against a background of Dantesque images on the night of 6 February 1934 in the Place de la Concorde, the militants of the extreme right-wing leagues and the ancient warriors of the Fiery Cross were presented as 'the French Hitlerites'. On the other hand, no scene could be powerful enough, no commentary lyrical enough to express the glory of the unions and the historical role of the working classes, to evoke the soup queues and to denounce the redundancies. The character of the capitalists is uniformly odious and ruthless, the speeches of the party leaders – Vaillant-Couturier, Duclos, Thorez and others – are thoroughly wooden, and there are plenty of special visual effects. The whole thing finishes with the Internationale. It is heavy-handed, demagogic, but efficient.

Henri Cartier-Bresson was not and in fact never became a communist. He resisted the efforts of one particular man to get him to join the party: Georges Sadoul, a surrealist and a connoisseur of painting and drawing, who had broken with the movement out of loyalty to Aragon; he came from the Vosges and had a simple but burning faith in politics. He was a film critic, and he was also Cartier-Bresson's brother-in-law. Without ever being a fellow-traveller, Henri certainly felt much sympathy for the cause – it was said that communism represented the world's youth, after all. His visceral anti-fascism, the very precarious situation of Europe in the mid-1930s, the need to choose 'against' rather than 'for' – all this frequently obliged him to take sides with the communists. But he had no illusions. These had been shattered in his youth by the tragedy of Cronstadt in 1921, when Trotsky had ruthlessly crushed the fleet's mutiny against the power of the Soviets.

Even if circumstances sometimes made him temper his criticisms, his views never changed fundamentally. Initially, communism represented for him something of a renewal of Christianity. It did not take long for him to discover the exact nature of its advocates when André Malraux, working for Gallimard, refused to publish Boris Souvarine's devastating book on Stalin.

La vie est à nous was a real film in the sense that it was made by a team of real technicians, had a real screenplay, and starred real actors – who were far from second-rate, since Jean Dasté, Madeleine Sologne, Gaston Modot and Roger Blin took the main roles. But it was only 66 minutes long, the producer was a political party, and the distributor only intended it to go to the very limited circle of communist supporters.

It didn't matter that nobody was paid. When Renoir was there, he would invite the whole team to dinner at La Mascotte, a restaurant on the rue des Abbesses. These evenings in Montmartre expressed the true spirit of the film crew, and chimed in perfectly with the whirlwind activities of the Popular Front. Such moments were ample compensation for all the frustrations. Rarely can a film have been made in such an atmosphere of joyful disinterest, crowned by the fact that the verdict of the ballot box eventually vindicated the whole enterprise. On 3 May 1936, after the second round of elections, the Popular Front coalition won a clear victory. Léon Blum, President of the Council, formed a government consisting of socialists and radicals, while the communists preferred to lend their support without being actually involved. It didn't matter that there were many differences of opinion on both political and economic issues; all that mattered was that at last the left had gained power, and the world was theirs.

By participating in the making of this film, albeit on a modest scale, Cartier-Bresson felt that he had made his entry into the world of the cinema. He was not mistaken, for he really had been accepted into the Renoir clan. This did not allay his concern about the future, since no one can guarantee whom the producers will decide to employ; but his mind was put at rest when he was officially engaged for the director's next film. He became closer to him, entered the inner circle, and finally got to know what Georges Simenon would call the 'naked' man behind the myth that would soon grow up around him.

At 42, in the eyes of most people Jean Renoir was still the son of his famous father Auguste. He could not escape the family legacy. It is impossible to be the son of a great artist and not be affected by his aura, particularly if the son is himself an artist following a parallel course and striving to transcend the burden of his heritage.

Jean Renoir worked with different methods, but with both men instinct held sway over intellect. They each followed the same precept: 'Down with the brain, long live the senses!' As visual as he was literary, Jean brought a poetic spirit to his films. The world of ideas was foreign to him, and that of ideology even more so (in spite of *La vie est à nous*). He lived in a world of intuition, sensation and emotion, which provided the colours of his cinematographic palette. He was keener on writing films than directing them, and had no interest in the technical side. He never interfered in matters of lighting or camerawork, and his greatest thrill came from the dialogue, from getting the words right. Listening to him and watching him, Cartier-Bresson soon became convinced that a director had above all to be gifted with a literary imagination. In this sense he saw Renoir as a great novelist who, despite the modern means of expression he had chosen, remained in essence a man of the nineteenth century.

Renoir was a force of nature. He was earthy and generous, blessed with powerful instincts, a rich humanity and an ability to understand others – full of life, in other words, even if the contradictions that dogged his private life were exhausting for his team. No one can be permanently assailed by doubts without upsetting those around him. It was impossible to form an overall judgment of a man who was clearly as fascinated by ordinary people as he was by aristocrats – two different worlds, to neither of which he would ever belong despite his middle-class education. He dressed badly, was prone to excesses, talkative, but uncertain of his own charm; full of contradictions, seductive yet awkward, naturally elegant yet embarrassed by his own body, avidly consuming life to the last drop, yet regularly drowning his melancholy in Beaujolais. Cartier-Bresson recognized a profound truth when he realized that Renoir's Achilles heel was not his passion for women so much as his weakness of character.

Light years away from propaganda, the new project was to be a proper film. *Partie de campagne* ('A Day in the Country') was an adaptation of Guy de Maupassant's short story, just a few pages long, about a summer Sunday in the country, set in 1860. A lower-middle-class family, the Dufours, who own a hardware store in Paris, decide to go on a picnic. Two dashing young men, Henri and Rodolphe, who are sitting at a table in the inn, become all excited at the sight of Henriette, the pretty daughter, and with smiles and winks and nudges gear themselves up for a bit of fun. Having got M. Dufour and his assistant out of the way by shoving fishing rods into their hands, they take Mme Dufour and her daughter for a boat ride on the river. The two rowers achieve their ends, but the focus is on the fate of the young girl rather than that of her mother. After a year, during which the two lovers-for-a-day have never stopped thinking about each other, they meet again at the scene of their brief and passionate encounter. But Henriette, who in the meantime has married her father's assistant, can this time give him no more than a look of intense regret. They chat, and then she leaves for ever, sadly resigned to her fate.

Of course, the story is much more than this thin plot-line, or an ironic, libertarian satire on the lower middle classes. What was needed for the film was the underlying excitement and tender emotions that would transcend the story and transform an individual fate into a hymn to nature. Only a writer with the soul of an artist rather than the skill of a technician could capture the joy and the sadness of this dreamlike experience, for beyond the universality of the story the film was about an earlier world – not just that which existed before the Industrial Revolution, but that of childhood.

The film was to be shot mainly outdoors. This in itself was unusual. After some reconnoitring, a suitable location, with a forestry worker's house, was found on the banks of the Loing at Sorques, near Montigny-sur-Loing. This spot, on the outskirts of the forest of Fontainebleau, was not only unspoilt countryside, it had the great advantage of proximity to the Villa Saint El, Renoir's property in Marlotte. The area had been a favourite subject for the painters of his father's circle. There was no escaping the benevolent shade of the great artist. On the walls, large rectangles marked the memory of pictures sold to finance his son's films. How could one not think of him when his grandson, the 15-year-old Alain Renoir, was out in the garden practising with the clapperboard in the company of his friend Jean-Pierre Cézanne?

Rowers, pretty women on the riverbank, picnics, lovers walking together... nothing could be more naturalistic. For the first time in his burgeoning career, Jean Renoir paid homage to his father, taking the risk of making what people would call an impressionist film.

Henri Cartier-Bresson was employed by the Société du Cinéma du Panthéon as second assistant from 26 June 1936, the eve of the first day of shooting. His fee was a lump sum of 1000 francs, with a bonus of up to 1250 francs depending on box office receipts. The previous month had seen the country paralysed by strikes, with factories being occupied by the workers and demonstrations aimed at forcing the government to implement the reforms promised by the Popular Front's election manifesto. Within a few weeks new institutions and social laws that were to become historic came into being: collective contracts, readjustment of wages, paid holidays, a 40-hour week. It was all a long way from Maupassant.

The credits of this film are full of Renoirs, and it needs no expert analysis to work out what parts they all played. This was Jean's true world, a poet's concept of his film as a family affair in which everyone is involved. To him, of course, fell the task of directing, and of writing the dialogue. Marguerite Houllé, with whom he shared his life, was responsible for the editing; she also wrote the script and played a cameo part as a servant. Claude Renoir, his nephew, was director of photography. Germaine Montero sang a song with her mouth closed, and the starring role was taken by the delightful Sylvia Bataille, who was having a passionate affair with the producer, Pierre Braunberger. Renoir, who had already worked with her in Le Crime de M. Lange, had no doubts: he had 'heard' her voice when rereading Maupassant's story, and she was Henriette Dufour. The rest of the cast included Jane Marken, Gabriello, Gabrielle Fontan and, of course, Renoir himself, who gave himself a small role as the bistro-owner.

Henri Cartier-Bresson was the second assistant in a team of six; the others were Yves Allégret, Jacques Becker, Jacques B. Brunius, Claude Heyman and Luchino Visconti. All of them would pursue careers in the cinema, for in France an assistantship was a school for directing, whereas in the US it was a job in itself. Henri Cartier-Bresson was the exception. Later, in his memoirs, the producer referred to him as the stills photographer for Partie de campagne, but he never took a single photo.

Being an assistant meant being a dog's-body. Cartier-Bresson loved a challenge, and this certainly was a challenge. Renoir was unpredictable. When he was in a good mood, everything went so smoothly that it was almost too good to be true. But when he was depressed, the atmosphere on set became brutally tense for the whole crew. It was not easy to follow someone who believed in the spontaneity of inspiration. The assistant never once put his eye to the viewfinder. At best he was invited to work with the Master on the dialogue, to polish and perfect it, and then to polish and perfect it again. At worst he had to attend to a thousand and one details, no matter how insignificant, not even getting so much as a thank-you or knowing whether they had served any useful purpose. These minor matters were not so minor either, because with the filming being done out in the remote countryside it was essential that even the tiniest prop be there at the moment when it was needed. The relationship between the two men could be affected by endless possibilities, not all of them to do with the cinema. 'At the right moment you had to suggest a game of table tennis, or going for a drop of Beaujolais. It was a continual psychological strategy. In actual fact, his assistant was his maid of all work,' Cartier-Bresson recalled.

In Renoir's eyes a good assistant had to combine total efficiency with the ability to subject his own personality to that of the director, the better to serve him. Cartier-Bresson threw himself into the designated role, feeling rather like the Renaissance assistant preparing the colours for the master painter. But there were assistants and assistants. Luchino Visconti was the one who did least. One of the props men, he never lifted a hand except to deal with costumes, while the rest worked themselves to a standstill. He owed his appointment to the recommendation of Coco Chanel – a close friend of his and Renoir's – and even if he tried not to draw attention to this, his whole attitude suggested that he was different from the rest. Like a student dropping in on lectures in another department, he was only there out of interest. He was a mixture of dandy, dilettante and connoisseur, though he would have denied this. He stayed at the Hotel Castiglione, which suited him perfectly. He kept himself to himself, and never seemed anxious to be involved in the film itself or the production, acting more like a privileged observer than a paid assistant. It took him quite a time to become integrated into the team, and he never fitted in to the places where they enjoyed this collective adventure together – the Villa Saint-El, the Hôtel de la Renaissance and the Café du Bon Coin. The gap between him and the rest of them never really closed. He was convinced that all these young Frenchmen were communists who looked askance on a fascistic aristocrat from a country under the thumb of Mussolini. He could see the bonds of solidarity, friendship and respect that linked them, but he wrongly assumed that these were politically generated. He misinterpreted the nature of Renoir's entourage, not being acquainted with the upper-middle-class environment that many of them came from, and not understanding that they inclined to be anarchists rather than Stalinists. In his own personal mythology, the rich and illuminating period that he spent with Renoir, six years before he made his first film, *Ossessione*, would remain engraved on his memory as a shock and a revelation on both a moral and an artistic level.

Jacques B. Brunius was a multi-talented will-o'-the-wisp. As well as his assistant's duties, which he performed down to the last chore, he played the part of Rodolphe under the name of Jacques Borel and, on a completely different level, supervised the team administration. Within the little group of Renoir's helpers he was one of the most striking characters. Although he was only 30 he had packed quite a lot in: he had acted in Pierre Prévert's 1932 film *L'affaire est dans le sac*, had assisted Luis Buñuel in *L'Age d'or*, and had made some surrealist films himself.

Of the six assistants, Jacques Becker was the one with whom Cartier-Bresson forged the most durable links. He remembered this jazz and sports-car fanatic as being quite exceptional – sensitive, with a natural elegance, deeply aware of other people's feelings. Bearing in mind Cartier-Bresson's own social background, it is understandable that he was drawn from the outset to this son of an upper-middle-class family, who was apparently predestined to become a manufacturer of accumulator batteries. It is, incidentally, interesting to note that, among this film crew, the bosses lived in the working-class areas (Braunberger on the rue de Charonne) or the suburbs (Renoir in Meudon), while most of the assistants lived in the bourgeois districts (Becker on the rue de Longchamp in the sixteenth *arrondissement*, Cartier-Bresson on the rue de Lisbonne in the eighth, Visconti at a big hotel on the rue de Rivoli). Jean Renoir was the first to mock Becker's cheeky tone, and he never lost a chance to tease his favourite assistants about the English influence that snobbishly affected their accents.

'Becker and Cartier, you're talking too much of *the the!*' he would often yell at them, imitating the worst culprits, though this did not stop him from always saying 'choual' instead of 'cheval' ('horse') with all the affectation of a former officer in the cavalry.

Work-plans and production notes give a good idea of how Cartier-Bresson spent his days: 'Go to Bontemps (in Paris, rue de Cléry) to get a skeleton key

with a head and a music box with six verses (to be heard by the Abbé Champly)';
'Buy a nightingale (Paris, quai de Gesvres)'; 'Arrange to hire a skiff, 15 francs a
day (Joinville, chez Elie)'; 'Get a horse-drawn wagon, fishing rods, a stove, para-
sols, posters'; 'Buy or hire barrels, straw hats for the horses, Pernod spoons,
old-style matches in Paris'.

Jacques Becker had the same sort of thing to do in Marlotte, near
Fontainebleau, while Luchino Visconti was asked to provide precise details for
hiring costumes: the types of dresses needed, the quality of the material, the
footwear.

Since the assistant had to be a jack of all trades, he was also called upon to
act. Directors sometimes succumbed to the temptation to appear before the
camera, though less from vanity than from a sense of fun. Renoir pushed his
assistants into this agonizing performance so that they would know what it was
like in front of the camera as well as behind it. And so, during *Partie de campagne*, Henri Cartier-Bresson made his first screen appearance in takes 17–20
of sequence 2, shot by Pierre Lestringuez, a lifelong friend of Renoir's, and by
the writer Georges Bataille, then married to the film's leading actress, but soon
to be separated.

This silent scene, filmed as a panned shot, is one of the shortest. A little
group of priests and seminarists comes into shot, and the youngest of them –
Cartier-Bresson, of course, since he always looked younger than his age –
glances at the girls. In cassock and biretta he looks 18, though in fact he was ten
years older. He is riveted by the brief vision of Sylvia Bataille's underwear as she
sits on a swing. There is a hesitant but glowing smile before the Father Superior
reprimands him with a stinging back-hand, whereupon he goes his way, head
bowed. The scene may not have been the pivotal moment of the film, but it was
his. And when his friend Eli Lotar, who was both cameraman and stills photographer for the film, immortalized the group of seminarists, little did he know
that his photograph would take on the status of an historical document.

In Maupassant's short story the weather is always fine, and so it is in
Renoir's screenplay; but the weather reports of 1936 told a different story. The
summer was particularly wet, and this dampened the spirits of a technical crew
which from the start was keen to become a group of friends. The atmosphere
soon deteriorated, and the climatic conditions – which were nobody's fault –
made it absolutely unbearable. What did not help was that relations between
Sylvia Bataille and Jean Renoir worsened as the skies grew darker. When a
director and his star actress are not speaking to one another in the midst of

making a film, while the camera crew are squelching about despairingly in the mud, there are bound to be consequences. The tension on this chronically inactive set reached breaking point. One day the producer, Pierre Braunberger, sacked everybody. This was a relatively simple matter, since they had all been employed for a fixed fee. In fact, what he did was to stop paying expenses, which effectively meant stopping the film.

A month later, when the fine weather returned and Braunberger wanted to resume in the hope of recovering his investment, everything suddenly became more complicated. Renoir was no longer available full-time. With his insatiable appetite for working at full pelt in creative chaos, he liked to run one project into another. He was turning away from Maupassant and tackling Gorky, making preparations for his next project, an adaptation of *Les Bas-Fonds* ('The Lower Depths'). In any case, he was now fed up with *Partie de campagne*, which had been so close to his heart only a month or so ago. There were too many problems, worries and clashes. Renoir was one of those men who, in such circumstances, want only a way out.

On 15 August 1936, *Partie de campagne* finally fell through. It remained unfinished for ten years, until someone realized that all that was needed to complete it was to supply the missing scenes with two cartoons. When the credits roll, it is clear that most of the assistants had departed to join the supernumeraries of posterity, since only two were left: Jacques Becker and a certain 'Henri Cartier'. Under the government of the Popular Front, it was not a good idea to use the name of the Pantin capitalists. (Robert Capa's photographs of the big communist demonstration of 14 June 1936 had the textile workers marching under the banner 'Cartier'. We shall never know if this discreet dropping of the '-Bresson' was due to technical problems or the goodwill of the photographer.) In the end the shoot came to nothing. In the circumstances nobody was paid, but the producer took the two assistants to one side and offered each of them a wallet as a parting gift. 'Thanks, but next time, put something in it,' remarked one of them.

Jean Renoir launched himself into *Les Bas-Fonds*. Two assistants would scarcely be enough for this task, but while Jacques Becker took it on, Henri Cartier-Bresson did not. For the moment, other urgent matters brought him back to current affairs, the press, photography and documentaries.

The main reason, though, was strictly personal. He got married. It goes without saying that the marriage was unconventional in the context of his middle-class background. In fact, however, the outsider he chose was quickly accepted and integrated into the family, thanks to her mother-in-law and one of her sisters-in-law – two women with whom she became close friends.

The clairvoyant had been right again. Cartier-Bresson remembered her prophecy word for word: 'You will marry a woman from the East, not someone from China, nor from the Indies, but not white either, and it will be a difficult marriage...'. They had met in 1936 in the street, near the Parc Monceau, when she was looking for a hotel. Then they saw each other again shortly afterwards on the terrace of the Café du Dôme. Her name was Ratna Mohini, known as Eli, and she was a Javanese dancer. At least, that was how she introduced herself. She was born Carolina Jeanne de Souza-Ijke into a Muslim family in Batavia, which was the name the Dutch gave to Jakarta when they ruled over the Indonesian archipelago. She had a full figure, big, sparkling dark eyes, and was four years older than Henri. She was unquestionably a strong character, attractive, even seductive, in her movements, with a sense of humour that could become witheringly sarcastic, an ironic intelligence, and a streak of toughness as marked as his own. After divorcing Willem Berretty, an influential Dutch journalist, she had come to Paris to study and practise dancing. Strangely, she was more inclined to the written arts than the visual, and in her spare time wrote poetry, well received by Jean Paulhan, writer and chief editor at Gallimard, and the Belgian poet and painter Henri Michaux, who both encouraged her to publish.

After they had lived together for a while under the family roof in rue de Lisbonne, the couple took a studio apartment on the rue des Petits-Champs, between the avenue de l'Opéra and the place Vendôme, a thoroughfare full of charming eighteenth-century buildings. Having finally left the rue de Lisbonne, Cartier-Bresson now wanted to be totally independent of his family, and for this, for the first time, he needed a regular salary. Neither Jean Renoir nor the cinema could guarantee this – which perhaps was a sign that his path would lead him elsewhere.

There were other reasons too, the principal one of which was war. Civil war is the worst of all, when a nation tears itself apart, and like every war it involves the nations all around, for when a country goes up in flames, it threatens to ignite a whole continent. The war in Spain might be called the real beginning of the Second World War.

Not so long before, Cartier-Bresson would have savoured every line of the following critique in the *Nouvelle Revue française* of summer 1936, for under the signature of his beloved André Lhote it reviewed a photography exhibition:

> Eternally dependent on painting, whose reincarnations it embraces with singular fidelity, beginning with Corot, Courbet and especially Manet, photography – after brushing lightly against surrealism without lingering for too long (though it will return) – is going through a crisis of virtue: it is aiming at the pure image, at form in itself, at crystal clarity, at the perfection of means.

Later, perhaps, he would return to this – but at this moment Cartier-Bresson felt himself being driven elsewhere by the spirit of the age. He wanted to be at the heart of the things happening now, for when you are 28 and have a left-wing political conscience, and the world is under threat from fascism, you cannot with any sense of decency devote yourself to recreating the universe of Maupassant. Cartier-Bresson seized on the symbolic import of the military uprising against the Spanish government on 18 July 1936, seeing it as an alarm call. At bottom, his reaction was not that of a political animal but simply that of an honest man. To ignore this would be to go back on everything he stood for, and if ever there was a situation that demanded engagement, this was it. It would be the first, though not the last.

The man who had made it a point of honour never to join anything now found himself in the AEAR (*Association des écrivains et artistes révolutionnaires*), as it was called by the 'non-conformists who want to fight side by side with the proletariat'. The Association of Revolutionary Writers and Artists had been established four years earlier by Paul Vaillant-Couturier. He made no secret of his communist background; his policy was openly to attract fellow-travellers and other 'useful idiots', whereas intellectuals who harboured any critical thoughts about the USSR were not welcome. André Breton was swiftly cast out, and others followed. But despite all this, the AEAR was powerful, it guaranteed the defence of culture, and it counted among its members a number of good people such as Elie Faure and the novelist Jean Giono. Its creed was a clarion call to engagement: 'There is no neutral art, no neutral literature'. And so this was the place to be if one wanted to make a difference. For action was urgent. The American writer Paul Bowles, passing through Paris in 1937, was struck by the sudden proliferation of anti-Semitic and anti-American graffiti on the walls, as well as by the pessimism of his friend Henri Cartier-Bresson in the face of mounting danger.

Louis Aragon, political activist, surrealist, poet and passionate communist, soon became the real head of the association, unofficially at first. His web stretched everywhere. There was scarcely a cultural or journalistic project initiated by the party that he did not immediately take charge of. In 1936, during a conference at the Maison de la Culture, he launched the debate on realism in art by contrasting two concepts: the one illustrated by Man Ray's studio photographs – a static form that could flourish only in a period of economic prosperity and social peace – and the other, which accurately reflected preoccupations in times of crisis and anxiety:

> Today crowds are returning to art by way of photography. With the passionate movements of children at play. With the poses of men caught unawares in their sleep. With the unconscious twitches of people strolling by. The heterogeneous diversities of the human beings who succeed one another in the streets of our towns. And here I have in mind particularly the photos of my friend Cartier.... This art, which is opposed to that of the relatively peaceful, post-war period, is the art of the period of wars and revolutions in which we are living, at the moment when its rhythm is quickening.

It was Aragon who gave Cartier-Bresson his first real opening when he appointed him photographer to *Ce Soir*. It was a job with a title and a salary. Behind it was the hand of the Communist Party and the spirit of the Popular Front, with all that this entailed. When he wasn't publishing his reportages in *Ce Soir*, they would be in *Regards*, a weekly that was quite similar to *Vu* in its basic concept, but was clearly more communist in its politics. Despite all this, however, he remained faithful to his old libertarian credo: neither party, nor Church, nor movement. It may have been paradoxical, but life is full of contradictions.

The first issue of *Ce Soir* appeared on 1 March 1937. Its policy was manifestly to offer the public a progressive alternative to two right-wing dailies that claimed to be neutral: *L'Intransigeant*, which was losing readers, and *Paris-Soir*, which was gaining them. The creation of an evening paper which would have popular appeal while remaining anchored to the left was the brainchild of Maurice Thorez, Secretary-General of the French Communist Party. Aragon, whom the party put in charge of the project, thought it a good idea to share responsibility with the writer Jean-Richard Bloch, a sympathizer but not a member. This might have helped to disguise the degree of support that the paper was relying on from the French Internationale. Between them they were able to recruit a number of well-known and talented people who would ensure a healthy circulation: Andrée Viollis for major stories, Paul Nizan for foreign affairs, Georges Soria for the events in Spain, Elsa Triolet for fashion.

In all, 120,000 copies of the first issue were sold, and the circulation kept growing. The daily paper was an immediate success, all the more so as it sometimes came up with commercial ideas that the bourgeois press could not have objected to. Paul Bowles recalls that Cartier-Bresson was given the task of photographing thousands of children in the deprived areas, and *Ce Soir* made a point of publishing a picture a day and giving a fee to the parents of each lucky child.

Quality, surprise and originality were the order of the day, since Aragon had never lost the taste for provocation developed in his early years among the surrealists. Of all the Parisian journals, his boasted the greatest number of writers among its contributors. In fact, it might have been *Paris-Soir* with an added dash of culture. It had borrowed the latter's very effective techniques for its columns and factual reportages, and offered other attractive features that simply could not be found elsewhere: revealing glimpses of the set of Jean Renoir's latest film, exclusive publication of extracts from Malraux's *L'Espoir*, moving photographs of the Spanish Civil War, sent by Chim, Robert Capa and Gerda Taro – all these were what made *Ce Soir* special.

Henri Cartier-Bresson was the owner of press pass no. 3112. He was proud of it. But he insisted that his photographs should be credited to 'Henri Cartier'. He was proud of that too. More than ever now, under the Popular Front, he saw his background as an impediment, and he did not wish to be castigated for his birth, his money or his family. The Cartier-Bressons had long since been perceived as one of the line of mythical bourgeois, capitalist, industrialist dynasties that had taken over the destiny of the French and were denounced by Edouard Daladier in 1934 at the radical congress in Nantes: 'Two hundred families are masters of the French economy and, in effect, of French politics.'

However, in none of the press campaigns and publications attacking this two-hundred-headed hydra did the name of Cartier-Bresson appear, unlike that of Thiriez, the rival company with which the Cartier-Bressons had merged. Perhaps this was the cause of the confusion, but the merest suspicion of wealth would have been enough to damn the suspect as a member of one of the famous 200 families so rudely denigrated by Jean Renoir and his associates in *La vie est à nous*.

The café-crème drinker who watched the world go by from the Dôme had become a hound for *Ce Soir*. He was a complete professional, awaiting the editorial board's decision at the morning conference and then spending the rest of the day on the chase. This did not stop him from seeing things his own way, but sometimes he would look at them from a different angle. When he photographed the festival at Connétable near Senlis, while he included every detail of the hunters' traditions and customs, he also immortalized a strange, surrealistic scarecrow on the square in front of the Hôtel de l'Oise. It was the quality of his vision that had really developed, and although once more he was walking the streets, his focus was now considerably sharper. All the same, he would never be like Arthur Fellig, known as Weegee, who transformed his van into a darkroom and drove around permanently tuned into the wavelength of the New York police so that he could get to the scene of the crime as soon as they did.

The vaguest, biggest and most universal section of the paper came under the heading 'diverse facts' – which no one was pedantic enough to rechristen 'social facts'. The all-and-sundry brief was the best schooling for a reporter, and no matter whether the items were big or small, once the photograph was in the can, the photographer would cry out, in the jargon of his trade: 'I've done a Fragonard!'

Cartier-Bresson often had to work with 9 x 9 plates instead of his Leica, as the technical department wanted these to make retouching easier. The advantages were not always evident in the field. In Montmartre, during a visit from Cardinal Pacelli a few months before he became Pius XII, while the crowd were crying 'Long live God!', Cartier-Bresson was obliged to hold his heavy camera at full stretch high above his head in order to get his photograph. The result was inevitably an unbalanced image which had to be recentred in the laboratory. He hated the whole process, but if you work for a newspaper, the newspaper calls the tune. The picture, as it happened, was a success: in the foreground was the cardinal, seen from the rear and identifiable by his skull-cap; facing the camera, amid a dark sea of humanity that included cheerful policemen and laughing onlookers, were two of the faithful confronting him with an intense and imploring devotion, the man reverently kissing his hand, the woman looking at him with all the hope and despair in the world. It was a Goya rather than a Fragonard.

In May 1937 he was given a major assignment: he was to go to London to cover the coronation of King George VI. He teamed up with a friend, a brilliant Ecole Normale communist who had swiftly given up teaching in favour of journalism. Paul Nizan was in fact the diplomatic correspondent for *Ce Soir*, but

Cartier-Bresson enjoyed his company less for his official position in the Communist Party than for his human qualities and the intellectual acuity that shone through his published work: his scathing *Les Chiens de garde* and two novels. A satirical tract entitled *Aden Arabie*, published in 1931, was to make a profound impression on Cartier-Bresson, but only later, because he did not read it until after the author's death. He would never forget the violence, or the poetry: 'There are highways, ports, stations and countries other than the daily kennel: it is enough one day not to go down into one's underground station.' This definition of liberty might have been specially written for Cartier-Bresson, and the quotations from his beloved Elisée Reclus might have been specially chosen for him. He felt a spiritual kinship with this dynamic, hypersensitive man, who dismissed bourgeois culture, mocking the pointless flame beneath the Arc de Triomphe and the old Europe that needed to be cleared away. An acerbic eulogy to flight and adventure, the book has one of the most moving openings in twentieth-century literature: 'I was 20 years old. I will allow no one to say that this is the most beautiful age of one's life.'

After the abdication of Edward VIII for love of his American divorcee, the coronation of the new king of Great Britain was no ordinary matter, focusing as it did on the future of a whole nation. The world's press would be there, and so *Ce Soir* had to be there too. Communists can still enjoy the spectacle of people celebrating, even if it is in support of the monarchy. Aragon's paper dispatched several teams of reporters, each dealing with a different aspect of the event. One covered the rehearsal for the procession in central London, another visited the slums of the East End. What was good for the journalists applied equally to the photographers – each had his own angle. The whole thing was a real team effort, and none of the photos was individually attributed, nor were many of the articles.

As the great day approached, Britain put out the flags. In the meantime, Nizan took the opportunity to report on the bus strike and on the Cup Final between Sunderland and Preston North End. On 12 May the coronation occupied a large part of the front page, abundantly illustrated, but it was not until the following day that virtually the whole of the front page was devoted to it: 'The King of England [*sic*] and Queen Elizabeth were crowned at 12.30 in Westminster Abbey'. There were eye-catching subheadings ('Five to six million spectators watch the procession') and a bold, rather un-Marxist-Leninist caption: 'The coronation ceremony, in the presence of representatives from an Empire of 100 million citizens and 400 million subjects, constitutes not only a

grandiose and romantic ritual but also an important political act for the domin-
ions.' The bombardment of Madrid, which on the same day claimed 217 dead
and 693 injured, was relegated to the bottom right-hand corner. *Ce Soir* or *Paris-
Soir*, left-wing or right-wing, the press is the press.

From the departure of the carriage from Buckingham Palace to the entry
into Westminster Abbey, from the 'Te Deum laudamus' to 'God Save the King',
the whole event was reported in every detail, without the slightest whiff of criticism. Cartier-Bresson himself was more interested in people's faces than in all
the ceremony, for he knew this was the best way to capture the soul of a nation.
He simply turned his back on the parade and looked for the reflections of the
coronation in the expressions and attitudes of the people watching it.

Others might be drawn to the pomp; for him it was the circumstance – a
fair division, since he was not going to change. If he had been an illustrator in
the Middle Ages, he would certainly have worked in the margins of illuminated
manuscripts. He was aware that it was on the periphery that social resistance
found its expression, while the centre was given over to the conventions. He
would have filled his Book of Hours with outcasts and exiles and little people,
leaving others to portray the mighty. It was always the side-issues that preoccupied him, and he expressed his nonconformism primarily by being
unpredictable, by seeing the reverse side of things. In this he was in complete
harmony with his friend Nizan, whose views were equally out of step with con-
vention. It was almost as if they had made a vow to each other, for the articles of
the one could have served as captions to the photographs taken by the other.
Paul could write literary prose that enhanced the poetic dimension of the
images. The following is pure Nizan – more tweed than ermine, more umbrella
than halberd:

> Night, and parks where lost couples forgot King and Empire were sur-
> rounded by a blaze of electric lights and by cries whose dissonance was like
> the concert of cockerels at dawn. Along the streets, the crowds – suddenly
> submissive to the prestige of the trees and the grass – fell silent. A negro king
> passed by with feathers on his head, but he was only a singer or a shoeshine
> boy; the true black kings of the coronation were waiting for the moment to go
> to Buckingham Palace. The fraternal bands of drunkards came staggering
> along. At the corner of Half Moon Street, big women in thick make-up made
> signs to passing cars.... On a pavement in Shaftesbury Avenue, a very old
> woman was dancing slowly, turning in on herself with her eyes completely
> motionless beneath the paper feathers of her hat. Towards one o'clock in the

morning, the fog descended.... It absorbed the phantom police cars that had come from the provinces, and the fire engines, the groups of first-aid workers, the St John Ambulance brigade with their flat caps and white bags.

Far away from the resounding organs and the splendid banquets, but still very close to Westminster and Buckingham Palace, Cartier-Bresson took some of his finest photographs while working on this assignment. Through his close attention to people and to the show on the streets, he was able to bring out the most extraordinary elements of ordinary life. There are three policemen carrying a young girl on their shoulders, a party reveller in Trafalgar Square dozing in an ocean of newspapers, first-aid workers carrying their stretchers in a kind of ballet. His England was rather like himself – full of surprises.

Whatever he did and wherever he was, Cartier-Bresson always remained true to himself as he absorbed the great spectacle of life. His capacity for absorption was so vast that he never ceased to gain from it, and he would immediately seize whatever his imagination and his sensibility latched on to. On his return to Paris, he photographed fishermen and picnickers on the banks of the Marne – a naturalistic reflection of the revolutionary political development of paid holidays for workers. In the pleasure of living that emanates from this superb graphic composition, it is hard to avoid seeing an echo of Manet's *Déjeuner sur l'herbe*, or the recent influence of Renoir's sets in *Partie de campagne*.

As events unfolded towards the end of the 1930s, different facets of Cartier-Bresson's personality continued to come to the fore. The painter in him discovered a highly accomplished artist in the person of Alberto Giacometti, and they became firm friends. Giacometti came from Graubünden in Switzerland, was seven years older than Cartier-Bresson, and was at a turning-point in his career. Having gone through periods of neo-impressionism, cubism and surrealism, as a sculptor he was now launching himself into research on representation of the human body. Cartier-Bresson developed a deep affection for him, admired him as a master, and respected him as a thinker. They knew that, despite differences of opinion and of art appreciation, their outlook was very similar, because they had played the game of three favourite painters. Each had written his choice separately. Two were identical (Cézanne and Van Eyck), and although their third choice was different (Uccello and Piero della Francesca), the discrepancy was tiny, given these two great Italians' obsession with geometry. Cartier-Bresson did not hesitate to add the name of Giacometti to the exclusive inventory of his ideal museum. In his eyes, this man in rebellion against his own time embodied better than any other contemporary creative artist the qualities of discipline and authenticity.

Now a recognized photographer, Cartier-Bresson scarcely mixed with any of his colleagues except Robert Doisneau, Robert Capa, Chim and Eli Lotar. A Frenchman, a Hungarian, a Pole and a Romanian – these were his brothers-in-arms, his chosen family. They talked, showed their work to one another, and influenced one another. If Cartier-Bresson's photographic style had now become less personal and more social, it was as much due to his circle of friends as to the spirit of the age and the demands of the chief editor of *Ce Soir*. He was not yet 30, but *Time* had already ranked the 'itinerant Frenchman' alongside Robert Capa, Walker Evans and the doyen of them all, Alfred Stieglitz. The American magazine in fact described them as the privileged members of an élite club whose members were 'truly and exclusively engaged in capturing through photography what they can find as instants of truth'. One of them was already considering an idea that would revolutionize their profession. This was Robert Capa who, during their conversations and correspondence, drew up the basis of what he called 'a sort of organization' designed to protect their interests – in other words, a 'fraternity' of photo-journalists.

Cartier-Bresson remained faithful to his youthful passion for surrealism. He still loved it as he had always done, and more than ever it seemed to him like 'shadow and prey merged in a unique flash', to echo André Breton. When Breton published *L'Amour fou*, he read it with shocked wonderment. He was transfixed by what was said about the 'convulsive beauty' and the 'odious order' created by the pathetic trinity of family–country–religion. One idea, carefully highlighted in italics, struck him most forcibly and fixed itself in his brain: 'The powers of objective chance that defy verisimilitude.' For this revelation alone, which was not without effect on his vision of the world, *L'Amour fou* joined *Nadja* in his personal pantheon – especially as Breton published a detail from one of the photos that Cartier-Bresson had taken in Seville in 1933. It was unfortunate that he committed an historical blunder by giving it a caption taken from his own text in which he referred to 'all the little children of the Spanish militia'.

The student in Cartier-Bresson still sought a mentor. To start with there had been his Uncle Louis, then Jacques-Emile Blanche, and to a lesser degree René Crevel and Max Jacob. Later, Tériade arrived from Greece and took over, to the exclusion of everyone else. Cartier-Bresson had enormous respect for him, and as he got to know him better, realized that this thoughtful man, far from being uncouth, was in fact merely reserved. People always thought they were bothering him, whereas he thought he was bothering them. Such misunderstandings do not make for easy communication. But Tériade was really his guide.

In December 1937 he was delighted when Tériade, who was devoted to the classical ideal, at last published the first issue of *Verve*, his own magazine, which was eventually to develop into a publishing house. He brought a degree of literary and artistic ambition to it, since his intention from the outset was to make it the most beautiful magazine in the world. In two languages and financed by the director of an American magazine, its content and style were conceived from beginning to end by its indefatigable founder; it was printed by the master printer Draeger and the master lithographer Mourlot, while the typography was entrusted to the National Printing Press. Tériade, who was clearly a catalyst, presented himself as a mere craftsman in the service of a magical union between painting and poetry. He even wished to give painters the chance to talk about painting! Cartier-Bresson particularly savoured his view of art critics, professional or otherwise. Their most brilliant analyses seemed to Tériade to be always less interesting than the most banal statement by any artist. His declaration of intent in this first issue was a credo which Cartier-Bresson found entirely congenial:

> *Verve* intends to present art intimately intertwined with the life of every period, and to provide evidence of artists' participation in the essential events of their time. *Verve* is interested in artistic creation in all domains and in all its forms. *Verve* refrains from fantasy in the presentation of documents. Its elements are validated by their quality, by the selection that has been made, and by the importance that they assume through their position in the magazine. So that the illustrations do not lose the quality of the originals, *Verve* uses the most appropriate technique for each reproduction: colour gravure, wood engraving, typography. It is not afraid to make use of the forgotten process of lithography.

The first issue of *Verve*, with a cover designed by Matisse, contained three photos by Henri Cartier-Bresson. They were notable, but they were a distraction from his purpose. Cartier-Bresson the anti-fascist was trying to work out how to serve a cause that was neither aesthetic nor artistic – that of the Spanish Republicans, which had to be that of every democratic European. He could do it through photography, but the photograph, by definition static and two-dimensional, seemed to him to be not quite appropriate as a means of reflecting the violence of the age. The documentary, synonymous with speed and movement, was far more suited to this extreme crisis. It was time for him to put into practice what he had learned in New York from Paul Strand's circle, and in France from Jean Renoir. If something was to be done, it had to be done properly. And so he did not hesitate to accept – for reasons more political than professional – the commission offered him by the American Medical Bureau in Aid of Spanish Democracy.

In French the film is called *Victoire de la vie*, in English *Return to Life*, both of which represent a powerful defence of this cause of all causes. The 42-minute, 16 mm sound film was made by Henri Cartier-Bresson – team-spirited individualist, camera in hand, more or less the director – and Herbert Kline, Spanish correspondent of the left-wing magazine *New Masses*, more or less the scriptwriter. The two of them worked together with the camera operator Jacques Lemare. The producer was Frontier Films, an association made up of friends of the 'Nykino' group. The project was a token of resistance, capturing the daily lives of Spaniards in their epic struggle. The aim was to give a prosaic account of the medical dimension of the tragedy: the setting up of field hospitals, the manufacture of sanitary ware, the transformation of the Ritz Hotel into Hospital No. 21, the surgical operations carried out in the most hazardous conditions, the rehabilitation of the seriously injured, emergency care and emergency transfusions, the repatriation of the wounded, the heroism of the stretcher-bearers.

The viewer would need to be made of stone not to be moved. But the public was to some extent used to such horrors. As early as 1860, in the wake of the Anglo-French expedition to China, Felice Beato had published his first photographs of corpses littering the battlefield. Immediately afterwards Matthew Brady sent forth his team of photographer-reporters to record the still smoking rubble of the American Civil War. Since then, there had been no let-up.

The film is sober, efficient, direct. There are more children playing than soldiers fighting. And yet the viewer is in the line of fire, even if he does not necessarily realize it. Armed with his Ben & Howell, a small portable camera using 30-metre reels, Cartier-Bresson worked with as much facility as with his Leica. Both cameras allowed him the movement and the geometry required to capture the fleeting scenes that pass across the screen.

There had already been several Spanish films about this aspect of the Civil War, showing virtually the same sequences, but the difference here lay in the commentary. *Return to Life* launched a direct appeal from the health services for action; it sought to make the American public aware of what was happening and to elicit its support. It was a perfect example of how international sympathy could bring aid to the 'good' side in Spain in its hour of need. The friends of the Republican camp were better versed in this kind of propaganda than the Nationalists, and in three years they produced about 200 such films – many more than their opponents. Most were made in Madrid, both capital city and symbol of the strife, the scene of an heroic siege and house-to-house fighting. The camera can itself be a weapon of war, and there could have been no more effective means of combating the disastrous effects of non-intervention and of mobilizing international support.

One of the very best of the films was made by Paul Strand, at whose New York home Cartier-Bresson had learned all about documentaries. *Heart of Spain* depicts the siege of Madrid from the hospital perspective; the details of blood and amputation make it more like a painting by Goya than anything else. Kline and Cartier-Bresson's film does not have the same impact, but nevertheless it achieves its purpose. The pair made a second film, also in 1938, *L'Espagne Vivra*, as a kind of postscript to the first. Even those involved in it later forgot about it. The *Lincoln Battalion*, about the bravery of the American volunteers who fought with the international brigades, was financed by public subscription. It was shown in the United States but then lost for ever, since no copy has as yet come to light.

The war was not over. Like many of his friends in Spain and elsewhere, Cartier-Bresson followed its ups and downs: the Nationalists' assaults on Madrid, the bombing of Guernica, the uprising of the anarchists and Trotskyites in Barcelona, brutally crushed, the capture and subsequent loss of Teruel by the Republicans, the reopening and reclosing of the French borders. He knew it was time to go home – he did not intend to join up as a volunteer.

The war was a dress rehearsal for the catastrophe to come. But in the heat of battle at the time no one was really aware of this. For Cartier-Bresson, the Spanish war was a shattering personal experience – an upheaval on a par with the revelations of Africa. It was the first time he had seen anyone die.

Everything to do with this period would leave its mark on his memory (though not *Espoir*, Malraux's film on the war, which Cartier-Bresson never saw). It was at this time that he got to know the painter Roberto Matta in Paris, and it became a lasting friendship, though one indelibly marked with the image of the Spanish war.

Nothing would ever be the same again, on a professional or a personal level. And yet Cartier-Bresson's true nature did not emerge into the open, even under the pressure of all these astonishing events. He was not like others: Albert Londres, for instance, whose report on the burning of Rheims Cathedral after a German attack in 1915 revealed as much of himself as of the conflagration; or François Aubert, portraitist of government officials, who came to photojournalism during an expedition to Mexico, when he reported on the execution of the Emperor Maximilian.

Although he did not like to admit it, for a long time Cartier-Bresson suffered from the fact that his two great friends Capa and Chim, but not he himself, went down in posterity as *the* photographers of the Spanish Civil War, even though the three of them had been at work there. To his eternal regret, he had never actually taken any photographs of the war itself, being preoccupied with raising money for the Republican hospitals with his propaganda film. But a documentary swiftly fades in the collective memory, whereas photographs endure. Editing a film can often be a long process, and by the time this one was finished the civil war was over. Next time, he would bear all this in mind before pandering to the needs of the moment. Henri the militant would take precedence over Henri the reporter.

Cartier-Bresson returned to Paris, to Aragon's newspaper and to photojournalism. But after one call from Jean Renoir, who was writing a regular film column for *Ce Soir*, he was ready to drop everything. It was now the beginning of 1939.

They had not seen each other for about two years. Renoir, who had a tendency to flit from one thing to another, had nevertheless made four more films: *Les Bas-Fonds*, his famous project based on Gorky; *La Grande Illusion*, which Cartier-Bresson hated for the way it exalted class affinities, exemplified by the bond between the French aristocrat and the German country squire; *La Marseillaise*, about the French Revolution, a film still very much influenced by the spirit of the Popular Front, though produced by the Confédération générale du travail – a French trade union; and finally *La Bête humaine*, based on Emile Zola's novel. With each film, the public had become more and more confused. It was as if the director refused to conform to any pattern, changing genres deliberately. And yet by nourishing his craft with other arts, this fiercely independent cinematographer was in fact constantly making the same points. It was just that the continual change of register entailed taking risks and, consequently, varying the degree of enjoyment.

He wore out his assistants, this man of exceptional generosity, humanity and simplicity, who would do anything except fight – he was too weak, too depressive, and too easily discouraged for that. But few directors treated their actors with so much tact and courtesy. If he wasn't happy with a scene, he would never say, 'No good, it's got to be done again,' it was always, 'That's marvellous, really marvellous. Now supposing we tried it this way?' Perhaps Cartier-Bresson had missed this warm human quality, the laughter and singing, the unique and timeless experience of film-making. Whatever the reasons, he accepted the invitation to work on a film which would, in the eyes of posterity, remain not only the great Renoir film, but also one of the masterpieces of French cinema. It was one of those rare films that attain the status of a classic, kick-start the careers of several directors, and stir the emotions down the generations.

The title of the film was *La Règle du jeu*; the story, a weekend of hunting in Sologne, finishing with a party. The amorous intrigues of the masters are echoed by those of the servants, though we do not know which outdoes the other in cynicism, treachery, hypocrisy and cruelty. Everyone deceives everyone else, A runs after B, X wants to be loved by Y, who doesn't love him, Z wants to convince us that he has an aged mother.... Again, the synopsis tells us nothing about the film's touch of madness. Nor does it capture the extraordinary density of the action, the inextricable tangle of emotional manoeuvres, the joys and sufferings caused by the fickleness of the heart, all this conveyed in broken rhythms that the popular cinema finds hard to accept even now. It required a dramatic technique that grew out of the film's paradoxes, even without a real hero to draw the viewer's admiration.

There was a great risk of confusing the audience, not helped by the fact that the budget was strictly limited, and everyone was afraid of overspending. However, the commercial success of *La Grande Illusion* and *La Bête humaine* had given Renoir a degree of self-confidence, though this could sometimes be a fault. His reputation would in future override such faults.

Shooting took place in the Sologne region, apart from the interiors and the steps leading to the château which were brilliantly reconstructed in the Joinville and Billancourt studios by the designers Eugène Lourié and Max Douy. From mid-February 1939, the crew stayed at the Hôtel Rat in Lamotte-Beuvron, south of Orléans. It rained, as usual. Those who had survived the making of *Partie de campagne* took it all in good humour. This time the assistants left the search for props to the props men, and the costumes to Coco Chanel.

The first assistant, André Zwoboda, had a major hand in the screenplay; much of it was written in advance, but some things were left open right till the end so as not to lose any opportunity of improving the script, especially through the spontaneous contributions of the actors. As for the second assistant, Henri Cartier-Bresson, when he was not slipping his own little gems into the dialogue (a habit he shared with Renoir), he was charged with various delicate assignments, both finding locations and supervising the actual filming. Despite his comparative youth, a kind of legend – the African jungle, the lower depths of Mexico, the perils of Harlem – had already grown up around him. He found the château of La Ferté-Saint-Aubin and its 40 hectares of parkland in Sologne; he showed one of the actors, Marcel Dalio, how to use a gun expertly; he organized the rabbit-hunting scenes, and stood in for the actor skinning the animal; he found ways to raise Renoir's morale during his depressions and to stop him drowning himself in alcohol.

Along with a select group of insiders, Cartier-Bresson was the privileged spectator of a film within a film. He was aware that Renoir was leading parallel lives, and that these were unravelling before their eyes both on and off the set: Marguerite Houllé was the editor and his official companion; Dido Freire was the continuity girl. His private life was reflected in the fictional château, behind the façade of which the masters and servants pursued their own double-crossing, double lives. As in the film, his life teetered constantly between comedy and tragedy.

To ensure that they got a feel for what was going on, Renoir liked his close collaborators to spend a little time on the other side of the camera, and so, as before, Cartier-Bresson was given a small part to play: that of an English manservant named William. The scene takes place in the kitchens of the château. The chambermaids, manservants and chauffeur are sitting round the dining-table. Cartier-Bresson, in formal costume, has to stretch out his hand and say in a strong British accent: 'Would you please pass the mustard?' And then in the same tone: 'Thank you.'

In the next shot, Germaine the cook says: 'All the same, madam is going a bit far with her pilot!' Then William, youthful as ever, turns to her and replies in an accent you could cut with a knife: 'When things get embarrassing, there's just no pleasure!' He makes her laugh. A little later he holds her in his arms as they perform the *danse macabre*, and protects her from the menacing spectre of death.

This was the true film début of Henri Cartier-Bresson the actor, but there was to be no sequel. It was clear that he was no actor, and this did not bother him. What was disappointing, and painful at the time, though ultimately fruitful as it shattered certain illusions, was the other obvious discovery. At the end of their third film together Renoir made him face the fact that he was totally devoid of imagination, and he came to realize that it would be pointless to continue as an assistant because he would never become a director. To make a film, you have to lead a team, give orders, exercise authority – things that Cartier-Bresson simply couldn't do.

Renoir had done him two good turns: first by engaging him, and secondly by letting him go.

La Règle du jeu was one of the last films of the old world. Afterwards, France and Europe would be torn apart. Cartier-Bresson was 32. These dark years marked the end of the carefree innocence of that world. Among the personal tragedies was the premature loss of Jacqueline, one of three sisters to whom he was very close.

5 NATIONALITY: ESCAPEE
1939–46

'Soft, very soft. Incapable of promotion to a higher rank.' On seeing the military records in which this remark appeared, Cartier-Bresson was shocked to discover exactly what the army thought of him. To get over it, on the eve of his mobilization he said goodbye to civilian life as others bid farewell to bachelorhood. With his friend Jacques Becker, who was at the wheel of his old Model T Ford, he embarked on a methodical tour of the bars and restaurants of the great Parisian hotels: Ritz, Meurice, Plaza Athénée, Continental.

It was farewell to the cinema too. In any case, Renoir – longing to make a colour film to compete with those being made abroad – had left for Italy, heedless of any offence this might cause to his communist friends. Despite the fascist regime there, he was said to have accepted an invitation to work with Count Ciano, Mussolini's son-in-law, on an adaptation of *Tosca*.

Events moved fast during the summer of 1939. The signing of a non-aggression pact between Germany and Russia outraged many fellow travellers as well as militant communists. Among the intellectuals, however, Paul Nizan was the only one to resign from the party in protest against this unnatural alliance. He did so in an article, without any fuss, and then withdrew into silence. The Communist Party, which never forgave him for this 'betrayal', proceeded to launch a vicious campaign of rumours purporting to give the real reasons for his resignation: he was a spy from the Préfecture de Police who had long ago infiltrated the party; he was a traitor. The accusation recurred, often indirectly and insidiously. A few months later Nizan, fighting as a liaison officer in British uniform, was killed at Dunkirk. His name was dragged unscrupulously through the mud by his former comrades, led by Aragon. Cartier-Bresson, at first stupefied and then sickened, never forgave Aragon for his appalling part in this affair. Until Aragon's death, he felt a sincere affection for one side of him, the surrealist and the director of *Ce Soir* who had given him his big opportunity; by contrast he felt the deepest contempt for the other aspect, the apparatchik, the VIP Stalinist who concealed all crimes, beginning with the ruthless and despicable smearing of the admirable Nizan.

In spring 1940 the Daladier government, whose 'cowardice' had been regarded as a huge let-down by many of the military, was forced to resign. Paul Reynaud, the new President of the Council, charged Philippe Boegner, who had previously been on the management board of *Vu* and *Paris-Soir*, with the task of setting up an army photographic service designed to counterbalance the many pictures of German generals now appearing in the press. Even the American magazines were full of them. Boegner realized to his horror that the French propaganda machine was using only eight photographers to cover the whole world. At once he drew up a list of 80 names, at the head of which was Henri Cartier-Bresson, at the time enrolled in the 'reserve' infantry. Eighteen of these photographers, of which Cartier-Bresson was the first, were summoned to his office in Buttes-Chaumont.

Cartier-Bresson was stationed at the Desvalières Barracks in Metz, where he teamed up with other conscripts in the Film and Photo unit of the Third Army. In addition to their light, practical cameras – American Cameclair 120 mm and Eyenos – the unit was equipped with a Ford van on whose doors was emblazoned the curious monogram *Oyez. Voyez* ('Hear. See').

Their mission was to film the so-called 'phoney war', to photograph soldiers in outposts or along the Maginot Line, and to provide pictures of heavy artillery in action. They themselves regarded the job as cushy, and in its way it was a perfect illustration of the phoney war. There were four of them: Cartier-Bresson himself, Albert Viguier, André Bac, a press photographer who hoped to break into the cinema as a head cameraman, and Alain Douarinou, who had already worked as an assistant cameraman for Jean Renoir, Jacques Tourneur and Marc Allégret, and as cameraman in some 20 films starring Sacha Guitry, Edmond Gréville and others.

On 10 May 1940 the 'French Campaign' began. The armoured corps of the Wehrmacht crossed the Meuse and reached Sedan three days later. Mandiargues was the only one to spot that among the generals who entered Paris at the head of their troops were one Von Kleist and one Von Arnim. Abbeville, Arras, Calais – one town after another fell under the advance of this steamroller force. Northerners fled south, and France became a nation of refugees. It was a débâcle.

Corporal Cartier-Bresson just had time to save his dearest possession: he buried his Leica in a farmyard in the Vosges. Then he performed a ritual that others would come to regard as sacrilegious but which he also carried out in peacetime when there was no pressure to do so: he destroyed most of his work and threw away the negatives he didn't like.

On this occasion, he cut out one by one those he intended to keep, in an act of intense self-criticism devoid of even the slightest complacency. Three quarters of those he examined were discarded, along with their negatives, the selection being made – as usual – purely on instinct. There was no appeal against this judgment: the rejects were destroyed, and the chosen few were placed in a Huntley & Palmer biscuit tin and dispatched to his father, who had the good sense to store them in a safety deposit box at the bank.

With his colleagues, Cartier-Bresson filmed and photographed the effects of aerial bombardment on the roads. They were forbidden, however, to film the major road and rail junctions, and this order remained in force until the Third Army, defeated and demoralized, was commanded to retreat. Initially they did so in orderly fashion, but subsequently there was chaos, with even the staff officers disappearing into the night. In the course of their retreat the troops found themselves surrounded by the Germans, while on the radio Marshal Pétain, the new President of the Council, called on all soldiers to lay down their arms.

On 22 June 1940, the day when the armistice was signed at Rethondes, Cartier-Bresson and his comrades were captured at Saint-Dié in the Vosges. The officers of the Wehrmacht informed them that they would be treated as 'prisoners of honour', and they assumed that they would shortly be released. They handed in their weapons, expecting that they would then be allowed to travel freely in their own country, but what they did not know was that the armistice would not come into force until 25 June. After the débâcle came the humiliation, all the more crushing because the nation put much of the blame for its plight on the soldiers themselves. Stunned though they were by the disaster of 1940, worse was to come. The soldiers now had to learn what life was like as prisoners of war.

Every prisoner that arrived at Stalag VA in Ludwigsburg was given a number and made to pose for a photograph – smile not compulsory. About 23,000 men were held there. A prisoner-of-war camp was not the same as a concentration camp or extermination camp, but it was a camp all the same. Cartier-Bresson, KG 845, found himself in the Black Forest, then in Württemberg, near Heidelberg, working in labour gangs. He laid railway sleepers, carted metal shavings into a munitions factory that specialized in crankshafts for submarines, quarried stone, manufactured cement, made hay, tore up cloths, ground up bones in the slaughterhouse.... In three years he did 30 different jobs, and in so doing he took on a new identity, even a new nationality: KG (*Kriegsgefangener*, prisoner of war). For the Germans, production was everything, and here was a supply of cheap labour every single day of the week. The experience was physically taxing and morally unforgettable for a young, aesthetically-minded middle-class man who was not even any good at sport.

Very few people in the camp knew of his photographs, but most of them made the connection between his name and the family business in Pantin. Here, even more than in the land of the free, he felt this to be a burden and preferred not to talk about it.

As everyone had to work, or at least to give the impression that he was working, Cartier-Bresson made every effort to fight his gaolers with the forces of inertia. He swiftly volunteered to practise 'work resistance', in domestic surroundings rather than in factories, since the former were ideal for getting away with the minimum, as well as offering the best chance of escape. No sooner had he arrived behind the barbed wire than he started planning how to get out – he never once even contemplated waiting out the war in such appalling conditions. The moment would come when he had to do more than merely stop himself shouting at the Germans, to think hard thoughts, to devote his energy to doing nothing, to upset his farmer host by constantly talking politics, to explain how it was that Gibraltar could be in Spain and yet belong to England. Nor could he bear just to sit and watch the farmer doling out the food: first for himself and the prisoner, then for the children, and finally – the smallest portion – for his wife. At such moments Cartier-Bresson longed to have his Leica in his hand, but all he could do was to take mental photographs.

When he was not shaving his head like the Russian prisoners in order to annoy the guards, or rereading Joyce's *Ulysses* – one of his few surviving possessions – or decoding the letters in Behasa Melayu from Ratna, his wife (thanks to his French-Malayan dictionary, probably the only one in the region), or drawing or painting, his thoughts would turn to escape. The Germans kept insisting that the prisoners could not get home because all the bridges had been bombed and not yet rebuilt, but he had no intention of waiting to test the truth of this.

The camp contained a huge cross-section of humanity. Where else could a middle-class Parisian, even one who admittedly had done a bit of travelling, have picked up such Polish expressions as *pizda* ('cunt') or *kurwa jego mac!* ('your mother's a whore')? In the camp, all normal points of reference went by the board. The non-life that the prisoners lived wiped out all conventional notions of time, and the knowledge that there was no way out, and that there was no known end to the ordeal, drove some of them crazy. In such a world gossip and rumour reigned supreme. Paranoia and cholera were equally rife, and everyone lived on a knife-edge. Deprived of mental stimulus, the prisoners felt their humanity slowly draining away, and began to believe that for no good reason they had been cast out from the land of the living. It was a long, long way from the camp in *La Grande Illusion*, for here the prisoners believed they were invisible in the eyes of the world.

The camp was a microcosm of society, with its own clans and networks, but without women and children. The only profession not represented was that of the President of the Republic. There was even an insurance agent who wrote books in his spare time, two published by Gallimard. Tall and thin, his sharp but myopic eyes framed by thick glasses, Raymond Guérin had the height and bearing of a literary giant. As a non-commissioned officer he was not subjected to forced labour, and people considered him condescending and arrogant, clever but stiff. But he too suffered from the cold and was undernourished, though he tried not to show it.

He said very little and observed a lot. When he was not to be seen writing, it was because he was writing in his head. *Les Poulpes* ('Octopi') was a sort of novel that transposed the whole fantastical experience of captivity into an unreality in which man was reduced to the level of the worm. The prisoners were the characters, but without names or numbers – only nicknames. The hero was Le Grand Dab (Guérin himself); other characters were given such names as Frise-Poulet, Tante Pitty, Domisoldo, Thorax-d'Ajax, Organisir, le Folliculaire or les Tordus.

Guérin maintained a certain degree of style, unlike Cartier-Bresson and Douarinou, who paraded themselves in their rags. But he had enough respect for them to decline to escape with them. With his weak sight, poor health, unnatural movements, insecurity, lack of German and indecisiveness, he would not have been an asset to the escapees. It did not matter that some people took his refusal as a sign of disdain or cowardice. His friends quickly realized that beneath his show of indifference escape, for him, was escapism. This did not prevent him from helping them as much as he could, by obtaining money and information. The two of them come out well in his novel, and they are easy to recognize in a long passage around the middle of *Les Poulpes*. Douarinou is La Globule, and Cartier-Bresson is Bébé Cadum, a French version of 'the little white man with shrimp cheeks', the nickname given to him by his Zapotec girl-friend some years before in Mexico.

The two boys introduced themselves. Bébé Cadum had a huge skull, already balding, jutting over the blue eyes of an archangel and the pink cheeks of a chubby child. La Globule, with dark hair and skin, his face decorated with impressive whiskers, was the spitting image of a Saint-Malo corsair.... As much through bravado as through bohemianism, Bébé Cadum and La Globule appeared in the nicest possible way to affect the look of a pair of degenerates. Their disguise was indescribable! Dressed in combat fatigues, which soot and spit had gradually polished to a yellowish filth, red scarves round their necks, rubber boots on their feet, they stank of the kitchen sink and the rubbish bin.... With Bébé Cadum and La Globule, Le Grand Dab enjoyed the double pleasure of intellectual communion with no mannerisms, and perfect harmony of thought. Having been moulded by much travel, having read a lot and being a refined expert on painting, Bébé Cadum proved to be a subtle partner.

Escape was not a mere pipe-dream. About 1,600,000 French prisoners were transported to Germany during the war, and 70,000 escaped. The propor-tion is small, even counting the much larger number of attempts that failed, not to mention the virtual escapes that were planned mainly in order to conquer boredom. Cartier-Bresson and some of his companions were obsessed with the idea, even more than with the food they waited anxiously for each day – bread for seven, nettle soup for all. The prospect of freedom was what kept them going and saved them from the depths of depression. Others were too shat-tered, morally and physically, to be anything other than resigned to their fate – it was all a question of character and the life force.

At their first attempt, the weather played a dirty trick on them. Their reward was isolation in the bamboo hut reserved for escapees. Together with Alain Douarinou, his 'travelling companion', Cartier-Bresson was sentenced to 21 days in solitary confinement and two months of penal servitude before he could return to base. It was a grim time, with one glowing exception. On a day of deep gloom, when the two of them were down in a dark valley tilling the earth on a farm, the man who had been his friend ever since the filming of *La vie est à nous* suddenly turned to him: 'Look, Henri, beyond that hill, imagine there's the sea....'

It was just a flight of fancy, but the sort that helps to keep one alive through the darkest hour. Under such conditions it was a priceless gift. With it, Douari-nou, son of a naval captain, gave him a new slant on life, for it showed him what really mattered: from now on, he would keep his eye on the horizon.

The second attempt took place when he was working in a bomb factory in Karlsruhe; once again he managed to slip away from the guards, this time with Claude Lefranc. His friend, as calm as Cartier-Bresson was nervous, took a mischievous pleasure in provoking him, and indeed they even came to blows. They were caught 24 hours later by the Schutzpolizei. It was late at night, and they had just got to the bridge over the Rhine. Once again, it was back to detention, solitary confinement, forced labour – the same old story – except that in the middle of this escapade, he had been surprised to find himself making different plans.

'When all this is over and I'm free, I'm going to be a fashion designer. What about you?' his friend had asked him.

'Me? I'm going to be a painter.'

Third time lucky: they crossed the border on 10 February 1943, going on foot along the Moselle canal. It was Claude Lefranc's birthday. They had stolen some civilian clothing from the STO (*Service du travail obligatoire* – compulsory labour, set up by the Germans during the occupation of France), and had acquired forged papers and railway tickets thanks to an SS man from Alsace. They travelled to Metz without any untoward incident – the guard had put them in a carriage reserved for German officers – and after that spent three months hiding on a farm near Loches, in Indre-et-Loire, along with ten others – escapees, STO dodgers, Resistance fighters and Jews.

This period of his life, which ended three lost years, was one of the few that Cartier-Bresson recalled with visible emotion. But to cover it up he would make fun of himself. Years later, when filling in the questionnaire devised by Proust, his answer to the question 'What was your favourite journey?' was 'Escaping three times as a prisoner of war'.

The escape was not an act of heroism, but simply necessary to his survival. A born nonconformist cannot abide confinement of any kind. Cartier-Bresson escaped without even thinking about the risks, or indeed the possible advantages of staying put. He had to get away because he had never been able to bear any restriction on his freedom of movement, thought, speech, reading-matter, career or anything else. It was in his blood.

He was an escapee. That was the only 'medal' he wanted, and he shared it with the 30,000 others who received it officially – not with conceit but with pride at being one of those who kept his promise to those he left behind, the friends who had been denounced, tortured, shot. The enemy had tried to turn them into animals, but they had remained human and had taken their fate into their own hands. Now he knew what could be achieved by solidarity between humans, even in a context of total humiliation, and how they could adapt to the most appalling circumstances. Alongside these people he had touched rock bottom in the form of hunger, beatings, the cold of the night, the mud of the ditch, and man's inhumanity to man.

Germany would always remain anathema to him, and on meeting a German he would find it hard not to ask the obvious question, 'What did you do in the war?', in the same tone as he wanted to ask the person getting out of a Rolls Royce, 'Where does the money come from?'

The war changed him, as it did so many others. The old world was now the world he knew before he was a PoW. His soul would always be marked by the experience. In any political discussion, he could side with only one camp – the prison camp. Nationality: escapee. He had learned things in the camp that free men would never know, one of which was that those who have been inside can never truly get out again, for the camp is not of this world.

Lyons, June 1943. In a house on the outskirts, where a secret meeting was being held among the senior officers of the French Resistance, Jean Moulin, the chief, was arrested by the Gestapo. Henri Cartier-Bresson was just a stone's throw away, but of course knew nothing of this, despite the fact that his brother Claude, who was opposed to Pétain from the outset, had been at the heart of the Libération-Sud movement since 1941 while continuing his industrial work. Under the pseudonym of Vincent, he was part of the general staff of the secret army in the Toulouse region.

As a prisoner on the run, Henri was due to meet a Resistance fighter who could get him forged papers with the help of Aragon, who had felt obliged to make contact with the MNPGD, *Mouvement national des prisonniers de guerre et déportés* ('National Movement for Prisoners of War and Internees') and to give secret aid to escapees. While waiting, Henri needed to find a way of averting suspicion in case a patrol should come by, so he sat down on the bank of the Rhône, took out his box of Windsor and Newton paints, and started work on a watercolour. More such paintings would follow, and they would not be mere alibis. In the camp he had said that when he was free he would be a painter, for that was his passion and his vocation.

So long as the war continued, however, he did not see himself returning to serious painting or drawing. He felt that it did not fit the spirit of the age, with its intensity and rapidity. Photography was the medium for that.

The first thing that Henri did with his freedom was to return to the farm in the Vosges where he had buried his Leica, and exhume it. For three years he had not taken a single photo, except in his head, but all the old instincts were still there; he still wanted to capture the world's harmony and record its invisible order within a tiny rectangle.

He was introduced by the art critic Georges Besson to the prominent Mulhouse printer and publisher Pierre Braun, for whom Besson worked. At the beginning of the occupation, Braun had held an exhibition of works by Bazaine, Manessier and others under the title *Vingt jeunes peintres de tradition française* ('Twenty young painters in the French tradition'). Now he wanted to launch a series of small monographs on different contemporary artists (Matisse, Braque, Bonnard, Picasso, Rouault and so on) and writers (such as Valéry and Claudel). Cartier-Bresson readily agreed to photograph them all for these books – he admired most of them. To photograph a master in the privacy of his own home was a rare privilege – the first known instance was Edmond Bacot's portrait of Victor Hugo taken in 1862 at his house on Guernsey.

Matisse was at the head of the list. The first sitting took place at the end of 1943, and others followed during the first few months of 1944. Matisse was ill with duodenal cancer, and thought he was dying, but his surgeon had given him a reprieve for the three or four years he needed to finish his work. The artist christened by his son-in-law 'the tailor of light' had left the Hôtel Regina at Cimiez for the villa 'Le Rêve' at Vence, as air raids had made it essential to leave Nice. He was now hard at work experimenting with *gouaches découpées* – brightly coloured paper cut-outs, which he arranged into abstract, geometrical patterns.

Matisse did not like to be photographed. He hated the very idea of posing, and had little sympathy for the intrusive curiosity of those who practised the profession. Furthermore, it took him away from his work. But Cartier-Bresson had a talent for making people forget he was there. He paid regular visits, and sat in a corner for hours without saying a word to either the artist or the model, Lydia Delectorskaya. Any sort of conversation would have been inappropriate and would have spoiled everything. When he took a photo he did so with the absolute silence and secrecy of the Invisible Man. Thus the subject forgot that he was the subject. Matisse did not pose but remained completely himself, pencil in one hand, pigeon in the other, oblivious to the world. It was precisely this moment that the photographer chose to capture, expressing the inexpressible link between man and bird.

One can well understand why Henri Cartier-Bresson was the first photographer that Matisse ever allowed to work with him, for he was content to remain in the artist's shadow. Later, art historians were to reap the benefit of this extraordinary privilege when, on examining all the photos, they discovered on the walls projects they had never known about, African cloths and paper petticoats, not to mention the composition 'Formes' for *Jazz*, and above all the panels that the great artist had rejected and wanted to destroy. It is a sobering thought that some of these irreplaceable photos almost disappeared for ever. On his return to Paris, Cartier-Bresson realized that he had left the negatives of the pigeon series in the hotel. The feelings of the escaped prisoner can be imagined, armed with forged demobilization papers, having to cross France again, passing through all the controls and the checkpoints, in the faint hope that he might find his films where he had left them. Fortunately for all concerned, the faint hope was fulfilled.

One day, when he was visiting Matisse, Cartier-Bresson felt sufficiently emboldened to show him one of his own gouaches. Matisse took a box out of his pocket, held it to the top of the picture, and said simply: 'My box of matches does not disturb me any more than what you have painted.'

Cartier-Bresson accepted the criticism. Matisse was just as direct when it came to himself. When Cartier-Bresson showed him the dummy of 'his' book, which was to be published by Braun, he ended up by refusing to give his permission. It was too soon for the cult of the personality.

Cartier-Bresson also photographed Paul Claudel, who took him on a guided tour of his château at Brangues; Georges Rouault in his Sunday best, just about emerging from the previous century, with a heavy crucifix hanging over him; and the charming Pierre Bonnard – remarkable men, with remarkable pictures to match.

Bonnard's home and studio were at Le Cannet (Alpes-Maritimes), where he had been living since 1925. He agreed to be photographed because, as he told his great-nephew, the photographer was young, shy, and evidently needed the money. He had suffered a double blow with the defeat of France and the death of his wife, and was in a particularly vulnerable state, but he was too dignified and modest a man to parade his emotions. Only his self-portraits betray the depths of his grief.

Cartier-Bresson was well acquainted with the work of the man dubbed by his friends 'the very Japanese Nabi' (Hebrew for 'prophet'), who readily acknowledged that his art had always veered between intimism and decoration. He had his doubts as to whether Bonnard would allow the fantasy and irony of his paintings to come through in the photo sessions. He was, however, totally unprepared for the artist's resistance to being photographed at all.

Bonnard at the time was 66 years old, but continued to work as if he were just beginning his career. The conversation flowed so long as Cartier-Bresson left his camera on the table, but as soon as he held it to his eye, even with his usual speed and discretion, Bonnard would shy away. It was a cat-and-mouse game. Sometimes there would be a truce, marked by long silences, but then suddenly Cartier-Bresson would raise his camera, and immediately Bonnard would pull his fisherman's hat down over his eyes and mask the lower half of his face with his scarf. 'Toothache,' he would mumble, a wicked glint flashing from behind his round glasses.

Then the game would begin again, and he would hide his face again, and chew on his scarf: 'The expression on my face – who on earth would be interested in that? All that I have to say is to be found in my works.'

The photographer would again put down his camera but then, nonchalantly, would manage all the same to capture the essentials: the artist sitting in a corner, the artist in distress, looking as if he wanted to disappear into the walls, the artist standing, in profile, all wrapped up as if it were snowing inside... and in the background, pinned to the wall, his *Saint François de Sales bénissant les malades* ('St Francis de Sales blessing the sick'), on which he was working for the church at Plateau d'Assy (Haute-Savoie). Cartier-Bresson himself was too shy and too respectful to photograph him full face, for that would have seemed like an act of aggression.

'Why did you press the button at that precise moment?' asked the painter.

Cartier-Bresson turned towards one of the unfinished canvases leaning against the wall, and pointed at a detail: 'Why did you put a little touch of yellow here?'

Bonnard couldn't help but laugh, but the point had been made. In both cases it was a matter of vision, and no other explanation was necessary.

Cartier-Bresson had nothing but admiration and affection for Bonnard, who in his eyes was the very embodiment of smiling modesty – a quality that is beautifully reflected in the portraits he took of him.

The meeting with Georges Braque certainly had the most lasting consequences. On 6 June 1944, they were deep in conversation at Braque's home, on
the rue du Douanier-Rousseau, when there was an announcement on the BBC
– which they had left on for background music – that the allied landings had
begun in Normandy. The magnitude of this news alone was enough to ensure
that Braque had a permanent place in his memory, but the painter, with a smile,
rounded off their meeting by giving him a present – something so simple that
no one could have imagined it would have such a lasting influence.

Braque gave him a book that had been presented to him by Jean Paulhan,
who in turn had had it from someone else. There are some texts whose effects
are so magical that they demand to be passed on like a baton in a relay. These
pioneering pages of surrealism had a profound effect on Cartier-Bresson, and
yet the book does not figure in any literary or philosophical anthology, is rarely
quoted, and is difficult to obtain. It is called *Zen in the Art of Archery*, and is by
the German Eugen Herrigel, a professor of philosophy who went to Japan to
study mysticism in the Far East, and practised this 'art' with a view to understanding Zen Buddhism.

Once he had recovered from the shock of the news about the invasion,
Cartier-Bresson felt that at last he had found a manual of photography ideally
suited to his nonconformist spirit. It set out the apparently simple principles
that he had long been searching for: be there, wait in anonymity, and disappear.
But gradually something even more striking began to emerge: a whole way of
life, a detachment from the world and a vision of it that seemed all the more
irresistible because it formed the perfect complement to the libertarian ethic
that he would always cling to.

Here he was, then, a 35-year-old Norman Parisian, in body free to wander
round occupied France, in mind still trapped behind the barbed wire in the
Black Forest, bowled over by a book that presented archery as a mental discipline establishing complete harmony with the unconscious mind. On reading
it for the first time, he realized just how ignorant he was both of archery and of
Buddhism.

Until now he had thought of archery only from the standpoint of the
hunter, as a matter of tension, precision of aim, release. The action itself – the
manner of breathing, of seeing, or of firing – was not enough for the soul to
develop an inner shield. But on delving into the essence of the action, thanks to
the teachings of Zen, he could now see the possibilities of *satori*, that intuitive
spiritual enlightenment which takes the acolyte beyond the traditional bound-

aries of the ego. By learning to wait, he altered his perception of time. New vistas were opened up to him by the dialogue between master and pupil, as reported by Eugen Herrigel:

> The perfect shot does not take place at the opportune moment, because you do not detach yourself from yourself. You do not exert your strength towards the accomplishment but you anticipate your failure.... The true art is without aim, without intention.... Liberate yourself from yourself, leave behind everything that you are, everything that you have, so that nothing at all is left of you except the tension without the aim.

Initially, the photographer in Cartier-Bresson was deeply impressed by Herrigel, but when he had read the book several times his whole vision of the world changed. The philosophy of life that came across consisted of immensely complex ideas expressed with an almost disconcerting clarity and simplicity: you must live for the present, because the future moves away like the line of the horizon as you approach it. To be yourself is to be outside yourself. By aiming at the target there is a chance we will hit ourselves. The outside world sends us back to ourselves. You must arrive with great force and depart forgetting yourself.

Forgetting yourself, abstracting yourself, with nothing more to prove: only when it is no longer a pastime but a means of life and death does archery become an artless art, and then the archer, in conflict with himself, is both Master and non-Master, since he is mentally capable of hitting his target without bow or arrow. Cartier-Bresson would remember all this when he eventually came to finalize his own concept of photography.

A few days earlier, in May 1944, he had sent his patron, Pierre Braun, a letter rather like a last will in tone. No doubt, in his situation as an escapee living illegally and secretly helping prisoners on the run, he was anxious that his work should be preserved should the worst come to the worst. The tension in the atmosphere had grown, what with the savage repression of the Occupation (hostages executed, Resistance fighters massacred, Jews deported); even the immediate future was uncertain. Cartier-Bresson therefore confided his most treasured possessions to Pierre Braun, giving him permission to publish all his old unpublished photos in the form of an album, if necessary including the work of other photographers whose ideas were similar to his own. He was afraid that otherwise his pictures might one day be scattered. He imposed two conditions, however: the reproduction rights were to be the property of Ratna, his wife, and it was imperative that the original composition, as it appeared on the negatives, had to be preserved. In his letter, he once more underlined this perennial aversion to cropping:

> I attach great importance to there being no changes to my compositions; refer to my proofs in the album for this; if they are missing, print the negatives in their entirety without cropping even a millimetre during either enlargement or printing. Do not use margins, because they all encroach – even if only infinitesimally – on the image projected by the negative. Or if the paper is 18 x 24, project the negative on to 23 and not 24, which will leave half a centimetre on either side to hold the paper without the frame encroaching on the image.

His finest negatives were packed into several small round tins of different colours: the shots of Cardinal Pacelli in Montmartre; the series with Claudel, Matisse and Bonnard, wrapped in silk paper; the coronation of King George VI; New York, the Ivory Coast, Greece, Poland, Mexico and Italy. There were even some family photos.

Pierre Braun finally had to abandon the idea of publishing monographs on painters, but the work was not wasted. Quite apart from the portraits that he had taken with his Leica, Cartier-Bresson had had the privilege of meeting the great artists in person, starting with Matisse. The memory of these happy occasions was marred many years later by the publication in 1971 of *Henri Matisse, roman* ('novel'), a barely credible art book in which, beneath a portrait of the painter, Aragon referred in snide terms to the famous sittings:

> The photographer, who arrived punctually, insisted that he put on his dressing gown and also that hat that works wonders. He had been advised not to leave without having photographed Matisse in his dressing gown. Little by little he had created an image of the great painters. There could be no lies. The public would be disappointed. It was, regretfully, necessary for Matisse to put on his 'dressing gown' [A note from Aragon: I do not know if this was actually the dressing gown that appears in photos taken post-war in Vence, or a camel-skin lining that H.M. sometimes wore for its light weight. But photographers entering into the private world of a great man always think they are with Honoré de Balzac] and his felt hat. It was lucky they hadn't asked for the palette – you know, if you give someone an inch....

When he read this passage, Cartier-Bresson was again furious with the man who had denounced his friend Nizan, and for all his gratitude that he had been taken on at *Ce Soir* this added to the hostility between them. Needless to say, he vehemently denied this version of events:

> Nonsense! A load of crap! This scenario is totally contrary to my concept of photography and to everything that I have always done. And in any case, can you imagine for a single instant that a man like Matisse would lend himself to such a charade – or that, at my age, and in my position with relation to him, I would 'insist' on him doing anything? What's more, I've never read any Balzac.

Cartier-Bresson's pocket diary for 1944 spoke for itself. The pages between 7 and 14 June were blank, as were those between 22 and 31 August. But these gaps were not like Louis XVI's famous *'Rien'* ('nothing'), the entry in his journal for 14 July 1789. In the first of these periods, before and after the historic landings in Normandy, Cartier-Bresson was meeting Braque in his studio. In the second he was witnessing the Liberation of Paris, Leica in hand. When General Leclerc's armoured Second Division advanced towards Paris, he left the farm in Loir-et-Cher where he had been in hiding, got on his bicycle, and took the country roads to Paris.

The atmosphere was extraordinary. He had never seen such jubilation, people so carried away that strangers were kissing each other and calling each other *tu* – a rarity among the French since the heady days of the Popular Front. Everyone was happy. The comparatively few photographers had no trouble finding people, whether civilian or military, who were only too delighted to pose for them.

In the rue de Richelieu, not far from the National Library, about 20 photographers had improvised a Communist Party press agency for the occasion. They were in contact with all the different command posts of the Paris Resistance, and Cartier-Bresson and his colleagues divided the city between them according to their specific knowledge of each area. Among them was Robert Doisneau. During the Occupation, according to his biographer Peter Hamilton, he had taken a series of portraits of great scholars and scientists, another of young sportsmen (for a government body), and others for magazines patronized by the pro-Pétain organization *Secours national* ('National Aid'); meanwhile he had secretly been supplying the Resistance with photos for false identity papers. Now he was standing on the bridge with the others. When they divided up the city, he took Ménilmontant, les Batignolles and Saint-Germain-des-Prés. With one hand on his camera and the other on the saddle of his bike to make sure no one stole it, Doisneau did not hesitate to take everything, including the treatment of former collaborators: shaven-headed, half-naked women, a prostitute dragged on a chain like an animal by a Red Cross matriarch, and other violent purges such as inevitably follow any civil war anywhere when the mob takes control.

The little group of photographers covered the city quarter by quarter, although they encroached on each other's territory if they had to. The bicycle was their only means of transport, and a shortage of film was their biggest problem. Although it was still possible to buy Agfa, Kodak was only available on the black market.

This time, for all his reluctance, Cartier-Bresson really did practise photojournalism, and it was of the very best quality. Circumstances had thrust him into a historic position where it would have been dishonourable not to record what was going on. He was driven not by the instincts of a reporter, no matter how good his eye, but by the gut reaction of the escaped prisoner anxious to facilitate the return of the companions he left behind.

He had teamed up with a colleague from France-Presse, and together they moved between the barricades on the rue de Rivoli, near the buildings from which the German administration had ruled Paris for four years. He was able to photograph the surrender of the Wehrmacht officers exiting with their hands above their heads. He was able to get on to the balcony of the Hôtel Continental, where the white flags of surrender were draped in symbolic counterpart to the swastika banners flapping on the place de la Concorde at the beginning of the Occupation.

He was in the rue de Castiglione when armed Resistance fighters, aided by enthusiastic students and schoolboys, ripped up the road surface and used everything they could lay their hands on to build barricades and stop the usurpers from escaping. Standing beneath the arches of the Palais-Royal gardens, he found the perfect perspective between the columns when the French Resistance forces, the FFI, came under fire from German snipers on the roofs. He was at the entrance to the Louvre when the passenger in an enemy sidecar fell at his feet in a welter of blood, a bullet in his forehead in spite of his helmet. For a moment he thought about taking a photograph at point-blank range, but decided to run away – just in time to evade a Wehrmacht patrol which would not have stood on ceremony. He was at the quai d'Orsay, at the Ministry for Foreign Affairs, when a group of dishevelled Germans came out guarded by some rank-and-file soldiers. He was on the Champs-Elysées when General de Gaulle marched triumphantly down the avenue. Many other photographers recorded this great moment, but Cartier-Bresson gave it his inimitable touch: in the foreground, just in front of the General, is an African infantryman. There could be no more potent symbol of what the liberation of metropolitan France owed to free France and its Empire. Such a detail, whether deliberate or not, is absent from most representations of this historic scene.

He was in the middle of an avenue when a Resistance fighter arrested a suspect and pushed him forward with his sub-machinegun. A complete sequence unfolded before his lens, from the initial interrogation to their departure through the streets of Paris. The two archetypal characters were a photographer's dream: the young freedom fighter wore a beret and a sheepskin-lined coat that looked as if it had been the rounds of the maquis; the suspect, a lot older, wore a soft hat and a flashy overcoat, and was trying hard not to look like a profiteer, though his suitcase and heavily laden backpack suggested an all-too-hasty attempt to leave.

He was at the siege of the Gestapo headquarters on avenue Foch when the occupants were arrested. But despite the intense pressure of events unfolding all around him, he remained true to his own principles. We can see this in the photographs he took immediately after these action shots: a still life in the abandoned apartments and offices, like a flower among the ruins. An open window creates a strangely poetic paradox between the foliage of the trees and the wrought-iron arabesque of the balcony. In the background of a stairwell, discreetly visible in the gaps, we see the disorder of another hasty departure.

Wandering around the streets as usual, but always on the alert, he happened to see the actor and dramatist Sacha Guitry, accompanied by an armed guard of freedom fighters wearing armbands. It was evident from their expressions that they were not autograph-hunters. He immediately fell in behind them until they reached the *mairie* of the seventh *arrondissement*, and followed them into a room where Guitry was interrogated in a form of summary trial. He was under suspicion of being a collaborator. Seated behind a table, side by side with his young inquisitor, who is leaning over his transcript of the interrogation, Guitry stares straight at the camera. In the foreground, right in front of him, is his hat. In the background, standing against the wall and in front of the door, are the temporary law-enforcers, ready to grab him if he should try to escape. Cartier-Bresson devoted a whole reel of film to this episode, taken from every possible angle. He had the perfect composition: the two principal characters seated, the three secondary characters standing behind them. But had he wished to select another perfect image from the contact prints, he might have chosen the one in which a young freedom fighter lights a cigarette for his famous prisoner, or other close-ups – but then he would have lost the overall atmosphere. He might have picked the moment when Guitry corrects his interlocutor with a gesture of the hand – a spelling mistake perhaps, or one of syntax. But no matter what the circumstances, Cartier-Bresson always put composition before story-telling. Given the choice, he went for the most powerful and least demagogic image, though it would have been easy for him to load the dice against a man who represented everything he hated: a collaborator with the self-importance of the élite, the middle-classness of boulevard comedy, a superficially clever wit.

Cartier-Bresson rarely took two, let alone three pictures of the same thing. Apart from the fact that it was not in his nature to repeat himself, there was the need to economize on film. Time too was a factor. In order to deliver his photographs as quickly as possible to the magazines, he had these precious reels developed by a friend, but in the rush the friend left the film for too long in water that was too hot. Some pictures came out excessively grainy, while others were so shiny that they were simply unusable. A similar disaster had struck Robert Capa two months earlier. He had had the honour of being appointed with three others to cover the Omaha Beach invasion. Three of the four reels of his historic photos of the Normandy landings had been destroyed by an inexperienced technician (during development, the emulsion had melted owing to a lack of ventilation), and only 11 photos had remained intact from the fourth reel. Capa had risked his life to record one of the most important events of the century, making a point of advising his younger colleagues: 'If your photos are not good enough, it is because you are not close enough.'

On 1 September 1944, when the celebrations had died down and normality had returned to the streets of Paris, Cartier-Bresson met Capa at the Hôtel Scribe. The fast-living Capa had resolved never again to depart from his morning ritual (reading the daily papers in the bath), and declared himself delighted to have become an unemployed war photographer at last. The two of them then met up once more with various friends, including Chim, at a party given by Michel de Brunhoff, chief editor of *Vogue*. Afterwards, Cartier-Bresson went alone to a rendez-vous that he had vowed not to miss under any circumstances:

a reunion at the café de Flore, boulevard Saint-German, with le Grand Dab and La Globule, two of his closest companions in captivity. Raymond Guérin, le Grand Dab, was indeed there, waiting with tears in his eyes. But their reunion with Alain Douarinou had to wait until the end of the war, as just before the Liberation he had embarked for Rava Ruska in Poland.

Back among the living after his long absence, feeling the need to link up again with the old world, Cartier-Bresson returned to the haunts of his youth. Accompanied by his wife and Chim, who took photos every inch of the way, he went back to the family château where he had spent his childhood, and gave them a nostalgic guided tour of Fontenelle. Then he set about trying to find out what had happened to everyone he cared about. What had become of them in the war?

Ratna had taken refuge with farmers at Chouzy, near Chambord (Loir-et-Cher), not far from where he himself had been hiding at the end of the Occupation. His brother Claude was a lieutenant-colonel in the French Resistance. Jacques-Emile Blanche had died in 1942 on his estate at Offranville. Jacques Becker had seized the opportunity during the Occupation to direct films of his own, instead of merely assisting; he had made two, and was now bringing out a third, *Falbalas*, set in the world of fashion. Jean Renoir was in Hollywood, making films in English. André Pieyre de Mandiargues, the childhood friend with whom he was now reconciled after a quarrel that had lasted for ten years, had finally, at the age of 34, stopped obstructing the publication of his work, and the result was a collection of poetic prose pieces entitled *Dans les années sordides*. Léonor Fini was making her début as a designer, doing sets and costumes at the Paris Opéra for Balanchine's ballet *Le Palais de crystal*. As for André Lhote, Cartier-Bresson heard what he had been doing from his own lips, as the two of them went together to the first post-war autumn Salon. The master and his former pupil were actually photographed contemplating an effigy by Henri-Georges Adam.

Cartier-Bresson had barely had time to enjoy the capital city when once again he was on his way. Paris was free, but France was not; the war was not over. He followed its progress as a war correspondent attached to General Koenig's army – a post he was obliged to take through force of circumstance. It was not that he looked down on this kind of work, but simply that it was contrary to his nature. Reportage, however, is reportage, whether in war or in peace, and he perceived in these war pictures the same kind of intellectual protest that he had seen in Jacques Callot's drawings of the seventeenth-century anti-

Protestant struggle in the south, the same rebellious attitude as in Goya's paintings when Spain was under the yoke of Napoleonic rule.

He found himself in the ruins of Oradour-sur-Glane, a village martyred and destroyed by the retreating Germans in July 1944, photographing the few survivors picking their way through the rubble like ghosts in search of ghosts. In his dual function as reporter and photographer – each aspect of which he fulfilled with equal thoroughness – he accompanied the inexorable onward march of the Allies through the wreckage of Europe. This time he would not commit the errors of the Spanish Civil War.

The great purge was in full swing. Often, even before the official legal process could get going, the rough justice of the jungle took control. There were more public denunciations, arbitrary arrests, summary executions, though this time the executioners were not those of a foreign, occupying power. But after so much hatred, how could the tide of vengeance be halted? It was hard to imagine that, at least initially, such terrible crimes would not be punished by further crimes. One day, Cartier-Bresson returned to the farm in Loir-et-Cher where he had stayed in hiding. What he learned there made his blood freeze. With the exception of Mme Nolle, the farmer's wife, everyone he had known there had been betrayed to the Gestapo, arrested and deported to Buchenwald. He himself, it turned out, had escaped the same fate only by a few hours. He was a survivor.

In Paris the purge was engendering so much suspicion that no one could do anything without authorization. If you did not have the support of the Resistance, you were nobody. It was a horrifying, almost primitive form of bureaucracy, and the fact that someone was a former prisoner of war made not the slightest difference when it came to opening the right doors. It was as if the French could not forgive the soldiers of 1940, not only for being defeated, but for allowing themselves to be taken away.

Raymond Guérin returned home to Bordeaux to find that his house had been looted during his long absence, and he wrote despairingly to Cartier-Bresson: 'I live in the saddest isolation. I've never been given a better lesson on the dishonourable nature of my 43 months behind barbed wire.'

The ex-prisoner was not considered a hero, but he was a voter. The politicians still remembered the political importance of the former fighters in the 1930s. It was therefore in the interests of the best organized parties, foremost among them the Communist Party, to set about wooing the vast numbers of repatriated Frenchmen, and they were welcomed not with flowers but with party propaganda. The stakes were high, and so huge efforts were made to rein-tegrate these outcasts back into the community, boosting them as patriots and Resistance fighters even though very few of them had even attempted to escape. On 8 September 1944 Cartier-Bresson succeeded in obtaining his first permit, countersigned by the Section Secretary and the General Secretary of the Syndi-cate of Technicians for Cinematographic Production:

> Monsieur Henri Cartier-Bresson, former escaped prisoner of war, appointed to the Committee for the Liberation of the Cinema by the National Move-ment of Prisoners of War and Internees, has been entrusted by Pierre Mere with the task of making a film about prisoners. Monsieur Cartier, having been living illegally until this time, has not been able to formalize his posi-tion within the union. Given the urgent necessity for this film and the impossibility of assembling the section of directors in order to give a ruling on this case, I take personal responsibility for granting Monsieur Henri Cartier authorization to make this film in his capacity as a trainee director, pending the grant of his normal union card.

Four days later this paper, worth its weight in gold, was countersigned by someone else – this time in the form of an order approved by Major Paillole, Director of Military Security: 'Monsieur H. Cartier-Bresson, attached to the National Movement of Prisoners of War and Internees, is instructed to go to the liberated territories in order to take cinematographic and photographic pictures wherever the interests of prisoners of war and internees are represented.'

When Cartier-Bresson went to see Raymond Guérin in Bordeaux to cheer him up, Guérin urged him not to give up the cinema but to make a film about prisoners of war. Not being a film writer, he had no idea what should be done, but he certainly knew exactly what should not be done – something like *La Grande Illusion*, a film that they both hated for what they regarded as its appalling tone, especially after what they had been through. Guérin thought the whole thing should centre on daily life in the camp, and should be a documen-tary, since reality far transcended fiction. To his innocent eyes the whole project looked very simple: all they had to do was to sit down round a table for a few hours with their surviving friends, and a script would arise spontaneously out of their memories.

Cartier-Bresson listened to him, but he had his own ideas. The camp was already part of history, but what he wanted to do was film history in the making, in 1945, the year of the liberation of Alsace, with French troops marching into

Germany, the occupation of the Ruhr and the final surrender of the Reich on the two thousand and eighty-sixth day of World War II. He would show the liberation of the camps and the homecoming of the prisoners of war and internees. On 8 June 1945, newsreels showed the repatriation of Jules Garron, the millionth man to be taken home.

Le Retour ('The Return') was a 35 mm film directed by Henri Cartier-Bresson, Captain Krimsky and Lieutenant Richard Banks, produced by the US Office of War Information. It was filmed by cameramen from the cinema section of the American Army (apart from the sequence in Paris, which was shot by Claude Renoir), with a commentary by the journalist Claude Roy, and financed by the American propaganda services. It opens with the process of disinfection and finishes with scenes of reunion. Between the hygiene and the tears there is a whole universe, bracketed off from the rest of the world for four years. Cartier-Bresson had 25 minutes in which to capture the re-entry into life.

At the beginning of winter 1944, he had intended to film the departure of the prisoners and internees from their camps. But by the time the producer, Noma Ratner, had managed to raise the necessary funds the camps were practically empty. It was therefore decided to begin the film with various current activities that would conveniently fill this gap.

Le Retour tells the story of a long migration. From first to last, it shows nothing but queues, lines, columns of people moving or waiting. Many of them have to learn afresh what it is to be free, and find themselves unable to move unless told to do so.

Apart from its qualities as a documentary and its historical import, the film tells us a good deal about the photographer's own vision, driven by his mysterious, inexplicable instinct. Cartier-Bresson scans a scene, launches into a tracking shot, and when he stops it is at a point where the picture forms a perfectly geometrical composition of great spiritual depth. He allows emotions to speak for themselves, especially when families and lovers are reunited, as in the scenes filmed by Claude Renoir at the Gare d'Orsay. Le Retour is one man's view of how other people see things, and we witness in turn hope, fear, happiness and hatred. On leaving the cinema, the critic from L'Ecran français commented:

> In fact this film is less a documentary than a cinematographic poem inspired by the most tragic current events – and it is an admirable poem as much through its simplicity of expression as through the sincerity of the sentiments that it expresses. Directed by Henri Cartier-Bresson, who demonstrates his sense of rhythm and his awareness of the 'prosody' of images.

In contrast to his previous experience in Spain, or maybe because of it, the documentary-maker remained first and foremost a photographer. As he had a team of technicians at his disposal, he left it to them to implement his instructions, which allowed him the freedom to take his photographs. Sometimes he even used his Leica to photograph the scenes that his cameramen were filming. One such scene in particular has become famous – because of his photos and not because of the film. It took place in Dessau, Germany, the home of Mendelssohn and of the Bauhaus. In the foreground is a writing-desk in the courtyard of a transit camp. In front of it is a woman suspected of being a Gestapo informer, her head lowered, her face haggard. All around her is the crowd. From the grey mass on the extreme left there emerges a man in the 'striped pyjamas' of the prisoners, his hands on his hips in a gesture that expresses more clearly than words a settling of accounts. Suddenly, a woman in black, dynamic, determined, recognizing the person who has denounced her, rushes out and hits her. From the contact sheet of images Cartier-Bresson extracted the photograph. It is striking to start with because of its composition, superbly structured by an invisible diagonal that runs from the cold expression of the interrogator below right, through the shifty look of the suspect in the centre, to the accusing stance of the internee above left. Then there is the violence that leaps out of the picture. The whole image is of absolute clarity, with each figure fixed in his or her pose, which accentuates the movement of the avenging woman's arm. Finally, there are the expressions on the faces of the people themselves: the grimace of the avenger, the instinctive self-protection of the one who is being attacked, the mixture of joy, fear and indifference in the crowd. All these things rush past too quickly in a film to be seen properly, but a photograph freezes them for ever. The two forms can scarcely be compared, especially when both are the work of Henri Cartier-Bresson, but it is clear that in this period of extraordinary intensity, even the most brilliant documentary could not capture everything.

When they reached the camps that they had come to liberate, vast numbers of American soldiers pulled out their cameras to photograph the internees. We shall never know the quality of those photographs, but what we do know is that, quite apart from his remarkable talents, Cartier-Bresson had a major advantage over all of them, just as he did over his fellow professionals George Rodger, Lee Miller, Margaret Bourke-White and other photographers from *Life*: he had been in this world himself. His experience of captivity stretched not over three days but over three years, and every one of his pictures reflects this. They bear the marks of experience, suffering and death.

When, for instance, George Rodger arrived at Bergen-Belsen, he noticed from a distance people lying down under the pine trees in a little wood. He calmly measured the light and chose the best angle to take his shot. But when he drew nearer, he realized that they were not asleep. When he had recovered from the shock, he took his photos as clinically as he could.

In the 13 years that he had been taking photos with his little camera, Cartier-Bresson had never been as much of a reporter as he was now. If the scale of the subject being tackled is uplifting, then there can have been nothing more ele-vating in the twentieth century than the liberation of the camps. He was able to work on every conceivable level. There was even comedy, when the soldiers passed the delousing machine under the dress of a woman who reacted as if she was being tickled. There was also violence: one photo shows a remarkable vari-ety of movements as a crowd attacks some traitors. All on one plane, a man has lifted his club in the air, another is wielding a stick, a third has his stick raised, and crouching in the middle is the traitor, buckling under the blows. There is a deeply moving picture of a man kneeling on a garden lawn in the embrace of a woman, cheek to cheek, as if they had thought they would never meet again, one from the east and the other from the west. These pictures are often filled with pathos and always richly informative.

For the first time, Cartier-Bresson wrote long and detailed captions to accompany the pictures he sent to the different newspapers and magazines. This was as much for his own sake as for theirs, as he did not want his work to be misunderstood or misrepresented. It became a rule, and from that time on his notebook was as much a part of him as his camera. He wrote down every-thing, even for the most anodyne of scenes, and did not hesitate to tell a story if it seemed necessary. Thus the photo showing two men on a motorcycle, a smile on their lips, cutting through a jubilant crowd, was accompanied by this:

> A Russian camp, American side. Some Russians are waiting to cross. Two Frenchmen on a motorbike, officers who have just gone through the Russian zone on the way to Paris. The driver is Lieutenant Henri de Vilmorin. Lieu-tenant Gendron is sitting behind him. Both of them were close to General de Gaulle in the FFR. The motorbike is called 'Caroline' and has carried them from Berlin. They were captured in the Vosges during the last battle of this winter. Lieutenant de Vilmorin was the last of his 7000 comrades to leave the Stalag. He was head of the Liberation Committee.

We can imagine the caption he might have written had he been present at Wetzlar on the day the French troops arrived. Before the military police could intervene, they had taken over the Ernst Leitz factories, and in due course staged the magnificent spectacle of 1000 tank-crew members emerging, each with a brand new Leica hanging round his neck.

In spite of all this, however, the uniform of war correspondent never really fitted him. He had donned it because he had to, but he could not see himself forever touring disaster areas or reporting with a Stendhalian eye from the smoking rubble of Germany. The quest for the invisible would always excite him more than the spectacle of violence. To take a snapshot of the soul would be his life's task, but searching for war would not be. He saw himself rather as a peace correspondent.

He did not return to painting or drawing either – not after what he had seen and lived through. His curiosity about humanity was as intense as ever, but it required a different kind of involvement now, as if the war and especially the camp had seen off the utopian photographer, who gave way to the secular reporter.

What's it all about? The question was more pressing than ever, and so he would seek to find out not by judging, but by sniffing and feeling, above all by seeing.

Once more he found himself where things were happening. His contact sheets reveal a variety of events: André Marty on the platform at a communist rally; Maurice Chevalier and Aragon arm in arm, all smiles, at a demonstration in the place de la République; Jacques Duclos and the actor Jean Marais trying on period costumes at the couturière Mme Grès's; Tériade sitting on the ground in the most unlikely position studying photographs; Maurice Thorez looking pleased with himself behind his desk; the dress designer Jeanne Lanvin; the art critic Georges Besson; children playing in the garden; fashion parades for *Harper's Bazaar*. He was going through a transitional phase now. The surrealist dreams belonged to the past, but while he waited to develop something more akin to reportage he enjoyed a spell of culture, initiated by his series on the great painters and prolonged during this fertile post-war period by a passion for portraiture.

Everyone who was anyone passed before his lens in 1945–6. It was as if he had vowed to catch up on the missing three years. Artists, journalists, writers, poets, intellectuals, designers – no one escaped. Edith Piaf, Jean Paulhan,

Hélène Lazareff, Sennep, Christian Dior, Jean Eiffel, Louise de Vilmorin, Léonor Fini and many others found themselves conscientiously recorded on his list, along with Paul Eluard on his balcony, Edouard Pignon in his studio, André Lhote among his students. Not all of them were public figures. Along with the designer Christian 'Bébé' Bérard, an opium addict gripping his arabesque bedposts as if they were prison bars, Picasso athletically jumping over the bed, and Stravinsky hugging his cat, there was a Mlle Toussaint, director of the Maison Cartier, an ex-maidservant of Sarah Bernhardt's who was now concierge at the Musée Auguste-Comte, and a Père Ricoeur, preacher at Notre-Dame, with hat on head, briefcase in one hand, the other Napoleonically thrust into his cassock at chest height.

Cartier-Bresson hated the concept of the 'celebrity'. It was not that he had never sought them out, as everyone else did, or that he ignored them, which was impossible. It might even be said that he knew far more celebrities than he ever photographed. But his liberal principles refused to put them into a special, élite category. One day, he found in his photo archives a series of well-known names that the archivists had deliberately put together for this very purpose, and he wrote in the margin: 'This list is an absurdity. Draw up a list only of good portraits.' And with a thick ring round the word 'celebrities', he added: 'Scandalous notion!' Then in black felt-tip: 'N.B. The names below mean that these people have their faces on a photo, and that does not mean that it is a portrait.'

Cartier-Bresson remained true to Cartier-Bresson.

Some of the portraits from this period became icons: Jean-Paul Sartre, with pipe and sheepskin-lined jacket, chatting on the pont des Arts; Albert Camus with an intimate half-smile, his coat collar up. There are scarcely more than a dozen prints of each occasion, and one can imagine the meeting or the chance encounter and the surprise, even when the photo was taken during an interview with a journalist.

When a photograph is part of a wider brief such as an interview, and there is therefore a prior understanding between the two parties, there is nearly always a fuss, and when the subject wants to have a say in the style of the photograph, there is scope for calamity. Paul Valéry could not simply let it happen, but set out to help the photographer by adopting his own poses: full-face, three-quarters, profile, the good side, the bad side.... It was a nightmare, especially as he could not see what he was doing wrong, for instance when he positioned himself opposite his own bust on the mantelpiece in front of the mirror, formally dressed as a member of the *Académie française* rather than as himself.

Such reactions were not just due to vanity but to fear: fear of the camera, and of losing control both of the photographer's work and of his own image. Every time he heard the shutter, he would ask nervously: 'Have you got what you want?'

He was perhaps thinking of what he himself wrote in 1939 about things seen corresponding to things tangible, thanks to the 'demon press photographer'. Or he might have been thinking of the work of his master Mallarmé, painted by Degas, who also sat just in front of him on the mantelpiece.

Every portrait is an adventure – it cannot be planned in advance. When he went to see Irène and Frédéric Joliot-Curie, the famous physicists who first produced radioactivity artificially, Cartier-Bresson had no doubt that this would be a difficult assignment. Chim had photographed them in 1935 – a classical portrait with no mystery and so no surprise. The government had just appointed these two militant communists to official positions, Frédéric as high commissioner for atomic energy, Irène as director of the Radium Institute. It was essential that Cartier-Bresson should not show them behind a desk or in front of a mass of diagrams.

He rang the bell, they opened the door, and immediately the photo presented itself of its own accord. They stand there side by side in the doorway, almost medieval in appearance, bathed in an aura of monastic austerity, awkward in manner, twisting their hands in embarrassment, trying to mask their apprehension in the presence of the intruder. Their expressions are so sad that anyone would think they were attending their own funeral. It is the solemnity of these figures, rather than their expressions or the interior behind them, that brings to mind Jan Van Eyck's portrait of the merchant Arnolfini and his wife. It was not the first or the last time that a Cartier-Bresson portrait unconsciously reflected a landmark painting in the history of art – the former student of the Lhote Academy was still in there. The shock, however, of this vision from another age made him forget his manners, and instinctively, even before a single word of greeting, he had taken aim and fired. He took several more photos afterwards, purely as a formality and so as not to upset them, but he knew from the start that he had already got the one that mattered. The first impression of a face or a figure is often the most accurate. Of all the portraits that he took, this one remained the favourite of his friend Mandiargues, precisely because of the emotions it stirred:

> The Joliot-Curies, both with their hands clasped, or virtually so, their faces tense, as if waiting for something nasty that is about to come but cannot be talked about, their eyes truly bound to the lens by an invisible cable. Never,

even in ancient paintings of the archangel Gabriel, has one seen such worried expressions.

The first meeting with the prickly Simone de Beauvoir, in the rue de l'Odéon opposite the famous bookshop of Adrienne Monnier, went smoothly, but the luck didn't last. A few years later, at her home on the rue Schoelcher, she was far less accommodating: 'How long is it going to take?'

Since he had to say something, Cartier-Bresson replied with his somewhat caustic humour: 'A bit more than at the dentist's, and a bit less than at the psychoanalyst's.'

To punish him for his temerity, she gave him just enough time to finish the reel. Tactlessness doesn't help either, though it is difficult always to rein it in. When he went to do a portrait of Coco Chanel, he intended to talk to her about Pierre Reverdy, a poet they both admired. Instead, for some unknown reason, he mentioned Marie-Louise Bousquet, her rival in the world of the Parisian salons. The great couturière let out a string of oaths and brought the sitting to a premature end.

By now, Cartier-Bresson knew from experience two or three things that were essential for his art, and these helped him to get behind the relentless tyranny of human portraiture. It is hard to talk and take photographs at the same time. He admired the director Satyajit Ray, both as a person and as a film director, and they often met, but it never occurred to him to take a portrait simply because they always had so much to talk about that he didn't want to spoil the rapport by pointing his camera. It was the same with the writer and journalist Robert Desnos, the composer Edgard Varèse and the dancer Rudolf Nureyev, whom he photographed on stage but never in private. It had to be either conversation or photography, but never both. He took a portrait of Carl Gustav Jung, the analyst of hidden human depths, and later greatly regretted never having told him about the predictions Pierre Colle's mother had made concerning his future. But when you are trying to capture the inner silences of a human being, you do not distract him by making a noise. The camera must, as it were, get between the subject's shirt and his skin without his noticing, for the whole point is to capture the inner vibrations and not the expressions of the face – that unknown internal picture, the essence of the soul contained within the outer frame.

There can be no portrait without a look, and we can only admire the dexterity with which Cartier-Bresson recorded, for instance, Braque's look, whose eyes were never directed towards the photographer but always towards the picture he was working on, placed just behind his visitor. Bonnard, as we noted earlier, was another whom Cartier-Bresson grasped, though he never dared to engage him face on. An infinite and unyielding curiosity has to be maintained to catch these 'looks', and the lines and wrinkles and hollows whose mysteries are impenetrable. Cartier-Bresson preferred to improvise rather than work to some grand design, because in order to plumb the depths of a person he had to snatch the moment from real life. Good looks and fine poses meant nothing – what mattered was the freshness and naturalness of the impression. It was even better not to know the subject too well. In the case of a creative artist, you should first study and absorb his works, then leave them behind so that instinct is not tainted by knowledge. You must read his books, look at his paintings, listen to his music – not merely skim, see or hear. But then you must put them out of your mind, adopt the subject's own surroundings, take in the atmosphere, but never intrude – be the invisible man. In this way, you will not direct him or make him pose. Ideally, he will not even know that he is being photographed. To achieve this, you must have the concentration of an archer and the swiftness of an arrow.

You have to realize that, regardless of fame or fortune, every individual may become a portrait. The face of the man in the street can be much more stimulating to the visual appetite than that of a celebrity, and that is what will impel the Leica to come out and stop at eye level.

One must always expect the unexpected, the fateful moment when the subject lets go or even betrays himself. One day, at one of Darius Milhaud's rehearsals, Cartier-Bresson stood just behind him in order not to disturb him. Despite the legendary discretion of his Leica, the tiny click was heard by the composer, who swung round and facetiously stuck out his tongue, proffering a once-in-a-lifetime chance of a photo.

A museum of Cartier-Bresson's finest photographs would be a gallery not of portraits but of chance encounters. It's true that sometimes a face-to-face meeting would become a *tête-à-tête*, but even then the picture would usually be in profile, for his subjects rarely look frankly or directly at the camera. These portraits are the result of a tacit agreement by which the subject keeps back part of his face and the photographer takes part of his soul. Among the hundreds of thousands of people who see these pictures, only a few are aware of this secret – it's not important, and it would be astonishing if it were otherwise, since the shadowy parts are not usually the most spectacular.

The portrait artist must be aware that his art is in a way a portrait of death, a true battle against time, for the portrait is the reflection of something unique which is destined to disappear. To know this at the moment when you press the button is to know all that is ephemeral in the human condition. But on the other hand all photos, all portraits are as timeless as anything can be. That is why Cartier-Bresson either didn't date his pictures, or did so unreliably except when they were part of a reportage, and then he was precise because they reflected something that belonged to a precise context.

There is no special trick or even formula behind these photographs, but simply an inner wisdom. Miraculously put together in 125th of a second, each of them reflects an instant of eternity. The people he portrays often seem to be in a state of isolation, and the Cyclops eye that has transfixed them seems to belong to an invisible man.

As a portraitist, Henri Cartier-Bresson could have ensured his place in posterity by attaching himself to a particular enclave of society, as Josef Albert did with the court and the gothic follies of Ludwig II of Bavaria, or Cecil Beaton with the British royal family. Instead, he chose to embrace the whole world.

6 FROM NEW YORK TO NEW DELHI 1946–50

It is rare for people to have the privilege of attending their own funeral. For artists, the equivalent is to take part in a posthumous exhibition of their own works, and Cartier-Bresson, who never did anything like other people, actually managed to do just that, though of course not without paying the price.

Set up in 1940, the photography department of the Museum of Modern Art, the most prestigious artistic institution in New York, showed an interest in his work from very early on – so much so that the first curator, Beaumont Newhall, decided to hold a retrospective. Since he could not get any information about Cartier-Bresson after the Liberation, he was convinced that the Frenchman had died in the prison camp in the Black Forest, or had been shot while trying to escape, and so the exhibition was to be posthumous. His wife Nancy, however, who also worked at MoMA and was uneasy about these unsubstantiated rumours, contacted some American photographers based in Paris with a view to getting a message through. And in due course one of them managed to reach the still very much alive Cartier-Bresson. When he learned what was being done in his honour, it was a real incentive to cross the Atlantic once more, especially since the people at MoMA were kind enough to carry on with preparations despite the resurrection of their hero.

Fascinated by the complexity of the USA, which he had known since 1935, Cartier-Bresson and his wife stepped ashore at New York in 1946. Together with his desire to breathe the air of the New World, his taste for reportage revived, because his curiosity was enormously aroused by the impact of the country.

This so-called posthumous exhibition was a shining example of the adage that 'a prophet is not without honour, save in his own country'. It was now some ten years since Julien Levy had mounted the first exhibition in New York, and Cartier-Bresson would remain ever grateful to America. A dedication written in old age – with typical self-deprecating wit – acknowledges that 'it is thanks to my American friends that I am known as a *foutugraphe*' (a 'phutographer', i.e. one who messes up).

Apart from the gallery-owner Julien Levy and the curator Beaumont Newhall, these friends were James Thrall Soby, an art critic, Lincoln Kirstein, who founded what was later to become the New York City Ballet and wrote essays on photography, and Monroe Wheeler. It was Cartier-Bresson's good fortune to have been recognized at such an early age by these brilliant and highly influential people – good fortune, but of course risky, since history is full of those who have risen too fast and come crashing down.

What did they see in him? Lincoln Kirstein attributed to him the typical qualities of the classical French tradition: a sense of proportion, clarity, economy of means, a frugality that did not preclude generosity. He discerned something almost Racinian in Cartier-Bresson's taste for invisible conflict, suggesting that his approach was what he described as 'Jesuit-Protestant'. Classical, however, did not mean academic, and for him Cartier-Bresson was an artist who had found a mechanical medium for his art. The left eye was for the internal world, the right eye for the external, and the grace of his work was a fusion of the two. He saw him as the heir to a line stretching from Saint-Simon to Jean Renoir, taking in Beaumarchais and Cézanne on the way. All of these contributed something to the photographs, with an extra touch of freshness, elegance and truth added that set them apart. Most of the American biographical references to Cartier-Bresson at the end of the 1940s ended with a not insignificant detail: 'In his spare time, he continues to paint.'

Beaumont Newhall, an art historian who had studied at Harvard, praised the sharpness, visual composition and intensity of the pictures. He was dazzled by Cartier-Bresson's virtuoso use of the Leica, and admired the almost casual manner in which this master of discretion applied his technique. At last, he said, here was a photographer who worked on tiptoe and hated the aggression of the flash, that most intrusive of lights.

The American press did not lag behind. Listing the impressive array of his reportages (the Ivory Coast, Mexico, the Spanish Civil War, the coronation of George VI, paid leave on the banks of the Marne, the Liberation of Paris, Germany in ruins), the critic of *Time* magazine had no hesitation in describing him as a painter turned 'historian'. The *Harper's Magazine* critic distinguished him from other 'documentary humanists' by virtue of the emotional intensity of his photos.

Such comments left no doubt in anyone's mind: the camera had been invented for Cartier-Bresson, guardian and virtuoso of the new vision. In April 1947, at the end of the two-month exhibition which had been such a landmark for him, his friend Robert Capa gave him a piece of advice that proved to be wise counsel:

> Beware of labels. They are comforting, but people will stick them on you and you will never be able to get rid of them. You will be labelled the little surrealist photographer... you will be lost, and will become precious and mannered. Continue on your way, but with the label of photojournalist, and keep the rest deep in your heart. That is the one that will always bring you pleasure from your contact with whatever is happening in the world.

'Mannered': that summed up everything he detested. That was all he needed to resolve to relegate the influence of surrealism to the realm of nostalgia. The advice had been brief but, coming at just the right moment from someone for whom he had the utmost respect, it had a lasting effect. Cartier-Bresson never ceased to be grateful to Capa, for on that day he opened up the whole field of vision.

Cartier-Bresson was totally at home in New York. He didn't feel the same about America as a whole, but New York was not America. Like many Frenchmen he was both fascinated and repelled by the country, admiring the pioneering spirit of the Americans but at the same time disliking their clumsy handling of ideas and their general lack of subtlety.

His passion for New York, however, remained unchanged, even if the great city was not quite as he had remembered it from ten years before. His pleasure at wandering through the streets and alleys remained unabated, and arose as much from the places as from the people.

Claude Roy, the journalist who had written the commentary for the film about returning prisoners of war, was in Manhattan at the same time as Cartier-Bresson; he had been teaching French Literature at a girls' college in California. Roy often went with him on his Sunday walks, but one day he was astonished to find him taking photographs in church, and wondered if he perhaps took his Leica with him to the bathroom. Roy was fascinated by the almost frenetic curiosity that his friend emanated, but watching him thread his way through people, photographing them, blissfully unaware that they might not like it, he couldn't help fearing that one of them might take offence and do something terrible. But nothing happened – no row, no attempted murder. It was as if there was some supernatural power at work, but Cartier-Bresson was merely practising his art – it wasn't even a technique, simply that remarkable faculty he had of forgetting himself and making others forget him. The Zen archer could be sensed in the photographer, but Claude Roy only believed in what he saw, and could not imagine the inner workings of his friend's mind, or the extraordinary alchemy that lay behind the moment of the click – the profound spiritual processes at work in the bending of the bow:

> I saw in a black church in Harlem the Reverend and the faithful in a trance, singing, clapping their hands, a woman confessing in a shrill voice, foaming at the mouth. Henri, the invisible man, flitted around among the worshippers. He captured them at close quarters without them even noticing the presence of this see-through seagull.

He saw Cartier-Bresson as a proud man capable of effacing himself when he was at work – a man of his time, tense, always in motion, impossible to pin down, a man who did not know everyone or everything but knew his own, more important world: the world of painters, poets and writers. To judge by his friends, he was not a photographers' photographer. It was he who introduced Roy to the Harlem Cantors of the Renaissance, such as the poet Langston Hughes – his great companion during the Mexican adventure and now a major figure among the black intelligentsia – and Ralph Ellison, who was hard at work on his masterpiece *Invisible Man*, and Carson McCullers, who was already basking in the success of *The Heart is a Lonely Hunter* and *Reflections in a Golden Eye*. She was a person of rare refinement and sensitivity, and they had become friends during a long photo session at her house in Nyack, which had produced some tremendous portraits that vividly expressed her delicacy and her profound anguish. Along with Faulkner and a few others, and jazz and the blues, but excluding their painting, which he did not think much of, these were the elements of America that he took to his heart.

Ratna continued to devote herself passionately to Javanese dance, giving performances and lectures; she was increasingly attracted by more modern choreography. They lived near Queensboro Bridge, on the east side of Manhattan at the top of 58th Street. Jimmy Dugan, whom Cartier-Bresson had got to know before the war at the Eluards' in Paris, gave them accommodation there, though he didn't actually own the flat. They stayed there before themselves offering a home to Nicole Cartier-Bresson, Henri's sister, a brilliant poetess whom Darius Milhaud had invited to join him in Oakland, California, where he was teaching. They also put up Claude Roy, and members of the Indonesian delegation to the United Nations.

The long and detailed entry devoted to him in *Current Biography* 1947 gives his professional address as 572 Madison Avenue – the editorial office of *Harper's Bazaar*, one of the Hearst Group's monthly magazines. It was his second home, thanks to Carmel Snow, the chief editor, and Alexey Brodovitch, the art director. In the ruthless rivalry between the two magazines, Cartier-Bresson had chosen *Harper's Bazaar* in preference to *Vogue* because graphically it was bolder and more efficient. So great was his admiration for and his trust in Brodovitch's eye, mastery of blank space, skill at fitting compositions round the fold and genius at designing pages integrally that, miraculously, he even allowed him to fit his photos to the requirements of the magazine. As for Mrs Snow, she was impetuous, knew nothing but sensed everything, dazzled him with her flair and independent spirit, and earned his congratulations on having made *Harper's Bazaar* into far more than a fashion magazine. She was matchless in her ability to unearth young writers and to put together partnerships that would never have seen the light of day without her stimulating and creative intuition.

Thus it was that Henri Cartier-Bresson found himself in New Orleans, in baking heat, accompanied by a hypersensitive 22-year-old homosexual with a coruscatingly sarcastic sense of humour, a former runner for the *New Yorker* whose big chance had come when *Harper's* published his first short stories – Truman Capote. The magazine had asked them for an account of 'an impressionist journey', which gave the team *carte blanche*: the new darling of the editorial board, who happened to have been born in Louisiana's largest city, and the 'photographer that Mrs Snow has imported from France', said to be a real expert. The young American writer, who knew nothing about Cartier-Bresson until then, was unstinting in his admiration, particularly for one quality which for him outweighed all the others: his independence in all matters, sometimes excessively so. Of this joint project he had memories that coincided disconcertingly with Claude Roy's, judging by the portrait he gives of Cartier-Bresson in *The Dogs Bark*:

> I remember the day when I was able to watch him at work in a street in New Orleans, dancing along the pavement like a frantic dragonfly, three big Leicas swinging on their straps round his neck, the fourth glued to his eye, click-click-click (the camera seemed to be part of his body), bustling about doing

his clickety-clicks with a joyous intensity and religious fervour that filled his whole being. Nervous and high-spirited, devoted to his trade, Cartier-Bresson is a 'man alone' on the level of art, a kind of fanatic.

Capote gives an hallucinatory description of New Orleans. According to him, it consists of nothing but long, barren perspectives, in its quieter moments bathed in an atmosphere that recalls the metaphysical townscapes of De Chirico, diffusing a raw light that confers an unexpected violence on the most ordinary figures and the most innocent faces.

Ten days in Louisiana, all expenses paid, should have been just right. It was for one of them, who had now discovered the biggest city in the South, but it was too much for the other, who had rediscovered it with some degree of malaise. The budding author, initially delighted at the idea, very soon couldn't wait to get out. Not only did the city transport him back into an unhappy childhood (his mother used to shut him up alone in his room), but he was in a hurry to get back to his new lover, the critic Newton Arvin.

Cartier-Bresson had a plan to form a partnership with an author to create a book in which photographs and text would be of equal importance – so much so that it would be impossible to tell which was illustrating the other. For a while he considered his friend Lincoln Kirstein, but as a specialist in dance and photography he was known above all as a critic rather than an author. In 1941, Walker Evans had combined with James Agee on the unforgettable *Let Us Now Praise Famous Men*, which provided a wonderful model, particularly as it had been put together under similar conditions: the writer had travelled across Alabama with the photographer on behalf of *Fortune*, in order to produce a reportage on the living conditions of the sharecroppers.

When the magazine eventually decided not to publish the articles, they formed the basis of a unique book. Cartier-Bresson saw no reason why he should not do the same. After his wanderings round New York, this excursion to the South could prove to be the catalyst for an ambitious work on the whole of America. All he needed was to find the right partner.

John Malcolm Brinnin was 30 years old, a poet who had won critical acclaim for his first collection of poems and who had since been fêted by academics and institutions for his subsequent work. When he was not writing, he taught at the universities of Boston and Connecticut. And when he wasn't teaching, he travelled, crossing the Atlantic at every opportunity as if he wanted to set some sort of record. Such a restless spirit was the ideal match for Cartier-Bresson, who had just received a transcontinental commission, to be carried out alongside a man of letters. It was for a series of reportages for *Harper's Bazaar* on the subject of creators in their universe. And, at last, it was to be published as a book. The setting was to be simply America.

The first time they met, Brinnin was struck by the physical appearance of this foreigner: he had apple-cheeks, china-blue eyes, and a convict's haircut. Otherwise the main impression was of a very shy man who expressed himself in an English that owed less to Shakespeare than to the autodidact's pidgin version, and who was constantly fiddling with his cameras in order to try and appear in control. He soon became convinced that his natural self-effacement had made Cartier-Bresson morally neutral and physically anonymous. It has to be said that Brinnin, who observed him very closely, was not exactly devoid of the critical spirit, and his caustic humour – often to be found in certain homosexual circles – could be quite merciless.

In mid-April 1947 the new colleagues launched themselves on a car drive of some 12,000 miles across the United States. It was a truly grand tour, from Baltimore to Boston via Washington, Memphis, Houston, Los Angeles, Salt Lake City, Chicago, Pittsburgh and so on. Cartier-Bresson's vision recognized no limits, and his Leica was always at the ready. He was more interested in people than in things, and more interested in faces than in bodies, because only the face can tell a whole story. This applied to New York even more than to elsewhere, because it was and still is a veritable melting-pot of races and cultures. Nothing, of course, is more fleeting than snatches of life, whereas buildings are rather more permanent. Cartier-Bresson's job was precisely to seize the fragment before it disappeared for ever. On the eve of his departure, he told a journalist: 'I like faces, their meaning, because everything is written there.... Above all, I am a reporter. But it's also a bit more private than that. My photos are my diary. They reflect the universal character of human nature.' When the interviewer asked him what he looked for through his viewfinder, he replied: 'What I cannot put into words. If I could, I'd be a writer.'

John Malcolm Brinnin might have taken offence at this, but he knew exactly what his colleague meant. Before they set off he had been to a Javanese dinner at the Cartier-Bressons', where a crowd of people spoke a host of different languages, maps and guidebooks littered the tables, and Max Ernst wondered how his daredevil friend would set about photographing the Grand Canyon in black and white. On the hunt for some juicy gossip, Brinnin approached Jan Leyda, a university specialist on Emily Dickinson, to make enquiries about the other guests:

'And him, who's he?'

'Cagli, an Italian painter.'

'Is there any chance of getting to see his work?' asked Brinnin.

'No, but Cartier thinks he's awful. He's his pupil.'

'Doing what?'

'You mean you don't know?' exclaimed Leyda in surprise. 'You don't know that Cartier regards photography as a diversion, and first and foremost thinks of himself as a painter?'

Right from the start, then, Brinnin was aware of his companion's secret ambition. On the other hand, it was not until they were on the road that he found out Cartier-Bresson's real opinions on America. On their return, he was alarmed at the tone of the collection. The choice was typical of the photographer, for out of about a hundred photos a large proportion was strictly of New York, with the consequent risk of imbalance. The rest presented an extraordinarily gloomy, pessimistic view of the country. It was as if he was interested only in things like trains arriving late, so that through these pictures he could counter the rather too idyllic image of America that had generally spread through Europe after the Liberation.

When he photographed the New York skyscrapers, he did so from the New Jersey side of the Hudson, so that in the foreground were the Hoboken docks, still smouldering after a fire; he was showing that in this society, where grandeur and violence were closely interwoven, everything burnt itself out. He never, for instance, missed a scrapyard.

It is true that there were a few smiles, but they were rare: young girls in New York vying with each other for the attentions of the boys in uniform; the manager of a café in Texas; a young bridegroom in Detroit kneeling in front of his Michigan Juliet; somewhat inebriated New Yorkers in a bar; friends and neighbours in semi-detached houses in Baltimore. He also visited some celebrities and made portraits of them: Jean Renoir in California; William Faulkner with his dogs; Robert Flaherty filming *Louisiana Story*; Stravinsky in his studio; Katherine Anne Porter in her bungalow in Santa Monica; Henry Miller in Big Sur; Darius Milhaud in Oakland; Frank Lloyd Wright in front of a stone dragon; Saul Steinberg sitting in the lotus position facing a cat. All these, however, were separate from the main project because they were generally commissioned.

What he really focused on was racism, poverty, injustice, exclusion, unemployment, crime, solitude, social inequality, religious hypocrisy, repression and the arrogance of the wealthy. Like most foreigners he had his prejudices, and he sought to fit reality to them. In addition, he was a left-wing Frenchman, so committed to the cause that he would vote communist out of solidarity, and his ideas emerged not only from his experiences but from his private conversations with American intellectuals. Here he would, on more than one occasion, ask where the money came from.

Brinnin, whose parents were American but who was born in Canada, was often struck by the Frenchman's deductions. In Saratoga he saw him return from a walk rubbing his arm after a policeman had given him a good shaking, repeatedly shouting 'No pictures! No pictures!' No reason had been given. Cartier-Bresson concluded that he must have photographed too many husbands with women who were not their wives. In Detroit, he decided that the city was the archetype of the American phenomenon. One has only to read his commentaries on these reflections of daily life in order to see just how critical he was. In New York, for instance:

At midnight went to a cafeteria in Times Square. The cafeteria has solved the meal problem for people of modest means or in a hurry. It's a sort of canteen where, with an abundance bewitching for the newcomer but to which the regular customer is sadly accustomed, at one end of a long counter a variety of hot dishes and portions of meat are simmering, while at the other end is a no less substantial variety of cold dishes, rather like a children's tea party, neatly laid out on crushed ice. Everyone comes with a tray to make his choice, but at busy times it has to be done quickly, and any hesitancy is frowned upon. If you find the advantages of collective life here, you must also sacrifice certain individual needs born out of sentimental habits.

In spite of all this negativity, Brinnin continued to admire 'this cosmopolitan foreigner' who could ingeniously capture a moment just when it turned into a mystery. In the car it was the writer who was in charge of the itinerary, but on foot it was the photographer. When, however, the writer tried to precede or follow the photographer, in order not to appear in the photo, he would inevitably be told that he was in the wrong place.

Brinnin was fascinated by Cartier-Bresson's multi-faceted vision; he seemed to be able to focus on one thing while aware that ten others were clamouring for his attention. As soon as one particular desire was satisfied, he would immediately turn to the next. And if there was nothing in view, he would become mute, tense and unapproachable. He seemed constantly to be on the alert, tormented by a barely contained restlessness. Brinnin did, however, recall a few rare moments when he appeared happy and smiling in his own way, even forgetting to keep his Leica within reach. One such occasion was in Sedona, Arizona, at the house of Max Ernst and Dorothea Tanning; another was in a projection room in Los Angeles, where Jean Renoir showed *Le Retour* to Man Ray, Charles Boyer and a few other handpicked guests. It was only in such places that he ceased to be on guard, because he was among friends.

Brinnin kept a diary of this journey, writing his notes religiously every day, and a large part of it is devoted to the 'phenomenon' of Cartier-Bresson. Even allowing for possible exaggerations or subjective feelings, the account is illuminatingly perceptive and true to character. In Washington, we see him enthusing over the geometrical sights of the city (long lines of cars, crossroads and junctions with complicated road signs, street perspectives disappearing into the mist, a system of complex, harmonious curves on a motorway) and exposing the trademarks of absolute power, in the vast imperial spaces of government buildings like mausoleums.

The two men got on reasonably well during their journey, but there were several occasions when the relationship became fraught. First of all, there was a fundamental clash between the time requirements for their modes of expression: the one was instantaneous, the other required long hours of dedication. Then there was Cartier-Bresson's sometimes difficult character, with his excitability and his individualism, which had already tested the patience of Mandiargues in Italy, even though Mandiargues was more used to him since they were already friends.

Right from the start, Brinnin had to put up with Cartier-Bresson's moans about speed limits and the car not having a sliding roof. But he stood up to it well until they got home, when everything turned sour. The publishers, Pantheon, rejected the book. They were not prepared to take the financial risk of publishing something in which the disparity between text and pictures was so huge. Brinnin was furious. He was convinced that the Frenchman had always intended to be the sole author of a book devoted exclusively to photographs, and that he himself had been used merely as a superior guide to the inner depths of America.

Each went his own way. Brinnin caused a sensation with the inside story of Dylan Thomas's lecture tour of the United States. Then, after writing a biography of Gertrude Stein and a description of life on the great ocean liners, he went back to his old love of gossip by writing his memoirs. Published in 1981, and packed with salacious details many of which proved to be inaccurate, they lifted the lid on such well-known personalities as T. S. Eliot, Truman Capote and Henri Cartier-Bresson, who was given a complete chapter of his own. These 60 or so pages stank of rancour and revenge, though their subject was apparently aware of them only through the comment they aroused. Truman Capote, who knew what he was talking about, denounced the book as vicious mythomania, and objected in particular to Brinnin's putting into his mouth a number of thoroughly nasty remarks about other people which he, Capote, denied that he had ever uttered.

Cartier-Bresson did eventually publish his book on America, on his own in 1991. Magnanimous to the end, he thanked both of his extraordinary travelling companions in his acknowledgments.

When he set off on his tour of America he missed an historic event: the official registration in New York, on 22 May 1947, of a new entity called Magnum Photos, Inc.

Even before the war, Magnum had been in limbo. When Robert Capa had been at the front in Spain, he had often referred to it in his letters and conversations. It was an obsession with him: photographers should never be made to part with their negatives, which represented their only capital. Everything else flowed from this one principle: defending the interests of photographers, making them the rightful owners of their negatives, allowing them to sell reproduction rights as and when they wished, ensuring their independence from greedy magazines, guaranteeing them control over how the magazines used their photos, authorizing them to refuse commissions if necessary, because in all 'commissions' there is an element of 'command'. The basic concept was not that of an agency, for these already existed, with bosses and employees – the latter being the photographers themselves – but that of a genuine cooperative belonging to the photographers, preserving the liberty of each individual and existing exclusively for their benefit. Under no circumstances, said Capa, was it to be an agency.

At the time such an association seemed to be a utopian dream, especially since Capa's reputation did not do him any favours. He was regarded generally as a great story-teller, very charming, prone to exaggeration and profoundly melancholic to the point of being depressive – particularly after the death of his great love, Gerda Taro. He was Hungarian by birth, and had recently acquired American citizenship; as a war photographer he was out of work from September 1945, but became the talk of the town when he had a passionate affair with

Ingrid Bergman. When his photography was not going well, he dreamed of taking up the cinema. The writer William Saroyan thought he was a professional poker-player who only did photography as a hobby. Cartier-Bresson preferred to see him as an adventurer with an authentically anarchist code of ethics, since he made no distinction between people regardless of their power or social position. In his eyes Bob certainly had his faults, but first and foremost he represented elegance, charm, gaiety, enthusiasm and vitality. In short, Capa was a magnet of irresistible attraction. It didn't matter that people considered him crafty and unreliable. His extravagance may have worried those around him, but when, thanks to his savoir-faire, he did get commissions, everybody benefited.

Cartier-Bresson had a deep affection for the two men to whom he was most closely linked. Their friendship of 12 years' standing had been interrupted only by the Occupation and his period of captivity. But if he regarded Chim as his friend, he saw Capa as his bosom pal. While the former was the embodiment of wisdom, moderation, depth, intelligence and acuity, the latter was all instinct, dash, excess and humour – to the extreme. One of them earned money, the other spent it; one of them wondered how to do things better, the other simply did them. Chim was the thinker, but Capa was the man with ideas – the tortoise and the hare. But if Chim hadn't been behind Magnum, the project would never have got off the ground. Cartier-Bresson himself took up the perfect Norman position, equidistant between these two East European Jews, between the poles of unbridled optimism and constructive pessimism. Intellectually he felt closer to the chess-player, but emotionally he was with the poker-player.

George Rodger – an Englishman, an outstanding representative of the photographic tradition of adventurer-explorers – joined them, but although his loyalty never flagged he always remained on the periphery, refusing to take responsibility for any of it. Perhaps this was because he was not at the historic lunch during which the decision was taken to create Magnum. But in all probability it came down to a matter of temperament.

Capa had got to know Rodger during the allied invasion of Italy. Cartier-Bresson thought he recognized him when they were introduced in New York. He went straight to his contact sheets of the Liberation of Paris, searched and searched again, and... there he was, chest covered with cameras, standing in a jeep facing General de Gaulle as he descended the Champs-Elysées. Cartier-Bresson had photographed him without, of course, having any idea that three years later they would both be involved in a remarkable project that would change their lives and those of their colleagues.

There were five co-founders of this adventurous enterprise: Robert Capa, David Szymin (Chim), Henri Cartier-Bresson, George Rodger and the American William Vandivert. After the latter withdrew, the five musketeers were reduced to four, but that was enough to keep the flame burning.

Gone now were the days of the leisurely photographer's stroll, head in the clouds, soul steeped in poetry. From now on, stories had to be told. It was no coincidence that, after several preparatory meetings in the restaurant at the Museum of Modern Art, Magnum came into being precisely when people were eager to throw off the restraints of war and embrace the world again.

As a co-founder of Magnum, Cartier-Bresson was now a full-time professional. One day, perhaps, he might abandon the business and become an artist again, although for him the distinction was surely social and administrative, imposed by other people. He still saw himself as a man of art, an enthusiast even if not an amateur, and his outlook and his love of photography were unchanged. But from now on, he would always have to bear in mind the client's deadlines.

The price to be paid for not being a mercenary was $400, advanced to him by Mrs Snow, who had tucked away a stock of his photos that were still awaiting publication. Accepting commissions implied the right to refuse them, and now photographers could work for themselves while still being engaged by others. Cartier-Bresson himself refused an offer from a magazine which, having seen how beautifully he was able to photograph litter bins, asked him to photograph models in the same receptacles. Magnum provided the fundamental liberty of independence: the photographer could now be autonomous without being isolated, and from this point of view it was the perfect association for an individualist with team spirit. It held three principles: to be there when needed, to be there of your own accord, and to put long-term interests before short-term. All that mattered now was to get things moving, not in terms of commercial projects but in terms of ethics. And so in 1947, in the heart of Manhattan, five good men and true, all of them with great futures ahead of them, came together to found a society for the benefit of all. It is perhaps worth pointing out that none of these co-founders was actually American (except Vandivert, whose involvement was short-lived).

Magnum: the name was carefully chosen. It had the dignity of Latin, the *joie de vivre* of champagne, the prestige of Smith & Wesson's finest gun, the etymological stamp of grandeur. From the start it fostered its own image of quality, along the lines of an élitist English club, but at the same time in the spirit of a cosmopolitan family that warmly welcomes its children's friends. It embraced the picture in Shakespeare's Henry V: 'We few, we happy few, we band of brothers.'

The world was their studio. They decided to recruit members of the Alliance Photo, a Parisian agency with which they had collaborated before the war and which was now trying to start up again, and Cartier-Bresson invited Doisneau to join him at Magnum. Doisneau refused, however, as he felt he would be out of place among all those foreign languages, and didn't relish the amount of travelling envisaged. 'You know, coming from Montrouge, I'm lost,' he confessed. There was no point in trying to persuade him.

With Magnum was born the list of the 'Five Ws' – the questions that every photographer must answer with his reportage: 'Where? When? Why? Who? What?' The principle was valid for all, and became so deeply ingrained in the unconscious that it became a natural reflex. For Cartier-Bresson, it was added on to the advice he had received from Capa, which he had never forgotten: to beware of labels, especially that of the surrealist, and to be a photojournalist and do what he wanted to do.

It was a typical Cartier-Bresson paradox that what freed him also constrained him. Photojournalism served him, but he also served it. His soul remained that of a poet, but he was now a sort of vagabond with the luxury of having his wanderings paid for. His main problem was to avoid falling into the trap of the documentary. How was he to reflect his time without supplying something that would be reduced to the level of mere testimony? What mattered to him as a photographer was not evidence but intuition: 'What counts is the small differences. General ideas mean nothing. Long live Stendhal and the little details! One millimetre makes the difference. And all that is proved by those who work with proofs is their resignation in the face of life.' To be a reporter while maintaining his poetic view meant forever juggling with the world of facts and the world beyond the facts.

Two years after the Yalta Conference, the founders of Magnum set about dividing the world. Capa and Chim took Europe, George Rodger had Africa and the Middle East, while Asia belonged to Cartier-Bresson. They didn't draw fixed boundaries, though, and the division was made mainly according to their personal affinities. Cartier-Bresson was drawn to Asia mainly because of his wife. In August 1947 he was appointed photographic expert to the information department of the United Nations (which had just replaced the discredited League of Nations), and he followed at close quarters the struggle for independence waged by those nations that were still under the yoke of Empire. His political convictions, his own character and his empathy with Ratna all told him that decolonization was to be the great cause of the post-war world. It was not only the spirit of the age, it was the lesson of history.

And so Cartier-Bresson stepped on board a freighter bound for India. At midnight on 15 August 1947 India had become independent, and the jewel in the British Crown had fallen to the nationalists. The Indian subcontinent had split into Nehru's Hindu India and Jinnah's Muslim Pakistan, but Mahatma Gandhi, the great man who had helped to turn a dream into reality, could not recognize his country in either of these. Partition was his personal defeat. No sooner had the wounds of history appeared to be healed than they burst open again. Twelve million refugees fled from one side to the other amid fear, hatred and bloodshed, and before the terrible exodus was over vast numbers had been massacred: Muslims in the Hindu lands, Hindus in the Muslim. Gandhi fell back on his only weapon: fasting. From September, in order to bring Calcutta back to its senses, he announced that he would stop eating, if necessary until he died. After a few days he had won his battle, and turned his attention to Delhi, the political and administrative capital, drenched in the blood of its refugees.

He was accommodated at the home of a wealthy Parsee friend, a colonnaded villa named Birla House, symbolically situated on the frontier between the two warring worlds. The comforts of this place in no way changed his way of life. He surrounded himself with adopted children and fell into deep melancholy, but received visitors. Among these was Maurice Schumann, a member of the French parliament whom the President of the Council, Paul Ramadier, had charged with a delicate mission: to persuade the Indians to respect the colonial status of the five French trading posts (Pondicherry, Chandernagore, Karikal, Yanao and Mahé). Schumann was the last Frenchman to have a lengthy interview with Gandhi, though not the last to have seen him at a moment of intense and prophetic emotion. Only someone who was a professional witness and an artist blessed with luck could have captured that moment.

The Cartier-Bressons arrived in India in September 1947, a month after independence. Their ship, a German boat taken over by the British during the war, had had problems with its crew, which had entailed interminable delays in Port Sudan and Aden. Not being under contract to any magazine, Cartier-

Bresson's time was his own, but he was desperate to get to work. He knew history was in the making, and the delays were galling.

India was more a world than a country. It was very far from the spirit of Hinduism that he had glimpsed in his youth when reading Romain Rolland, the biographer of Gandhi, Ramakrishna and Vivekananda. From his very first days in Bombay he was hooked. As Delacroix said of Morocco, the pictures were already there; all he had to do was to reveal the soul of the place and at the same time conserve its mysteries. His photos showed some of the 600,000 refugees camping in Kurukshetra, some stretching their legs and walking as if in a trance; nationalist leaders haranguing the faithful at fiery meetings; cholera victims being cared for in hospital; processions moving round the temples; guests being lavishly entertained on the Maharajah of Baroda's 39th birthday; Nehru and the Mountbattens laughing on the steps of the palace; Untouchables, still relegated to the fringes of society in spite of the decrees abolishing their pariah status; gentlemen indulging in civilized conversation in a beautifully manicured garden; refugees crammed together in the train from Delhi to Lahore; people in rags waiting in Bombay's streets for the distribution of food.

Wherever he was, Cartier-Bresson always remained true to his compositional vision. He was somewhere in Kashmir, but it might have been anywhere in the world as he waited for the precise geometrical congruence between the patterns on the ground and those of the saris. He took four photos in succession, but ended up by discarding them all. In Ahmedabad, the graceful sight of women washing their clothes in the river and spreading them out to dry offered him an array of curves and parallels and perpendiculars hitherto undreamed of. Further on, he would have come across the perfect composition if only the three men had been as shrivelled as the three trees beside which they were sitting. He secretly took his photographs, trying not to disturb the scene, and went on his way. Next he stopped to capture the patterns of walls. It even happened, quite exceptionally, that instead of viewing a scene at eye level he perched high up on a ladder to capture the movements of a worker cleaning the outside of a palace. Sometimes his obsession with composition was completely satisfied, but he would nevertheless drop the photo from his final selection because it lacked the spiritual dimension that made all the difference. One such picture was a meeting between two leaders who sat side by side and looked each other straight in the eye, while in the background two flags hung on a wall, arranged crosswise as an invitation to reconciliation.

Everything that Cartier-Bresson was able to grasp of the complexities and subtleties of the East, its cultural traditions, its struggle against colonialism, was thanks to his wife. There was no better guide than the Javanese Ratna to introduce him to India's high society, not just because she wore the sari and knew the local languages. Although she was a Muslim, she had studied the *Bhagavad Gita* closely. A Hindu who took them under his wing introduced them everywhere as *ksariats*, members of a warrior caste in Java-Borneo. But quite apart from understanding a world so profoundly foreign to a westerner, there had to be a degree of empathy without which the visitor would always remain alien to the people and their way of thinking.

Ratna was able to do a great deal for her husband. She even offered to take photographs herself where there were veiled women and no man was allowed near them. But he declared himself incapable of explaining how the Leica worked. The fact was that he didn't want her to take his photographs. He was not in the least interested in scoops or sensations. All his work was based on the idea that a photo was not a view but a vision.

Ratna, who now began to study traditional Indian dance under Uday Shankar, was a close friend of Krishna Hutheesingh, one of Prime Minister Nehru's sisters. This contact proved important when Cartier-Bresson turned from the subject of India in general to focus on the man who epitomized the nation, Mahatma Gandhi. It was inevitable that their paths would cross.

When he was not accompanied by Max Olivier from Agence France-Presse, Cartier-Bresson toured around with James de Coquet. A brilliant special correspondent with *Le Figaro*, De Coquet was writing a series of articles on 'India Without the English', and the two went together to the wedding of the Maharani of Baroda. Then De Coquet went to Srinagar in Kashmir, a land which aspired to be the Switzerland of the Indian subcontinent, but which force of circumstance had turned into a kind of Sudetenland. He went on to visit the man who had become almost the mythical incarnation of India. His report, experienced and written in the spirit of the explorer Albert Londres, is a classic of its kind:

> I am before the last fakir in India. He is squatting on a thin horsehair mattress, and his skinny body is draped in a white cotton cloth. He greets me in the Hindu manner, hands together, then he reaches out and invites me to crouch down opposite him. The welcoming fakir is Gandhi. And the trick that he has accomplished is far more difficult than throwing a rope into the air so that it remains suspended there. He has made 400 million subjects disappear from the English Crown.

On 13 January 1948, this man with power over souls began a new fast to stop the threat to the Muslims and their property. It was, as always, the only weapon he had to shame those who used their strength not to protect but to destroy. The Indians and Pakistanis had to reach a financial agreement at least, even if they could not learn to love one another. As usual, Gandhi would only break off this process of slow death in exchange for a written promise. After five days he got what he wanted. The following day a Hindu extremist threw a bomb at his home while he was conducting public prayers. Nine people were injured, and some damage was done, but the Mahatma simply continued with his prayers. It needed more than a bomb to subdue the inner strength of this man.

January came to an end. The owner of Birla House registered the unease that had marked the last few days, as if the tension were pressing in through the very gates. The garden was full of people of all kinds who had come for an audience, advice, help, a blessing. The Mahatma was seated at the back on a platform situated inside a sort of red stone kiosk. When he was not praying, he was commenting on current affairs in a voice so gentle and weak that the scribes had to strain their ears so as not to miss a word that fell from the lips of the sage.

Cartier-Bresson arrived on a bicycle. He had at last been given an appointment. The previous day he had already walked round the outside of the house in order to take in its atmosphere: the poet rather than the film director in search of his location.

On 30 January he was duly admitted. He had already taken photographs of Gandhi supported by Abha and Manu, his two great-nieces, but now he was after more than just a toothless smile snapped from the midst of a worshipping crowd. For a while he watched him receiving a westerner in his kiosk. The two men faced each other, Gandhi apparently doing the talking. He could only be seen from behind, but in fact it was just his hand that was directly visible. The hand seemed to be saying, 'And now what?' while the forearm stretched out parallel to a bottle of water. It was a magical composition. A hand can sometimes tell you as much as a face. These fingers, which told a whole story and summed up a whole life, were the last portrait of Gandhi.

Before leaving, Cartier-Bresson showed him the catalogue from his 'posthumous' exhibition at the Museum of Modern Art in New York. The Mahatma was very interested, and took his time to leaf through it without saying a word. Then suddenly he stopped, leaned back and stared at one particular picture. 'What is the meaning of this photo?' he asked, in English.

'The meaning, I don't know. It's Paul Claudel, our great Catholic poet – someone preoccupied by the last days of mankind. It was in 1944. We were going along a street in the village near his château de Brangues when a hearse came towards us – empty but harnessed, drawn by some horses. I quickened my pace in order to get opposite him, with the church in the background. He turned round to look, and then....'

To have said more would have meant going into technical explanations – always anathema to him. And to have added that this was the actual spot where Julien Sorel had shot at Mme de Rénal in Stendhal's *Scarlet and Black* would have been absurd. But Gandhi seemed to be transfixed. At last he spoke: 'Death, death, death...,' he murmured, pointing at the photo.

He did not say anything else. The audience was over. Cartier-Bresson left on his bicycle in the middle of the afternoon. Less than an hour later, when he arrived home, it was to find people running through the streets in panic, shouting and screaming: 'Gandhi is dead! They've killed Gandhi!'

While he had been crossing the garden, he had been shot three times at point-blank range by a Hindu fanatic. Witnesses said afterwards that when he collapsed into the arms of his great-nieces who were standing beside him, he murmured the name of God with his last breath: 'Rama, Rama...'. There was no photographer.

Cartier-Bresson got on his bicycle and pedalled furiously back to the house. It was the start of a long, sleepless night, to be followed by many others. This was a time of extraordinary emotion. No fires were lit in a country that was plunged into a shocked silence. The remains of the Mahatma, covered in roses, were laid out on the roof of his last abode, so that the faithful could pay their last respects. They came in dense crowds to see him. Cartier-Bresson managed to elbow his way as far as the windows of Birla House before being swept away in the human flood. Nevertheless, he was there when Nehru left the house after kneeling beside the corpse of his friend. He addressed the crowd in the street, improvising a speech that was relayed by All India Radio: 'Friends and comrades, the light of our lives has gone out, and there is darkness everywhere. I don't know what to say to you or how to say it. Our beloved chief, Bapu as we called him, the Father of the Nation, is no longer....'

The Prime Minister was perched on the wooden gate that barred entry to the house. Immediately to his left, a uniformed officer of His Britannic Majesty's army leaned on his elbows, a last reminder of a past that was still present. Opposite him was a seething mass of Indians numbed by the appalling news, their eyes looking upwards imploringly. On a level with him, poking up out of the tide of this orphaned crowd, was the head of a street-lamp. It was a scene of indescribable intensity, bathed in haloes of light from all directions. Despite the constant jostling and impossible technical conditions, Cartier-Bresson managed to take some photos. They were mostly a little blurred, but there was one – dark and light, lit as if by a miracle – that stood out. It is a masterpiece, so unpremeditated yet so inspired that the viewer might feel its author was touched by grace. The artist has once more taken over from the photographer in a manner that recalls the great paintings of the Italian Renaissance, such as Filippino Lippi's *The Vision of St Bernard*.

For the next few days Cartier-Bresson was everywhere, too caught up in the maelstrom of events to be conscious of the danger. Hundreds of people were trampled to death as the crowds went out of control. He was one of two million that followed the funeral procession, attended the cremation and accompanied the train that took the ashes to be scattered in the Ganges and the Jumna. Although he refrained from preparing a reportage on the assassination itself, he did one in his own style on the shock waves that manifested themselves in people's faces and behaviour, assembling a portrait of a nation at the moment of its deepest distress. His visual record captured the rhythms of the crowds and their different expressions of grief, from the ordinary folk that had clambered on to pylons to the Mahatma's secretary, unable to contain his tears as the flames crackled.

In the eye of the storm, Cartier-Bresson caught details at all levels. And when life began to return to something like normal, it was the same story. He was invited to spend a week in Rajputana, to attend the wedding of the Maharajah of Jaipur's daughter to the Prince of Baria. Amid showers of petals, an orgy of feasting, processions of orchestras, elephants and camels, Cartier-Bresson focused on the shoes of the principal guests. He had noticed that they were wearing common black shoes such as any middle-class westerner might wear on a Sunday, rather than the sumptuously embroidered sandals that are the tradition in India. This same passion for the tiniest detail no doubt led him to note that, despite their aristocratic background and awe-inspiring titles, the young couple called each other 'Juju' and 'Mickey'.

During his years in Asia, life was so intense that he never had time actually to see his own photos, except when he was sent copies of the magazines that had published them. Most of the time he was content just to look at the contact sheets, make his choice with a red pencil, and send them off as quickly as possible to Magnum. There was no time for him to dwell on what he had already done, simply because there was always so much still to do.

When magazine editors heard that Cartier-Bresson had covered Gandhi's funeral (for of course no one had been able to cover the assassination), they besieged Magnum's offices in New York, fighting for exclusive rights to the 20 reels of film he had taken. *Life*, the *Saturday Evening Post* and *Harper's Bazaar* were prominent in the queue.

As well as his friend Max Desfor from the Associated Press, Margaret Bourke-White, *Life*'s correspondent, was in India at the same time. Although they appeared to ignore one another, they complemented rather than rivalled each other, since they were so different in character and approach. She was American, efficient and aggressive, a journalist to her fingertips and a devotee of the flash whatever the circumstances. He was the exact opposite.

No one knew this better than Satyajit Ray. At the age of 27 the budding film director, who had just founded the Calcutta Film Society and was yet to have his decisive meeting with Jean Renoir, was a fervent admirer of Cartier-Bresson. In his first film, *Pather panchali*, as in his subsequent works, he never ceased to demonstrate this, banning long-distance shots and, in true Cartier-Bresson fashion, making maximum use of the daylight.

As he looked through the catalogue of the New York 'posthumous' exhibition, Ray could tell that this was the same 'Cartier' whose pre-war photos in *Verve* had so impressed him. He was in fact confused, because he associated them with Mexico whereas they were actually taken in Spain, but this in no way detracted from their impact, whether they were of a woman in black carrying a child, or an out-of-work father looking like a hunted wolf, holding his sleeping son in his arms. When Satyajit Ray saw the images of his own country in its hour of grief, he was particularly struck by Cartier-Bresson's avoidance of all sensationalism, story-telling or politics; he seemed to dwell on matters that others might judge insignificant, and on ordinary people whose disorientation we can all understand. The drama is conveyed to us soberly, and yet with poetry and human warmth. Satyajit Ray recognized this unique gift for making the ephemeral into something monumental, and saw Cartier-Bresson as an artist who, instead of creating beauty, removed the veil impeding us from seeing beauty.

For the first time Cartier-Bresson had covered a live event of worldwide interest, and it was at a time when the demands of a flourishing newspaper and magazine industry fitted in perfectly with the dynamism of the new Magnum agency. Now aged 40, he adapted to the requirements of his profession, though he still insisted on his right to choose his own limits. When he went to the front at Hyderabad just after the armistice between India and Pakistan had been announced, it didn't bother him that he was not allowed to witness the signing of the treaty, although he had stuck to the protagonists like a leech. He knew that these pictures were ephemeral, whereas the truth lay elsewhere, in the images and faces of these countries and their people that would embed themselves naturally and enduringly in the memory. No matter what others may have expected of him, he would follow his own instincts and initiative. When the American journalist Ed Snow asked him to take a series of photos showing twelve different aspects of Nehru, he knew that he could not do this without overtaxing the Prime Minister's patience, and so he declined the commission.

One thing did change, however: every evening he would type out his impressions of the day, or at least those that he had not been able to capture with his Leica. This was primarily for his own satisfaction, though it would prove useful later for other purposes. A photojournalist should keep a journal, while a reporter simply reports. He would then send off his film and his contact sheets accompanied by detailed captions, written in English on onion-skin paper.

All these writings, done on the spot and without embellishment, create a vivid record of the daily life of a photographer in self-imposed exile, working on a continent in turmoil. They are astonishingly rich, not only for the information they impart, but for their insight into their author's state of mind. If his descriptive powers failed him, those of others would come to the rescue; once he recommended that the recipients of his captions should look at the fine description of Jaipur in one of Pierre Loti's books.

Although Cartier-Bresson left India he did not go very far, and it was India that remained his home base, particularly on an emotional level. It was another adopted motherland, like Mexico, and even in the 1990s, when he looked back on that time, it brought a glow of nostalgia to his eyes.

In September 1948, after spending a year there, he went to Pakistan to observe the consequences of partition. He had a long interview in Karachi with the head of state, Mohammed Ali Jinnah, and then travelled round the country using his Leica as a visual notebook. He went to the ruined city of Lahore, where the arrival of spring was still celebrated with clowns and acrobats in the gardens of Shalimar. He wandered into the bazaar in Peshawar, where everyone was armed except himself. He was received in a valley near Kashmir by a warlord who governed the state from his bedroom, with a telephone, a Winchester, a spittoon and the Koran all within easy reach.

He returned to India and saw the sacred Sikh temple of Amritsar, Bombay in the hurly-burly of municipal elections and Delhi in the throes of its devotions to the goddess Kali. He visited the south of the country: there had been a flare-up of communist violence there, which he took to be a general uprising.

By November he was in Burma, liberated from British colonialism less than a year before but now a victim of internal strife. After suppressing the violent opposition of the communists, the government was confronted by the Christian minority of the Karens. Cartier-Bresson found the country in a state of confusion; he photographed the leading figures in their homes, accompanied the negotiators on their missions without understanding a single word of their political dealings, and watched police being trained on the shores of the royal lake in Rangoon. As usual, he took risks, poking his nose behind the scenes, always expecting to find the unexpected – whether it was cock-fighting, young girls practising the art of hairdressing, the significance of each tiny movement in traditional dance, snake-charmers, women smoking cigars, or the essential literary pilgrimage to the famous Pegu, a club once reserved for whites only, where Kipling wrote some of his stories.

South-East Asia seemed to have become his home, and every time he left one spot he dreamed of returning. After staying with the popular but mysterious Razvi, the head of a private army of Rasakars, all Muslim extremists, he wrote down his impressions in his notebook, but urged editors using his material to exercise a degree of caution: 'It would be better if these notes did not appear under my name, because I am returning to Hyderabad in two months to do some non-political reportages.'

This was not so much a strategy as an instinct. He always tried to penetrate through to the cultural dimensions of a situation, whatever the context, and whatever the tensions, which would soon develop into open warfare. Photographing people, places or objects, he always sought to uncover the traditions from which they emerged, for that seemed to be the only way to reveal and understand the darker sides of their existence.

Cartier-Bresson lived in Burma for three months, travelling freely despite the dangers all around; he visited monastic communities, attended a firework display and so on. He was somewhere near the pagodas of Mandalay when a laconic telegram arrived from *Life* magazine: 'The Kuomintang can't last for much longer. Can you go to China?'

The news was couched in vague enough terms to arouse his instinctive curiosity, and he hurried back to Rangoon and took the first flight to Peking. For three years China had been torn apart by civil war, with Mao Tse-tung's forces constantly advancing. They took Manchuria while the Americans, preoccupied with Europe, gradually abandoned Chiang Kai-shek, who committed a number of strategic blunders. Military defeat was imminent, and all the signs were that the days of his regime were numbered.

At the end of 1948 Cartier-Bresson was ready and waiting for the end of one world and the beginning of another. For twelve days and twelve nights he was privileged to witness the downfall of nationalist China as it turned into the triumph of communist China. It was a kind of intoxication, to be a foreigner in an unknown city on the eve of what everyone knew to be an historic revolution.

In moments of intense excitement like this, when crowds can easily be overcome by collective madness, it is essential not just to be there, but to know when to get out. You have to save your films, and you have to save yourself. At a time of endless rumour and counter-rumour, each in itself enough to make anyone panic, to stay in Peking and face the unknown consequences of a brutal change of regime would have meant taking unacceptable risks. In such an atmosphere of frenzy and hysteria, who was really willing to stop and see if the Kuomintang general would or would not surrender the imperial city without a fight?

Any acquaintance could turn out to be an informer, but foreigners living in China, whether posted there as correspondents or exiles who had long blended in, proved to be invaluable when it came to potentially life-saving information. At those moments when the tenseness of the situation could cloud all judgments, a tiny detail or a last-minute hunch could change the course of a life.

In addition to Jim Burke of *Life*, Jean Lyons of the *New York Times*, Bob Ford Doyle of *Time* and Sam Tata from the Black Star Agency, Cartier-Bresson was on particularly friendly terms with some French journalists that he had teamed up with, including Jacques Marcuse, the France-Presse correspondent in Shanghai. Outside the immediate circle of his colleagues, his other friends were a well-known theorist on semantics, M. Vetch, who ran a bookshop in Peking, Alphonse Monestier, a former journalist who had a collection of old photographs of Chinese celebrities, and Jacques Guillermaz, military attaché to the French Embassy in Peking. The latter may well have saved his life by warning him that under no circumstances should he board the *Amethyst*, as he had been asked to do by *Life*, in order to photograph the crossing of the Yangtse by the communists. The *Amethyst* was a British escort vessel which the communists proceeded to sink with all hands.

Just before the communist army entered Peking on 31 January 1949, Cartier-Bresson managed to get on the last plane to Shanghai, while the communist troops were surrounding the airport. From there he tried to gain access to the areas controlled by the People's Army, in the regions of Tsing-tao and Shantung. On foot, pushing his luggage on a wheelbarrow through thick snow, he followed the route taken by the missionaries rejoining their followers – after all, if they had got through the snow he could, he reckoned. Fortunately, a journalist and a businessman whom he met by chance took him with them in their jeep. It was all a great deal of effort for very little reward. He spent several weeks holed up in a village, and was not allowed to take any photos even when he walked towards the soldiers with a white flag in one hand and his French passport in the other. 'No pictures!' was the order of the day.

He returned to Shanghai, and left again with a group of Buddhists going on a pilgrimage to the shrines of Hangchow. But *Life*, which had commissioned him to cover the Chinese Civil War, expected something else, and so he caught the last train to Nanking, the headquarters of the Kuomintang, to observe the final stampede of the nationalist forces, whose leaders had fled to Taiwan. He was there for the symbolic crossing of the Yangtse by the communist troops, still glorying in the epic achievement of their long march. He spent four months in Nanking without letting his two Leicas out of his hands for a single second, continually recording details of daily life there. He again went back to Shanghai, which had now become exorbitantly expensive owing to the huge rise in the value of the dollar; he and Ratna were lucky enough to find accommodation with friends so that they only had to pay for board and lodging. But then came the day of the great European exodus.

Cartier-Bresson had to go too, but, as if he wanted to turn out the lights before leaving, at the last minute he went back to some of the places where foreigners had lived, sometimes for decades. The British Country Club had never seemed so desolate as on that Sunday morning in September. The only relief was the incongruous presence of a young man who broke off from reading his book in order to inform the dumbfounded photographer calmly that 'The English are not afraid of solitude.'

On 24 September 1949, a month before Mao Tse-tung's proclamation of the People's Republic of China, Cartier-Bresson and his wife left for Hong Kong aboard the S.S. *General Gordon*, the only liner allowed to sail through the blockade. Its principal mission was to repatriate employees of the State Department and other American citizens, but any remaining vacancies were offered to refugees from other countries. Before embarking, he had had to develop his photographs and submit them for censorship – a risky business, since many of the pictures would be the last images of old China, but as it turned out he had no problems.

Despite the background of war, these pictures express a kind of serenity, at least initially: eunuchs of the imperial household deep in conversation, Kuomintang officers doing their morning exercises in the gardens, second-hand booksellers in Peking, diplomatic receptions. An unnaturally peaceful society in the circumstances, this strange vision is counterbalanced by images of beggars and blind men being led by young people in rags, the bodies of children abandoned by their families, women screaming or weeping when the coffins arrive after the bombing of their huts.

The gradual increase in tension can be sensed as the all-conquering armies come closer. We do not see them, but we can already taste the fear and feel the panic – there is misery everywhere and, above all, suspense as people wait for the inevitable. Some intellectuals in the West wondered if the Chinese were now enduring history rather than making it.

The violence is hidden in these photographs, though not in the way you might expect. It lies below the surface, in the all too evident struggle for existence which comes across through a tiny gesture or a furtive glance far more vividly than through overt force.

Once again Cartier-Bresson seemed to be in all the right places, though he was never obtrusive. As always, he steered clear of story-telling, preferring the private truths of individual people – but now both Magnum and *Life* obliged him to combine his fascination for a society's culture with the demands of current affairs. Pressure of events, however, never prevented him from devoting maximum attention to the sculpture, paintings and drawings that he encountered during his three years in Asia.

He was in Nanking for the last session of the nationalist parliament, on the Bund (waterfront) in Shanghai when students demonstrated against the black market, in front of Madam Sun Yat-sen and Madam Chou En-lai at the Liberation meeting in the grand theatre in Shanghai, on the Yangtse when the communist troops crossed over, in the streets of Nanking again to register the numbed expressions of the shopkeepers preparing to face their new masters, whom he described as a Spartan army of peasants from the north, in Zikawei to see if the thoughts of Mao Tse-tung were really being taught at the newly reopened Jesuit College, and at the home of the French consul in Shanghai, Monsieur Bouffanais, to celebrate 14 July between two governments.

In all this hectic travelling and turmoil, he remained as obsessed as ever by the principles of composition, as if he had an in-built framing device in the retina. One of his Chinese photographs, entitled *Les derniers jours du Guomin-dang* ('The Last Days of the Kuomintang'), appears on the surface to be unspectacular, but it is generally considered to be a masterpiece. The painter Avigdor Arikha, who was reminded of Caravaggio's *The Beheading of St John the Baptist*, described it as follows:

> In a horizontal space, a perfect set square, two men. One is motionless, look-ing away, the other eating, looking into his bowl. The black on the left and the white on the right create tension. The corner of the black shadow on the left is balanced by the door on the right, level with which a second enclosed rec-tangle forms a hypnotic rhythm. On the left, a door leading to a black void, the opening being an inverted rectangle, frames in counterpoint the motion-less Chinaman who is looking away. Balancing his silent stillness is the seated man who is eating. He is situated precisely at the harmonic juncture of the golden section. He is holding a bowl in his hands. Another bowl, standing on the bench, echoes the first. The black skull cap is their counter-point. Hatched and diagonal shades run from top to bottom and from right to left, disturbing the peaceful horizontality of the scene. It all borders on the miraculous.

Cartier-Bresson's colleague Jim Burke was struck by the energy and agility with which he moved about – worthy of an acrobat or dancer. However, by his own confession, Cartier-Bresson did not always feel at ease:

> I had the impression that I was on an island within China. The people are so lively, and I was so curious about everything that it made this country the most difficult of all to photograph. To work properly, a photographer needs at his disposal about as much space as a referee has around the boxers. But what would he be able to do if he had 15 kids between him and the ropes? At the bird market in Peking, I had 50 under my feet, and they never stopped pushing one another and pushing me.

With the photos that he took in China, he was extremely precise in the phrasing of his captions, as if conscious that the historic nature of the events he had witnessed made it essential to avoid any chance of misinterpretation. His typing was slapdash and his English syntax only approximate, but his vocabulary was rich and colourful. His aim was above all to get things right. His descriptions of the scenes of his reportages ensured that there could be no ambiguity with regard to the meaning of what he had recorded. At the head of his reportage on life in Shanghai and Nanking after the defeat of the nationalists, he wrote: 'This photo may only be reproduced if accompanied by its caption or by a text written expressly in the spirit of the caption.'

He ordered Magnum to have this text stamped on the back of every photo in his reportage, as Bob Capa had done with his photos from the Soviet Union. To make his intentions crystal clear, he added:

> I want the captions to consist strictly of information with no sentimental comments or irony of any kind. I want them to be honest information, and there are sufficient elements of that in the pages I am sending you. I have complete faith in you, but I would be very grateful if you would make everything perfectly clear to our clients in this regard. Let us allow the photos to speak for themselves, and for the love of Nadar [the great nineteenth-century photographer], don't let us allow the people sitting behind desks to add on things they have not seen. I regard these captions as a personal matter, as Capa did with his reportage.

It was, then, a question of principle. But such demands were not justified solely by the political aspects of the reportage. Cartier-Bresson devoted the same energy to ensuring the integrity of his captions whether they concerned the equivocations of political leaders or the bare breasts of Balinese dancers (he was anxious for such pictures not to be interpreted in any way as a manifestation of eroticism). Being married to a Javanese, he had the greatest respect for other cultures. It might be a matter of a single detail. Once, for instance, he was about to photograph a young Chinese girl in a rickshaw when a gust of wind uncovered her thighs. She saw him, and immediately covered her face! Modesty takes on different forms in different cultures.

Cartier-Bresson did not have very happy memories of his reportage on the Pondicherry ashram (a retreat for the practice of Hindu disciplines) of Sri Aurobindo, shortly before the latter died. A syncretist philosopher, author of *The Synthesis of Yogas*, he had not left his room for 30 years, but four times a year he allowed his 700 followers an audience. Needless to say, it was not easy for a foreigner to gain access to this living god, in the heart of one of the most respected religious communities in India. Sri Aurobindo's divine consort was a lady named 'Mother', who in another life had been a Tunisian Jewess married to a Mr Richard. She was now a hale 75-year-old who looked after the grain and had such a hold over the leader that everything had to go through her. In his captions Cartier-Bresson seems to have mixed feelings about her – admiration for her organizational talents and energy, but exasperation at her officiousness and the way she over-dramatized everything. The impression is that he had difficulty in taking her seriously. One evening a Bengali devotee tried to excuse 'Mother's' lateness in attending a public session by nonchalantly announcing that she couldn't come straight away 'because she must still be in a trance'. Cartier-Bresson wrote in his notebook: 'I should have been less surprised if he had said that she was making an *omelette à la mère Poulard* for the deserving disciples.'

He was probably more interested in the general secretary of the ashram, a gentleman named Povitro who, when he was still Monsieur de Saint-Hilaire, had been a brilliant mathematician at the Polytechnique. Impressed by his calmness and affability, Cartier-Bresson saw him as a kind of local St John the Baptist. He certainly wasn't the one causing problems – they were 'Mother's' fault, since everything had to pass through her hands.

On the day of his arrival at the ashram, she made him swear not to take any photographs of the great man. By the time he had taken a whole series of pictures of the buildings and all the activities he was as tired of the architecture as he was of the gymnastics, and finally managed to persuade 'Mother' to let herself be photographed from a distance among a group of disciples. Taking one picture after another, he gradually inched closer to the group until finally the good lady actually agreed to pose in front of the camera, together with Sri Aurobindo himself, just like any middle-class couple on the banks of the Marne. But there was one condition: their faces must be enclosed in an artistic halo, to convey the atmosphere of veneration that pervaded this holy place. Cartier-Bresson, who felt that he was simply in the midst of a sect, kept his cool: he was first and foremost a photographer, a Frenchman and a pragmatist. It turned out that 'Mother' did not want the disciples to realize that God had wrinkles and a double chin, and so the next day he took her aside and explained that the photos were so 'soft' that any additional softening would result only in disappointment.

When she understood that his reputation as a portraitist was at stake, she allowed him to go ahead and do what he had to do. But again she set a condition: every print must be submitted to her before publication. Then she suggested that he should discard any negatives where the wrinkles were too obvious. In the end, on the advice of Bob Capa, the negatives and rights to all the stories in which 'Mother' appeared were sold to the ashram in order to guarantee her complete control. History, however, was to play an ironic trick: a year later, on the day after Sri Aurobindo's death, the head of a major magazine in Calcutta wrote to Cartier-Bresson expressing his regret that the portraits of the philosopher were so badly shadowed that his expression could not be made out. And so he asked the photographer to do a reprint and lighten the eyes, which after all, he pointed out, were the windows to the soul.

The memories of this adventure were not all bad. Thanks to the sale of the negatives (the only time he ever took such a step), he was able to buy a country house in Saint-Dyé-sur-Loire, near Chambord. Capa was a good negotiator.

Some of Cartier-Bresson's captions were concise to the point of dryness. They might consist of just two factual lines, perhaps translating the Chinese inscription on a panel in the picture. Others drew comparisons between people or situations, which must have caused some consternation among editors, since the captions were so full of French references. For instance, in describing the features of Buddha 34, his favourite rickshaw driver, he invoked 'the mischievous smile of Max Jacob', or wrote that 'the presence of the former ambassadors is a sign that Shanghai has not always been as provincial as it now seems', or stated that the asceticism and prudishness of those who praised the new China reminded him strangely of the first Christians.

Occasionally, in passing, he defined his own concept of his profession. While giving a detailed critique of some sketches by a soldier, he allowed himself the following revealing digression: 'Let us raise the level of discussion: I have never been interested in anything but "*la vérité des petits faits*" [the truth of small facts] as we say in French, and the expression 'picture story' implies a dramatization of facts that has always been repugnant to me.'

At other times, when circumstances were more exciting, the captions would be no longer, but would acquire a more lyrical tone, as for instance with one of his most famous photographs from this period:

Shanghai, December 1948. The gold rush. Outside the banks on the Bund vast queues have formed, spilling over into the neighbouring streets and blocking the traffic. About ten people must have died in the crush. The Kuomintang had decided to share out certain gold reserves at 40 grams per head. Some people waited more than 24 hours to try and exchange their banknotes. Order was half-heartedly maintained by a police force whose assortment of equipment was acquired from the different armies which for 15 years had had an interest in China.

The photo was published in France on 29 March 1949 in the first issue of a new weekly, *Paris-Match*.

The effect of these captions, and the penetrating political analysis they often contained, must have come as a surprise to the editors-in-chief, who would not have expected such things from a mere photographer. The publication of his reportages in the American press confirmed Cartier-Bresson's standing as a witness of history as it happened. He was a sort of key contemporary, as was Gide – the writer with his journal and Cartier-Bresson with his contact sheets. Both provided unique temporal records of the Fall of Man.

The only previous occasion when Cartier-Bresson had been caught up in such a fever of emotion had been in India on the day after Gandhi's assassination; but there had never been such a turmoil of events as he experienced in China during the months leading up to the old regime's collapse in the face of the Revolution. At certain moments he felt that everything culminated in a single second, exploding at the speed of his shutter. He felt a physical exhilaration, as if balancing on the crest of a great wave, his camera in his hand.

By the end of summer 1949 he had spent two years in the Far East. He was in Lahore, Pakistan, when he received a cable from Talley, of the *New York Times*, asking him to sum up his impressions of these years in 500 words. For the uninitiated, such concision may seem ridiculous. Rather than an essay, Cartier-Bresson would have preferred to send him 'a big picture of history', since he did not feel able to translate images into words – especially just 500 of them. Any coherent synthesis would have seemed fraudulent, because he had seen history only in flashes, and felt that no one sentence could possibly recapture truths grasped in a fraction of a second. He refused the request but, by return cable, delivered something no less revealing – some keys to his vision of the world.

These lines drew a self-portrait of a westerner who had been bowled over by the ceaseless waves of humanity, a million mouths crying out for something to eat. He was convinced that World War II had changed the order of things here more than anywhere else. The myth of the all-powerful white man had crumbled, the rise of nationalism was inexorable, and empires had failed to find the words and actions that would facilitate a dignified transition. This failure was primarily the fault of our forebears, guilty of blindness because they had no desire to see or even imagine that the colonial system would not last for ever. But Cartier-Bresson remained faithful to his own vision in his continued belief that the former colonial subjects' attitude to art was the best indicator of the evolution of minds. It was better than any political or social programme, for it was all bound up in the clash of cultures. Nothing was more significant in his eyes than the fact that in Bali, for instance, where there was a mixture of Chinese, Cambodian and Indian influences, an artist such as Rembrandt was regarded as an alien from another planet. That is why he considered it to be just as urgent for the East to re-establish its own culture as to ensure its economic survival. Only by reviving its own traditions could it acquire sufficient confidence to understand and appreciate the West.

When he departed from the new China, Cartier-Bresson had still not quite finished with Asia. It was as if he found it difficult to leave, especially as Ratna was always by his side, or acting as his guide. There followed two weeks in Hong Kong, observing the capitalists at work and play, a week in Singapore, several weeks travelling all over Indonesia observing the last days of Dutch colonialism, back to Singapore, then on to the plantations in Sumatra. There was a pilgrimage to Ceylon, a visit to the ancient Jewish community in Cochin, a few days at the foot of the Himalayas, where rich Indians would now spend their holidays exactly like the British before them, a short stay in the Baluchistan desert, two months in Iran photographing the Shah in his palace and the mystical Zoroastrians, a brief trip to Baghdad, and three weeks on Damas to see the oldest street in the world.

But then it was time to go home, particularly after they had a car accident near the Iranian border. The accident was not serious, but the consequences were. Thanks to a careless lorry-driver, their convertible car overturned. Instead of trying to help them, the driver went off to find a lawyer. They finally managed to extricate themselves, but Ratna had a splinter of glass embedded in her fingertip, and when a local doctor attempted to take it out he was so clumsy that he severed a nerve. By thus destroying her ability to make gestures with her hands, he also destroyed her career as a dancer.

It was now summer 1950, and Cartier-Bresson was 42 years old. He had been awarded the US Camera Prize for best reportage of the year for his coverage of the death of Gandhi, and he won another award from the prestigious Overseas Press Club for his pictures of Nanking and Shanghai. At the end of his dry, factual chronology of his three years in Asia, he noted:

> I must have taken some 850 films with my Leica, and written down all my impressions recto and verso in my notebooks. It is therefore impossible for me to recount everything in three pages. Our only secret was to move slowly and to live with people. Furthermore, I benefited from one enormous advantage: the help of my wife.

7 THE WORLD IS HIS STUDIO
1950–70

Cartier-Bresson's work was by now widely recognized: published, exhibited, awarded prizes, quoted, reviewed, admired and envied. In France and elsewhere, he inspired others to follow his lead. Some were jealous of his fame; he himself both enjoyed it and shunned it, as ever faithful to his own contradictions, his middle-class liberalism, his philosophy, a kind of Norman Zen archery, his driving curiosity about the outside world and his quest for inner wisdom.

Magnum aimed to be the Rolls Royce of photography, with all the pride and efficiency that this implied. Cartier-Bresson was unknowingly paid the most flattering of compliments, as reported in the gossip column of the *New York Post*. One evening, when he and his Leica were pirouetting between the tables of a fashionable jazz club, Dixieland, the clarinettist leaned over to another member of the Duke's band and said: 'That cat is to the photo what Louis [Armstrong] is to us.' That was true recognition. The rest was mere words.

The debt that Cartier-Bresson owed to books made it inevitable that one day he too would become involved in creating them – but, as always, in his own way.

An author should never allow anyone else to impose a title on his book, for the title can take over and affect the real substance and spirit of the book. Cartier-Bresson, who never chose the titles for his books, was in this position right from the start with his first, *Images à la sauvette* ('Pictures in a Rush', or 'Pictures on the Sly'), published in 1952 under the prestigious label of *Verve*, in a format similar to that of a magazine, with a green and blue cover specially designed by Matisse and printed by the brothers Draeger.

The art editor was Tériade, his mentor from pre-war days, who for this project collaborated with the New Yorker Richard L. Simon of the publishers Simon & Schuster, himself a photographer. They wanted Cartier-Bresson to allow them full freedom in the selection and layout: 126 photographs taken over the last 20 years, to be published in large format with no additional material – even the most succinct captions were to be jettisoned – and in no order, other than an arbitrary distinction between East and West. But over and above this, he wanted Cartier-Bresson to write a substantial essay on the subject of photography, which would serve as a foreword. It was to be a kind of personal reflection on his concept of the profession.

'How do you make your pictures?' they asked, with the same naivety as Gide asking Simenon how he created his novels.

'I don't know. That's not important.'

'Oh, come on, why have you been doing it for 20 years? Write it down, put your ideas on paper, then we'll see.'

It was a somewhat brusque approach, but knowing his dislike of all explanations it was the only way. Still Cartier-Bresson hesitated. It just wasn't him to talk about the whys and the wherefores, and now they wanted a long essay from him about something he had always avoided discussing. All the same, he was tempted by the prospect of publishing his photos in a book along with his own text, not just the brief captions he normally wrote. Bob Capa, whose practical sense was not the least of his good qualities, added an extra bait: 'If it brings you some money, you'll spend it. But if it brings you prestige, that'll help you.'

Tériade gave him an assistant, Marguerite Lang. Having commissioned the essay he forced him to write it, and snatched it from him as soon as it was ready – within a week. Ten pages long, the preface was entitled *L'instant décisif*. When the book appeared in the United States, the translator didn't bother with the linguistic subtleties of *Images à la sauvette* but, at the instigation of the publisher, used the title *The Decisive Moment*, combining the sharp precision of the first term with the more poetic 'soft focus' of the second.

From then onwards, Cartier-Bresson was established as the photographer of the decisive moment. Thus are legends born. The effect was to blur his image in the United States, for by radicalizing his ideas in so restrictive a manner, the description had fixed him once and for all.

'There is nothing in the world that does not have its decisive moment.' This sentence by the seventeenth-century Cardinal de Retz is highlighted in his text, as if meant to shed its light on the whole preface. Cartier-Bresson had read it one day by chance, had memorized it in isolation, and had never been able to put it back into its context. Its truth had been tried and tested, and as he understood it, the secret was to discern and to fix those moments:

There is nothing in the world that does not have its decisive moment, and the masterpiece of good conduct is to recognize and seize the moment. If you miss it in the revolution of states, you run the risk of not finding it again or of not perceiving it.

Everything in this preface – the didactic tone, the choice of words, the sporting metaphors – reveals his mental approach. After this very *grand siècle* epigraph, the beginning has a somewhat Proustian flavour: 'I have always had a passion for painting. When I was a child, I did it on Thursdays and Sundays, and I dreamed about it on the other days. I had a Box Brownie, like many children...'.

After a short autobiography, he develops his ideas in six directions: reportage, subject, composition, colour, technique and client. In addition to his well-known obsession with form and his professional principles, which he applied to his private life, we find here his taste for the well crafted, disciplined formula – all the more effective because to the very last Cartier-Bresson resists intellectualizing the activity which is his life and his livelihood, even though it too is a kind of mental exercise. Because this preface is the only major theoretical text that he ever agreed to write, certain passages have been quoted over and over again. It is a professional's profession of faith, and with its practical content as well as its deeper reflections it is as much a handbook as a breviary:

The reportage is a progressive operation performed by the head, eye and heart in order to express a problem, fix an event or impressions.... For me photography is simultaneous recognition, in a fraction of a second, of part of the significance of a fact, and on the other hand rigorous organization of the visually perceived forms that express this fact.... The subject does not consist in collecting facts, for the facts in themselves are of scarcely any interest. The important thing is to choose among them, to seize the fact that is true in relation to deep reality. In photography, the smallest thing can be a great subject, and the little human detail can become a leitmotif.

Stripped of its technical aspects, this still gives nothing away. Everything in it invites us to contemplate the ineffable elements of such a strange human activity, a kind of poetry, with its close links both to time and to death. The decisive moment appears here as an extraordinary confluence of reality and sightline, issuing from the ideal of purity that we retain from childhood and project on to memories of that childhood.

Without a certain state of grace, Cartier-Bresson would not be Cartier-

Bresson. Such grace is found only when you don't look for it, although you must be open to it. The right moment comes when you have understood, without knowing why. These collected moments of eternity, the *images à la sauvette*, never resolve the mystery of their creation; they only augment it.

The warning which the author felt he had to issue separately makes no difference to the impact of his book: 'The pictures in this book do not claim to give any general idea of the appearance of this or that country.'

Behind such cautiously prudent words the hand of the scrupulous caption-writer for the photos of Bali and elsewhere can be sensed. But even if the reader knew nothing about the author's character, anyone looking through his book would soon recognize that it represented his own personal vision of the world.

It could be said that the book is one man's view of half a century, and certainly that was how the critics saw it. The article in the *New York Times* began with an anecdote. One evening, around midnight in Manhattan, the writer had agreed to go for a drink with Cartier-Bresson in a drugstore at the corner of the street. He was surprised to see him carrying his Leica.

'Are you going to take some photos?'

'No, but I never leave my Leica behind.'

Only such total dedication and permanent readiness can allow for the decisive moment, which otherwise might disappear for ever. The article finishes with a paean of praise, ranking the famous preface among 'the most intelligent and most lucid' texts ever written on the subject. The full significance of this only becomes clear when we realize who is bestowing such praise: another great photographer, Philippe Halsmann, portraitist of leaping celebrities, responsible for more than a hundred covers for *Life*.

The other major article that heaped praise on the book was by another photographer, also writing in the New York Times. He was one of the few colleagues whom Cartier-Bresson admired without reservation. Walker Evans was not content merely to emphasize the intelligence underlying Cartier-Bresson's talent for freshness and originality. After raving about the pieces on the coronation of George VI and the portrait of Sartre on the pont des Arts, he refers to the spirit in which the preface is written in a manner that would certainly have delighted its author: 'It has something that is rather rare in a piece of this nature: it is totally devoid of inanities and of ego.'

Philippe Halsmann and Walker Evans were not the only ones to sing Cartier-Bresson's praises. On the publication of *Images à la sauvette* and its English edition, *The Decisive Moment*, the press was unanimous in its enthusiasm.

Nothing, however, counted for more in Cartier-Bresson's eyes than the articles written by his peers, for they after all were the true experts. There was admiration from younger colleagues, accolades from older ones, and not even Cartier-Bresson could remain indifferent to such recognition.

This first experience must have given him a taste for the genre, because three years later he again teamed up with Tériade for a similar project. This time, though, the 114 photographs printed by Pierre Gassmann had been taken during the previous five years. Under the title of *Les Européens*, and with a gouache cover by Joan Miró, the photographs were preceded by a short essay which contained nothing theoretical, written by Cartier-Bresson himself, with a poem by Charles d'Orléans as an epigraph. The rest consisted of self-contained pictures that were arranged according to countries. The captions were relegated to the last pages, and were in any case of exemplary brevity: 'Seminarists walking in the vicinity of Burgos'; 'A pub in a London suburb'; not to mention the famous picture of a small boy proudly carrying a bottle of wine in each arm under the admiring gaze of a little girl: 'Paris, provisions, Sunday morning rue Mouffetard'.

Images à la sauvette and *Les Européens* were the only books that Tériade published on the work of a photographer. This is all the more of a compliment when it is borne in mind that for *Verve* he published 26 books of artists' own work (that is, not illustrating someone else's text). Thus Cartier-Bresson took his place in the catalogue of the most prestigious art publisher in Paris alongside Bonnard and his *Correspondances*, Chagall with Gogol's *Dead Souls*, Picasso and the poet Pierre Reverdy, Léger and his Circus, Matisse rereading the *Portuguese Letters*, and Matisse again with his famous *Jazz*.

Realizing that Cartier-Bresson was the only photographer in this galaxy of talent, his fellow photographer Brassaï vented his jealous spleen on Tériade, who, however, had no intention of giving way; he had made an exception for Cartier-Bresson, but his priority otherwise remained painting. The exception shows not only the immense respect that Tériade had for Cartier-Bresson, but also the prestige which reflected upon himself and which had a symbolic significance transcending the public and critical success of the two books.

The success was enhanced, after the publication of the second book in 1955, by an exhibition of Cartier-Bresson's work at a venue not normally associated with photography: the decorative arts section of the Marsan Pavilion at the Louvre. True to form, he welcomed friends in the corridors rather than among the 200 works on display, because he wanted to smoke. The reporter from *Lettres françaises* drew a closely observed pen-portrait of him:

Tall, pale, with hair cut very short and tending to lose its original colour, a sharp profile and a very mobile gaze behind the lenses of his spectacles, he looks like a shy and studious schoolboy on prize-giving day, an only son who has grown up too quickly and will always look on the world with the eyes of a wonder-struck child, while possessing all the experience of a man.

Ill at ease with the usual gathering at such openings, and not urbane enough to cope with the subtle comments of the writer André Maurois or the painter Félix Labisse, Cartier-Bresson was able to relax and smile only in the company of his fellow photographers – not so much colleagues as brothers amid this crowd of strangers.

The show was a kind of canonization. What had long been evident was now beyond doubt: Cartier-Bresson was a true artist. He who had cherished dreams of becoming a painter was, thanks to his exceptional qualities, now acknowledged as such. All that was required for him to achieve the status of a modern classic was to grow older.

Tériade was the first to incorporate Cartier-Bresson into the history of art, but he was not his only publisher. In 1953–4 he came into contact with a young man who would become his principal publisher, organizer of his exhibitions, and one of his most faithful friends.

Robert Delpire was a medical student whom he met one day at the Parisian office of Magnum, in the faubourg Saint-Honoré, when Delpire came to choose some photographs for 9, a lavishly illustrated magazine that he was putting together for the medical profession. Cartier-Bresson noticed his excellent taste and gave him a warm welcome. Always demanding the highest quality himself, he was never willing to grant rights to any publisher whom he did not consider worthy. When Delpire chose to go into publishing rather than medicine, he gave him his full backing.

Danses à Bali (1954) was their first book. It contained 46 photographs with a commentary by Béryl de Zoete. Especially noteworthy was the preface, an essay written in 1931 by Antonin Artaud on the intricate gestures, poses and geometrical costumes that transform Balinese actors into animated hieroglyphs.

In the same year, Cartier-Bresson and Delpire collaborated on an even more ambitious project. They were in perfect harmony on a personal level, but professionally young Delpire was far more impatient. He was constantly badgering Cartier-Bresson, who would usually respond in his typically cool way: 'It's not ready – there's no hurry...'.

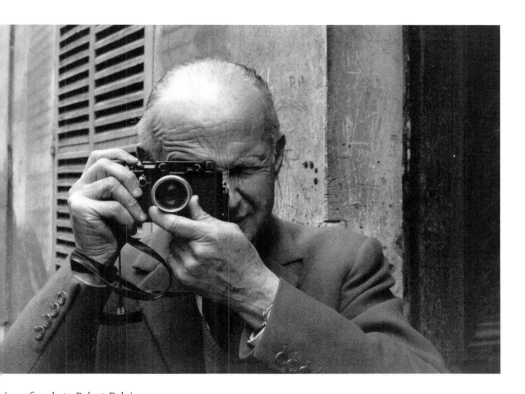

is, 1967; photo Robert Delpire

He could almost be mistaken for part of the Goya painting at the Prado, Madrid, 1993;
photo Martine Franck, Magnum (above) The draughtsman trying to make a self-portrait
at home in Paris, 1992; photo Martine Franck, Magnum (below)

e indispensable eye of Tériade, the mentor, publisher and friend to whom the artist Cartier-Bresson
»wed his drawings in 1974; photo Martine Franck, Magnum (above)   Henri Cartier-Bresson
tching in the Natural History Museum, Paris; photo Martine Franck, Magnum (below)

In Provence, 1987; photo John Loengard, courtesy of Life

Henri Cartier-Bresson with Ferdinando Scianna in Bagheria, Sicily, 1986; photo Martine Franck, Magnum

With Martine Franck, 1980; photo André Kertész, taken with Martine Franck's camera, All rights reserved

*ıri Cartier-Bresson and his
ghter Mélanie, France, 1974;
to Martine Franck, Magnum
)*

*ıri Cartier-Bresson with his
ghter Mélanie and
nddaughter Natasha,
tzerland, 2001; photo Martine
nck, Magnum (top)*

*ıri Cartier-Bresson with his
nddaughter Natasha and a
rait of his mother Marthe,
2; photo Martine Franck,
gnum (right)*

Julien Levy and Henri Cartier-Bresson, Provence, France, 1976; photo Martine Franck, Magnum

At the Combe de Lourmarin, Vaucluse, France, 1996; photo Martine Franck, Magnum

Cartier-Bresson finally gave Delpire his *D'une Chine à l'autre* ('China in Transition'), though not without some reluctance. He saw it as a visual record of the eleven months he had spent in China, half of them under the nationalist government and half under the communist regime as a privileged witness to an historic transition. It was indeed well worth a book.

Once they had agreed on the choice of pictures and the layout, they had to find a writer for the preface, and Delpire thought of Jean-Paul Sartre. Sartre then was one of the most prolific, most generous and so most sought-after writers of prefaces in Paris, contributing to works by Roger Stéphane, René Leibowitz, Nathalie Sarraute and Jean Genet among others. Nine years after taking the famous portrait on the pont des Arts, Cartier-Bresson set off to see him, heart in mouth, with the request that he write the preface to the new book.

'But I've never been to China!' protested the philosopher.

The photographer was not to be put off by such a minor detail, and responded with the first thing that came into his head: 'So? Priests don't get married, but they know a lot about women.'

'In that case...'.

Cartier-Bresson told Sartre all about China, so that the writer could comment on the photographer's vision of this distant country – he himself would not visit it for the first time until a year later.

Sartre's text is surprising. It begins with the commonplace notions with which he was brought up, the kind found in a children's story-book, continues with a reference to Henri Michaux, who so successfully revealed 'China without lotus and Loti', and ends by praising Cartier-Bresson's demystification of the country. The photographer, he says, does not like his photographs to be 'talkative', preferring them to stimulate ideas rather than claim to embody them. His Chinese are so natural and so ordinary that it is disconcerting. Sartre praises the iconoclasm of the book, which deliberately avoids the picturesque, the exoticism and all the clichés that for so long have distorted the western view of China:

> Cartier-Bresson's snapshots capture man at great speed, without leaving him time to be superficial. In a hundredth of a second, we are all the same, all at the heart of our human condition.... The crowds of Asia. We must be grateful to Cartier-Bresson for not having got it into his head that he must convey their swarming.... Cartier-Bresson makes us sense this phantom multitude everywhere, divided up into tiny constellations – this threat of discreet and omnipresent death.... Cartier-Bresson has photographed eternity.

His books sold – particularly *Images à la sauvette*. But, by a strange paradox, he made hardly any money out of them. Some time after his return from the Far East, where he had lived on very limited means, he asked Magnum for the accounts, since they collected his royalties and held the money for him. Bob Capa's response was: 'There's practically nothing left – we are, so to speak, bankrupt.'

There was a silence while this shock news sank in, and then he added with his characteristic irrepressible cheek: 'Anyway, this money, what would you do with it if you had it? Another fur coat for your wife? And you don't even like cars, so....'

What was a bit of money between friends with mutual interests? There could be no better illustration of the spirit of a cooperative, at least during its early, pioneering years. This could not really be thought of as a golden age when financially these were such lean years; but the fact is that when Edward Steichen hung the walls of New York's Museum of Modern Art with *The Family of Man*, a monumental exhibition of photojournalism comprising 503 pictures by 273 photographers from 68 countries, Magnum – with only eight members – was credited with 15 per cent of the total exhibits.

The agency had become Cartier-Bresson's home from home. In 1954, it went into mourning: just when he had at last become a naturalized American citizen, Robert Capa, who was covering the war in Indo-China on the day after the battle of Dien Bien Phu, stepped on a Vietminh landmine. His death left a gap that could never be filled.

In June, the stalwarts of Magnum met in the Cartier-Bresson family apartment on the rue de Lisbonne for a get-together that was certain to be a gloomy affair. By an extraordinary coincidence, on the very day that Capa died, another Magnum photographer, the Swiss Werner Bischof, who had joined in 1949, was killed in a car accident in the Andes.

From this sad gathering of image-makers there emerged no papal smoke signal announcing the election of a new supremo, but instead there were three vice-presidents: Chim for finance, George Rodger for the Paris office, and Cornell Capa – Bob's younger brother, an experienced laboratory technician before becoming a reporter for *Life* – for the New York office. These three, along with Cartier-Bresson and Ernst Haas, constituted the membership of Magnum. But it very soon became clear that they would have to choose a president who would have at least nominal responsibility for the agency. All eyes turned towards a friend of Cartier-Bresson's who had been giving them much good advice – a businessman named Jean Riboud. But although he was tempted, he finally declined, and so the presidency of Magnum fell to Chim, one might say by default, although he was possessed of all the necessary qualities for the post.

In many respects the organization soon found itself on shaky ground. George Rodger, the irrepressible Londoner based in Paris, was itching to go back to Africa and find unknown tribes to photograph. He proceeded to do just that, and left his vice-presidential chair to Cartier-Bresson, whose nature was no more suited to administration than was Rodger's. But cometh the hour, cometh the man, and so now he assumed more assiduously than ever the mantle of intellectual and aesthetic guardian of the agency, a role Capa had always assigned to him. He was not put off by one of the last conversations they had had together, when Capa had foreseen that all photographers would be turned into television reporters and was almost resigned to what he feared was the inevitable. As guardian of the flame, Cartier-Bresson, ever preoccupied with quality, fought ceaselessly to ensure that Magnum would never renounce its own philosophy, with its mixture of liberalism and respect for reality, and he wanted it to remain a small-scale organization, with few employees and fewer than 40 associates. Some regarded him as a bore, a moralizing pedant, but he never lost a chance, even when dealing with the most trivial administrative matters, to remind people of crucial principles which they might otherwise tend to forget: 'Actuality and the need for rapid delivery should never be to the detriment of our quality; we founded Magnum in order to present our photographic impressions in the way that we feel them,' he wrote.

In 1956, two years after Capa's death, it was Chim's turn to die an equally pointless death: he was covering the Suez war when he was killed by a burst of machine-gun fire from an Egyptian soldier several days after the ceasefire.

Cartier-Bresson was overwhelmed with grief. One after the other he had lost the two great friends who had shown him the art of telling a story in pictures – the type of photograph that was closest to his heart. In his depression, he reproached himself with not having given them more help, not having been more sensitive to their problems and fears. It was the kind of guilt adult children feel towards their parents when it is too late.

Three great men had gone – men who had represented Magnum's finest hours, each having their place of honour in Cartier-Bresson's memory.

Werner Bischof's humble humanism had shone through his reportages on the famine in India, and on Japan. He had been as good a draughtsman as he was a photographer.

Bob Capa would always be remembered as a charismatic adventurer who eventually became a photographer but could just as easily have turned to television or video if he had lived. 'For me Capa always wore the shining cloak of a great torero, but he never killed; a great gambler, he fought generously for himself and for others in a whirlwind.'

Chim was modesty personified, intelligence in action, a man whom Cartier-Bresson could never recall without a lump in the throat:

> He had the intellect of a chess-player. With his maths professor's demeanour, he applied his vast curiosity and culture to many different spheres.... The sureness of his critical mind soon became indispensable to everyone around him. Photography for him was a pawn which he moved around the chessboard of his meticulous intelligence.... Chim would pull his camera out like a doctor taking his stethoscope out of his bag, and then pronounce his diagnosis on the state of the heart. His own was vulnerable.

These open wounds were only partially healed by the long succession of new encounters that Cartier-Bresson experienced through the 1960s. It was people first and places second, for humanity is fleeting while the earth remains. Portraits were his main focus, and in this field he gained a reputation for being lucky – erroneous, because luck could not explain the sheer number of coincidences. It would be less romantic but more pragmatic to fix on the notion of availability, because when eyes and ears are constantly on the alert and Leica constantly in the hand, you are bound to intersect with lives at the moment of destiny. You simply have to have the instinct for the time, the patience to wait without expectation, and the awareness to seize the decisive moment. Cartier-Bresson had all those qualities in abundance.

Ever since he had been one of the last persons to talk to Gandhi he had had this 'lucky' reputation, and it is true that there were other coincidences that were strangely disturbing.

In 1946 he had photographed Alfred Stieglitz, stretched out on his sofa at home in New York, without knowing that this would be the last photo ever taken of him. A month later he died at the age of 82. It was their first and last meeting. But generally, Cartier-Bresson did not take portraits of people he scarcely knew. Of course he was familiar with Stieglitz through his work, but he had simply had a feeling that this was an occasion when he should ignore his self-imposed rule. Was that luck, or flair?

In 1968 he photographed Marcel Duchamp playing chess with Man Ray, exactly as they had been doing in front of René Clair's camera for *Entr'acte* in 1924. It was an insider's mischievous wink of the eye that all three would have enjoyed immensely. Marcel Duchamp died that same year, aged 81.

Between these coincidences, he had covered William Faulkner's visit to the military academy at West Point in August 1962. It was not a particularly important event, but he wanted to be there. The two men had not met since Cartier-Bresson's 1947 reportage from the home in Oxford, Mississippi, of the only American writer to style himself a farmer. Literature, he had said, was all very well, but farming was the thing to do.

In 1962, at the request of General Westmoreland, he had come to give a talk. Showing signs of fatigue, the 65-year-old Faulkner read an account of a horse-race from *The Reivers*, which he had just finished writing. Then, in his most sarcastic vein, he proceeded to regale the officer cadets with a speech that was as anti-militarist as could possibly be conceived in such surroundings. But he managed to perform this feat by condemning war and yet praising the army at the same time. Carson McCullers, despite being ill at the time, was at this gathering, but Cartier-Bresson was so engrossed that he failed to notice her.

'Is there any connection between the military and literature?' asked a cadet.

'If there was,' replied Faulkner, 'there would be no literature.'

And so it went on, amid thunderous applause. It was a triumph for Faulkner, and Cartier-Bresson's photos revealed him in a completely new light. He had abandoned his customary old tweed jacket for a formal tailcoat. The black and white were all the more striking as he had dug out the red rosette of his *Légion d'honneur*. These pictures were among the last to be taken of him. He died three months later.

These disturbing coincidences fascinated Cartier-Bresson, who could never have enough of such signs of destiny. They were a permanent spur to the imagination, though he did not take them for indications of any kind of blessing. They had punctuated his whole life, but his reactions were those of a surrealist, not a mystic. The links seemed to embrace both omnipotent chance and the demands of reportage. This obsession with objective chance, which had been with him ever since as a young man he had devoured *Nadja*, governed many of his attitudes and reactions, whether consciously or not, but it would be wrong and even contradictory to say that chance was the governing factor behind his photography. His portraiture, refined throughout the 1960s, is the enigmatic illustration of this. He always preserved the element of mystery, for regardless of the flair, the availability, the opportunism, the intensity of vision, the frenetic translation into the brilliant picture, what was always the essential factor was that he touched on the soul of the person he was photographing – that all-important, indescribable element that defies explanation. Chance played no part in this.

Even when he attended formal occasions that were also covered by his colleagues, Cartier-Bresson always managed to take at least one photo that would be uniquely his. In 1960, when John Huston was filming *The Misfits*, six photographers from Magnum were on the set. Despite the plethora of pictures, he succeeded in taking one of Marilyn Monroe, right under the eyes of the others, that stood out for its composition, its irony and its tenderness. Perhaps the actress was herself not altogether a stranger to this form of magic. While the crew were having dinner, Cartier-Bresson had put his Leica down on an empty chair next to him. Marilyn Monroe arrived late. She glanced at the camera, then at Cartier-Bresson, paused to make the connection, and at once he seized the initiative: 'Would you like to give it your blessing?' She pretended to sit on the Leica, just brushing it with her behind, and then gave him a mischievous smile.

At the beginning of the 1960s Cartier-Bresson was commissioned by the British magazine *Queen* to do a series of portraits of 15 famous people. It was to be entitled *A Touch of Grandeur*. Although he was very much at ease with the art of portraiture, this was something different, because he was expected to 'cover' each person as one would cover an event. The problem was how to combine his notion of the decisive moment with what would now be premeditated shots.

He observed the great conductor Leonard Bernstein in the intimacy of his family and at rehearsals with the New York Philharmonic Orchestra, noting his pyrotechnics and the Dior leather jacket he wore, in stark contrast to the austere clothes of the Soviet pianist accompanying him.

In Britain, he photographed the Russian-born ballerina Svetlana Beriosova in various dressing-rooms at the Royal Opera House in Covent Garden when she was rehearsing *Ondine*, *Baiser de la fée* and *Antigone*, and became friends with her husband, an eminent psychoanalyst originally from Pakistan. Cartier-Bresson refrained from describing Beriosova as beautiful or sexy, preferring to see her as someone who had deliberately subordinated her feminine side to the demands of her profession. Watching her move, he was reminded of what Paul Valéry had written in *L'Ame et la Danse* ('The Soul and the Dance') about the body's natural power and ability to change the nature of things better than the mind could do.

His next subject was the bearded, patriarchal-looking painter Augustus John, who reminded him of an apostle from one of Dürer's paintings. His expression was naturally serious, not because he was a sad man, but because he reserved his rare smiles for those people whom he particularly liked. He was not a man who looked lightly at things. He would gaze with intense concentration, avoiding anyone who irritated him, and terrifying hangers-on. The fact that he was prepared to receive the photographer and his wife at his home in Fordingbridge, near Salisbury, was a good sign. Even better was his permission for Cartier-Bresson to remain alone with his Leica in the painter's private rooms. His love of the French language, which he spoke perfectly, and of the wines of the Médoc, which he imbibed with equal facility, were the best possible ice-breakers, and since he was swiftly disarmed by the warmth of Ratna's personality, he was soon regaling them with jokes and stories. For all that, though, nothing could be trickier than taking a portrait of a portrait-painter who was generally on the defensive anyway. Cartier-Bresson concentrated mainly on the untidiness of the house, the painter playing with his cats, his hands, his delicate fingers releasing the pencil or brush and taking hold of his pipe.

The British architect Denys Lasdun talked in a high voice about his profession. When Cartier-Bresson tackled him, he was working on a refectory and chapel for a Cambridge college. He conceived the construction as a spiral, so that it could be extended if required. In Cartier-Bresson's introductory text he said he was reminded of the Bauhaus, of African villages, and of the Roman architect Vitruvius. He finished by noting, in a manner that shows his French spirit never became Americanized:

> His wife is delightful. He lives near Bayswater in a Victorian house which he has transformed. He has three extremely lively children. I don't think it's of any interest to know if he plays golf, if he kills butterflies, or if he slaughters partridges. What matters is the loftiness of his thought, his humanism.

The Boston poet Robert Lowell seemed to Cartier-Bresson to be the quintessential American aristocrat, if there is such a thing. Although Lowell had rebelled against his origins, he had retained a Puritan asceticism that was typical of New England, even if it took a European to be aware of it. He was so polite that he was continually fussing over his guest, which did not help Cartier-Bresson's commission at all. The meeting actually took place in New York, in the apartment where the Lowells spent their winters. Fortunately their three-year-old daughter Harriet was also there, and her mischievous presence made the poet unwind a little. A blurred figure in the background, she managed to extract a paternal smile from the man on the sofa. After the portrait was taken, Cartier-Bresson joined the little family on their Sunday walk in Central Park, accompanied Lowell to a meeting, where he was introduced to Allen Ginsberg, and later went to a public reading of extracts from the poet's new collection *Imitations* before an audience of devoted fans. Observing him in these surroundings, Cartier-Bresson understood that this man, so awkward and so shy in society, could only achieve self-confidence through the medium of his poetry.

Next came the writer of the moment, Alain Robbe-Grillet. The publication of *Les Gommes* ('The Erasers'), *Le Voyeur* and *La Jalousie* had established his reputation, and he was regarded as the leader of a new school of literature. When Cartier-Bresson met him, he was working on the screenplay and dialogue of a film by Alain Resnais, *L'Année dernière à Marienbad* ('Last Year at Marienbad'). The photographer realized straight away that the writer needed absolute peace and quiet, and could not possibly be disturbed while at work. The trick was to catch him when he was editing the script – a much more technical, mechanical process than the actual writing, and therefore less dependent on isolation. Cartier-Bresson was not satisfied, however, with the shot he had taken, even though he thought it was good enough to justify his trip. He proceeded to follow his subject to his flat in Neuilly, to a house in Bourg-la-Reine where the novelist picked cherries with his in-laws, to the offices of *L'Express* for an interview with a journalist, and to the offices of the publishers Minuit, where Robbe-Grillet talked with young Philippe Sollers about their respective concepts of the novel. Cartier-Bresson, who was listening in when not dancing around them with his camera, was surprised to hear their ideas, which fitted in perfectly with the conclusions of contemporary scientific thought. He wished he had been able to take notes. Even when he had been photographing him at home, he had regretted not knowing shorthand. There had been a sudden leak from the water-pipes, and Robbe-Grillet had telephoned the concierge and given him such a learned technical discourse, with such mounting anxiety, that it would have been worthy of inclusion in one of his novels.

There were other celebrities in this portrait gallery for *Queen*: the journalists Hugh Cudlipp and Scotty Reston alongside the choreographer Jerome Robbins, the archaeologist Jean Papadimitriou, the playwright Arthur Miller, the composer Gian Carlo Menotti, the US Attorney-General Robert Kennedy and the architect Louis Kahn. But there were two who deserved special treat-ment – not by the magazine, but by the photographer, because he had ties of friendship with them going back over many years.

The first was André Breton. Cartier-Bresson had seen very little of him since the Liberation. He found him among his collection of amulets neatly arranged in his study, and accompanied him out to buy his newspaper, *Paris-Presse-L'Intransigeant*, which carried the highly surrealist headline '*Debré lance le Plan Breton*' ('Debré Launches the Breton Plan'), following a demonstration by farmers in the west. Next they went to La Promenade de Vénus, a café in Les Halles where a group of young followers hung on his every word, just as they used to do in place Blanche. They went to the mythical apartment in rue Fontaine, and made a pilgrimage to the house in Saint-Cirq-Lapopie in the Lot, where people would walk along the banks of the river, stop at the village inn and eat under the pergola. Some four years previously, in *Le Surréalisme, même*, Breton had revealed his love of collecting minerals. Cartier-Bresson could not resist photographing him in the grip of this passion, searching for agates in his garden beside the stream. But he had to be even more discreet than usual. He waited until he was about 20 yards away before producing his camera with one hand while pretending to run the other hand through the soil. But despite the sounds of the outdoors, Breton heard the click. He turned and pointed at Cartier-Bresson: 'Don't you let me catch you doing that again!'

He did not take more than ten photos, of which he liked only half. But men-tally he took many more, especially when Breton began, wild-eyed and shrill, to read Baudelaire. But it would have spoilt everything if Cartier-Bresson had raised his 'spying machine', the very sight of which would have wiped the smile off Breton's face.

It was a day when the pope of surrealism was not excommunicating, but rather granting indulgences. Cartier-Bresson drew a portrait of contrasts: in the picture, a rounded man, arching movements, curls of smoke from his pipe, and a lion's mane; in the text, a shy but intimidating man, upright and honest, polite and punctual, but unpredictable; basically a man who judged others by their attitudes and their moral principles. Usually he did not have a good word to say about Italy, but today, sitting at the table, his *bête noire* was a painter. With an accusing finger that seemed to stretch right across the table, he pointed at Cartier-Bresson: 'You who like Cézanne, that gentleman who did not have the courage to tell his wife that in order to paint the bodies of women bathing...'.

The other great man to whom he was personally close and whom he was to photograph for *Queen* was Alberto Giacometti, a friend and kindred spirit. They had known each other since the end of the 1930s, and he admired the sculptor unreservedly, both as an artist – whom he placed at the very top – and as a man. He was intelligent, lucid, honest, thorough, lively and utterly straightforward. Cartier-Bresson could talk to him about anything and everything, even about photography, and the conversation would never descend into banality, which was as foreign to him as affectation. There was nothing conventional about him, either in his thinking or his appearance. His face resembled one of his own works – in capturing him on film, the photographer could not help but feel that the lines and furrows were Giacomettian, as if he had painted them himself. Cartier-Bresson went to photograph him with his mother in his native village of Stampa, a stone's throw from the Italian border. He had kept the 1938 photographs of the Paris studio, and those of his wife Annette, and of Tériade taken in 1952. He had of course been a quarter of a century younger when the 1938 photos were taken, and now the lines and hollows of the face told their own story. But beyond the mask, lit up by the eyes and warmed by the smile, was a man whose image is engraved on our memories by moments of grace captured by the photographer: one when he was preparing for an exhibition at the Maeght Gallery and was moving one of his sculptures; another walking along the rue d'Alésia with his coat over his head to protect him from the rain. Whether he was between works or between trees, he seemed to merge with them and become one of them. In the first instance, the tentative movements of his body are extraordinarily poetic, accentuated by the hieratic appearance of the bronze creatures all around him, which seem somehow to fit in with his rhythm. In the second, the poor man picks his way between the lines of trees that are so like himself, and finishes up on the pedestrian crossing, between the raindrops. This is how Cartier-Bresson fixed his image – Giacometti, the walking man.

Strangely, Cartier-Bresson was never able to get close to the man generally considered to be the greatest twentieth-century Frenchman of all. It was not for want of trying, but their paths never crossed. We can only imagine what sort of portrait he would have made of General de Gaulle, for if ever there was a man with the touch of grandeur so dear to the editors of *Queen*, it was de Gaulle. He came close, but never close enough. In April 1958, a month before the general's return to power because of the crisis in Algeria, Cartier-Bresson wrote to ask for a private session. The answer came by return:

Your letter has had my full attention. I take note of the request that it entails, the interest of which does not escape me. However, for the time being at least, I think I must stick to the rule that I have made for myself, not to agree to any photographic reportage.

Cartier-Bresson's timing was unfortunate, for de Gaulle had just finished crossing the desert. He did not, however, give up. In September 1961, when the President of the Republic was getting ready for his twelfth tour of the provinces since becoming head of state, Cartier-Bresson once more asked for the privilege of photographing him. He received a reply worthy of a senior officer addressing a non-commissioned officer. The letter expressed his willingness to display the public person but not the private man, for he did not wish to break his self-imposed rule. Magnum Man then pursued the hero of 18 June as he travelled round shaking hands in Aveyron, Lozère and Ardèche. But the photographer was not satisfied, and vowed that he would not be beaten. In summer 1963, he sent de Gaulle a copy of *Images à la sauvette* in the hope of swaying him. On 22 August he received a handwritten reply which was anything but formal:

> Very sincerely, I have admired the photos that are your work, as well as many others that are also yours. Furthermore, I have read with great interest the introduction in which you explain your ideas. You have 'seen' because you have 'believed'. You are therefore a happy man as well as a great artist.

But it went no further than this subtle allusion to the Gospel of St John. The private session never happened; there was no portrait, to his everlasting regret, but the rare failure did not stop Cartier-Bresson from covering General de Gaulle's funeral in 1970.

When Cartier-Bresson had applied for a post as Jean Renoir's assistant, he had shown him an album of his photos. Now, more than 20 years later, the album was in print. This was not the world in majesty, but his vision of it captured, as it were, on the sly. *Images à la sauvette* opened many doors, even if it failed to gain him access to de Gaulle. Sergei Yutkevich, a Russian film director whom he met at the Cannes Film Festival, was so impressed that he hastened to share his enthusiasm with the authorities on his return to Moscow.

In summer 1954, Cartier-Bresson was therefore the first western photographer to obtain a visa for the Soviet Union since the thaw in the Cold War 15 months after Stalin's death. There was, however, one condition: he had to develop his films in Russia so that the censors could see them before he returned to Paris. He and his wife travelled by train, going via Czechoslovakia. Air travel was too quick for his liking – he preferred to take his time. Once he arrived, he realized that there were other conditions as well: he was free to photograph everything except military installations, rail networks, bridges, panoramic views of towns and certain public monuments. It was not a problem. He was interested in the people, in *homo sovieticus* in all his manifestations.

He took advantage of every second when the interpreter – who stuck to them like a leech – was distracted by the need to explain things. He missed no opportunity to photograph tourists in the Kremlin, passers-by in the street, crowds shopping in Gum, workers at the Zis factory, collective farm workers in the tunnels of the Underground. Nor did he miss out on atmosphere: Tolstoy's house, the Tretyakov Gallery, the Bolshoi. He took nearly 10,000 photographs in ten weeks. It all bore little resemblance to Dostoyevsky's *From the House of the Dead*, which had imprinted itself on his mind as being synonymous with 'Russia'. Towards the end of his stay, he even caught a glimpse of Khrushchev and his cabinet colleagues in a grandstand applauding a march-past of sportsmen and women. This Soviet Union was a revelation for Cartier-Bresson, who like most Europeans had had little or no accurate information throughout the years of the Cold War. His own surprise, in these pictures that were so different from the hackneyed images, conveyed this different reality to the public in the West. He showed them that Soviet Russia was far from being a country of Bolsheviks with knives between their teeth. His exclusive reportage brought in $40,000 for Magnum; *Paris-Match* alone published 40 of the photos.

There were to be many other long journeys in the course of time, although he always said that since his return from the East he had done nothing but escape. He was indeed extremely gifted at the art of flight. Sometimes he would spend months on a subject because he felt it was necessary, and because his sense of time expanded; sometimes the period necessary would shrink. In a single week he attended the anniversary of the Chinese Revolution, a commemoration of the Russian Revolution, and the proclamation of a new pope in Rome. He was thoroughly at home in Spain, Greece, England, Ireland, Italy, Belgium, Switzerland, Portugal and Holland. In typically contradictory fashion, he was happy not to travel but liked nothing better than to stay somewhere else for a while.

During the 25 years following the war he was here, there and everywhere. He was in Vallauris with Picasso and in Barcelona with Miró; he followed the wine route through the Loire Valley and went to the Führer's house in Berchtes-gaden; he joined the audience on the lawn at Glyndebourne during the interval of *Ariadne auf Naxos*, and went backstage at Fanni's little circus in the suburbs of Paris. He was under the baroque arches of Viennese churches for *Harper's Bazaar*; he went with Mandiargues to Venice, which he had been so rude about, to seal their reconciliation. He was at the wall in Berlin, and at the funeral of the victims of the Charonne métro disaster. At Saint-Dyé-sur-Loire, near Cham-bord, he was with Ratna in the country house they had bought for their friends to come and visit them, and he was with his father when he died in his sleep from emphysema. In Quebec he attended the funeral of a member of the inde-pendence movement who had committed suicide after being suspected of anti-American terrorism, and in Paris he was at the burial of the militant left-winger Pierre Overney, who had been killed by a watchman outside the Renault factory. He was at Princess Anne's wedding in London, and at a demonstration against General Franco in Spain. He watched the Olympic regatta in Kiel, and the demonstrations in Paris in support of the Chilean leader Salvador Allende. He was always on the move, either for himself or for the agency.

This was his job, but it was also his state of mind, his vision of life and the world – a profession of faith in the blink of an eye.

The United States remained one of his favourite hunting-grounds. This coun-try could never be reduced to a single, definitive vision, and every time he went there, he found new contradictions. Curiously, in spite of his ceaseless wander-ings, there were two other continents that he stayed away from: Latin America (apart from the notable exception of Mexico) and Africa (apart from the equally notable exception of the Ivory Coast). Had it not been for his youthful passions he might never have gone there at all. It was not through lack of opportunity. He actually went back to Mexico in 1963, on a nostalgic and emotional pilgrimage, when the subjects of his photographs included cock-fights, bourgeois country club members, the painter Nacho Aguirre, celebrations on the anniversary of the death of Zapata, and the former president Miguel Alemán Valdés, who had sent him an official invitation. But he never crossed any borders. He also returned briefly to North Africa in 1967, some 30 years after his adventures in Tangier, to follow the experiments of the astrophysicist Bernard Autier at the Amaguir base in the Algerian Sahara, but he did not go any further.

Elsewhere, he was open to more adventures in India, Turkey, Japan, Egypt, Iraq and Israel, but wherever he went, he would always look at the world through his own eyes, seeing it as it was and not trying to adapt it, like others, to characters or conditions. At Churchill's funeral in January 1965 he was like a teenager with a new toy, leaping around on the steps of St Paul's Cathedral before the arrival of the cortège in order to get a better view. 'There was a dance and, simultaneously, a battle against time,' he said.

At Churchill's funeral, just as he had done 30 years earlier at the coronation of George VI, he focused less on the pomp and circumstance of the official ceremony than on its reflections in the streets: a woman in a station reading a newspaper with a portrait of the old lion on the front page; a man selling *The Times*; the sad faces of ordinary people. He liked nothing better than to be on the fringe of the fringe. His observations were never lost, because even if they were not recorded in the photos, they would inevitably appear in the captions. How many other photographers would have noted that at eleven o'clock the first person to enter Westminster Hall, where Churchill's body lay in state, was a New Zealand vagrant who had slept all night outside the door?

He had the eye, but he took a mischievous pleasure in turning his critical gaze on everything that did not meet the eye. He liked to focus on the unpredictable, to bring something unexpected into a routine situation. When he covered the 24-hour race in Le Mans in 1966, hardly any cars can be seen in the picture. Mechanics are having a drink while they wait, VIPs are enjoying a cocktail, spectators stretched out on the grass, lovers in their tents.... On the rare occasions when we do see the machines, they have been opened up and disembowelled. And they are not moving. Speed is the one thing that is missing from this reportage.

Nine years after leaving China, he returned to observe the changes that had taken place since the Revolution. For four months he travelled by train and boat, and occasionally by plane, the length and breadth of this vast country from Peking to Manchuria, to the great dam over the Yellow River, into the Gobi desert, through the gorges of the Yangtse, to the village where Mao was born, to Shanghai, and back to Peking to be present at the National Festival. Were the new Chinese of new China any different? 'In a nutshell, they are hundreds of years old and a few years young,' he said.

He also refused to attack the system. He preferred to describe their concept of liberty as 'relative' – their concept of photography, too, though that would not make him change his methods one iota. The problem was that in China, as in the Soviet Union, he was dogged at every step by an interpreter. The only difference was that the Chinese, of no matter what generation, were possessed of an insatiable curiosity, and this sometimes made it difficult for him to take his snaps. Also, the one thing they hated was to be taken unawares. The restrictions on his liberty, however, were not always what might be expected – apart from military installations, of course:

> It's a rule of the game of photographic hide-and-seek that he who sees first wins, but with them you lose if you're unfortunate enough to stop for a fraction of a second. It's really difficult to catch them by surprise, especially because of one small detail that I had quickly forgotten myself: I'm a white man. It reached a point when one day I called my interpreter over: 'Yu, come and see!' And along with the other Chinese from all around, I stared straight at a Soviet. For once I was not the centre of attention, and I was able to take my photos 'freely'.

The man who loved to merge into the crowd and to be as quiet as his Leica could not avoid drawing attention to himself simply by his very presence. Such a situation required a change of tactics. His actual movements were a disturbance, and rarely fitted in with the atmosphere. When he was in Wuhan, the cultural delegate, always very considerate, warned him that it was not the done thing to photograph passers-by without their permission.

Cartier-Bresson therefore had to learn about Chinese etiquette. He was not prevented from taking certain photos, but was politely asked to take others. Sometimes he had to perform a tricky sidestep in his desire to establish a parallel between the vestiges of the past and the outlines of the future. Why, they asked him, was he so interested in the ancient when the modern was so much more attractive? Cartier-Bresson, who was not born yesterday, gave the following interpretation of the efforts of his guides to convince him and not force him: 'They wanted to help my realism.'

His method of taking notes remained the same as ever, regardless of the event or person he was concerned with. He would spontaneously record his impressions in a pocket notebook with spiral binding, writing in pencil or ballpoint, in French or English. The spelling and grammatical mistakes bear witness to the urgency, though nothing could curb his caustic wit. In 1962, for instance, observing people taking what little sun there was in Blackpool, he scrawled:

> The reserve of the English gives these people, coming from the industrial towns in the region, a downtrodden look of ancestral labour. When they

leave, they queue up at the station like deportees; the first sign of tension will disappear when, sitting in the carriage, the mother says: 'At last we'll soon have a decent cup of tea.'

Humour always had its place, even if it was purely for his own benefit, since he himself was meant to be the only reader of these notebooks. Attending a beauty contest, he observed the disappointment with which all the typists and shop assistants sportingly conceded defeat as they returned to their seats because they did not conform to the judges' taste. He wrote: 'I must confess that for once I did not turn my camera towards the audience. One is French, *môssieur!*'

His notes were far from bland, for they were the source of material for his captions when the photographs did not speak for themselves. He absolutely insisted that these captions be respected – a principle he shared with the much missed Bob Capa – and time in no way softened his intransigence on this point. The caption was not a half-title or a sub-title, but a piece of writing about the picture. That was why it had to be written by the photographer himself. In addition to the sacrosanct stamp on the back of each photo ('This photo may only be reproduced if accompanied by its caption or by a text written expressly in the spirit of the caption'), Magnum sent a letter to its clients in six European countries when the subject merited further stipulation:

> The text and captions to Henri Cartier-Bresson's work on China must be respected to the letter. We wish to be certain that only an exact translation of the words will be published in your magazine. Any change that is neither in the spirit nor true to the meaning of the text and captions will not be permitted.

Experience and past disappointments had taught Cartier-Bresson that one can never be too careful in such matters, even if it means being considered a pain in the neck. Afterwards is too late, for nobody reads the corrections published in the next issue. Sometimes, as in the case of China, the Soviet Union and some other countries with strict censorship rules that are niggardly with their visas, his fussiness was justified by the need to obey conditions that only he was aware of. But at other times his purpose was simply to prevent his photos being used in a manner that would offend his deeply held principles, whether moral or political.

In November 1965 he was covering political life in Japan as expressed in the streets, where there was opposition to the war in Vietnam, to the Sato government, and to ratification of the peace treaty with South Korea. He covered the violent clashes between socialist and communist demonstrators on the one side and on the other a group of extreme left-wing students who advocated direct action and were known as Zengakuren. It is not hard to guess that the libertarian's sympathies were with the young people in white caps, who were well versed in street fighting. With his left bicep encased in an armband on which his friend Yoshi Takata had written 'French photographer' in Japanese, Cartier-Bresson proceeded to photograph the clashes, and as always he demanded strict adherence to the captions he wrote for his pictures. In a postscript to the letter he sent to the agency along with the negatives, he made his position crystal clear:

> It is important to say that not all the Zengakuren are so violent; it is those who have too much force that they need to get rid of, like a kind of active volcano – in more common terms it's called 'letting off steam'. It has to be said that in a country that is so conformist and so respectful towards authority, we must put ourselves in their place and not stay in our own as quiet little chaps, well-informed and well-fed bourgeois gentlemen.

This character trait explains his choices better than any statement – he remained a man of the left, always involved, never militant, faithful to the principles of his youth and of his conscience. He reacted instinctively against injustice and was always physically and mentally impulsive, acting first and thinking later.

In actual fact, nothing further need be known about the Zengakuren or the whys and wherefores of their actions, because the most arresting image to come out of Cartier-Bresson's long stay in Japan had nothing to do with the unrest. The picture was taken at the funeral of a kabuki actor. Some people were in tears, though with the dignity expected of them, showing their grief in the light or hiding it in a handkerchief, turning their backs with a sense of rhythm and movement apparently orchestrated only by the banner situated exactly in the middle, which read 'Funeral' in Japanese. There could not be a more impressive apologia for black and white than this miracle of emotion and composition. Only an artist could thus combine poetry and prose in such an instant of eternity. The vagaries of Japanese politics seem far, far away.

Although Cartier-Bresson did not set out to cover the events of the moment it often happened that he was there – at the liberation of Europe, for instance, and

the revolution in China. He simply took them as they came, in his own inimitable manner. When he gained access to totalitarian countries he adapted
himself to their restrictions, even managing to turn them to his own advantage.
He always achieved his ends, even though there were complaints that any
account of daily life in a communist country – especially a superb account presented under a prestigious name – was in itself a piece of propaganda for that
country.

Cartier-Bresson didn't care what the critics said. He simply went on, with
the words of Kant in his head: do what you must, come what may.... More often
than not he went alone, armed only with his reputation, though his own legend
often preceded him. It opened doors, but it could create difficulties. It was this
that lay behind his abstention from the burning issue that tore France and the
French apart more radically than anything since the 1940–45 war: Algeria.
Cartier-Bresson refused to go there, yielding to friendly pressure from Roger
Théroud, the editor-in-chief of *Paris-Match*: 'Don't go, you are too well known,
you will be grabbed by the military police, and they'll keep their eye on you so
that you won't have any freedom of movement.'

Other journalists, who were just as famous and even more vulnerable
because of the committed tone of their articles, nevertheless went to Algeria
frequently. But no one was forced to cover a particular event, and Cartier-
Bresson certainly had no need to justify this 'gap' in his c.v., especially since he
never went out of his way to cover any war.

The gap was more disturbing within Magnum. It had set out to be the
memory bank of the world, but, curiously, it had failed to fulfil its mission in
relation to the current history of France. There was nothing in its archives about
the Algerian war. And yet in 1957 a young Dutchman, Kryn Taconis, had covered the conflict from the side of the FLN (*Front de libération nationale*), and had
offered them an exclusive reportage which, however, the agency had refused to
distribute on the grounds that there might be government reprisals. Three
years later Taconis left the agency. It was not an episode that Magnum could be
proud of. Excessive deference to the authorities was perhaps one of its major
weaknesses. It was also said that the OAS (*Organisation de l'armée secrète* – a ter-
rorist group opposed to Algerian independence) had threatened to blow up
their offices, but this applied to all newspapers and magazines hostile to the
extremists of French Algeria. It is true, though, that these did not have archives
consisting of millions of negatives and prints – a photographer's only assets –
and it is also true that Magnum's Paris office was at 125 faubourg Saint-Honoré,

adjoining a police interrogation centre where torture was known to be common practice. The fact remains that the dyed-in-the-wool anti-colonialist dormant in Cartier-Bresson did suffer a gnawing feeling of guilt, less as a photographer than as moral guide to this mythical cooperative of photographers.

Some communist countries were hostile to him at first, even going so far as to refuse him a visa, because they had confused him with Raymond Cartier, the writer of editorials for *Paris-Match*, whose name was associated with the somewhat right-wing slogan *La Corrèze avant le Zambèze!* ('the Corrèze [a *département* of France] before the Zambezi'). Such misunderstandings were soon cleared up, and generally when Cartier-Bresson was received by government officials they did know exactly who they were dealing with. He didn't always need to send them a dedicated copy of *Images à la sauvette* in advance.

People feared his judgment. Pictures are as powerful as words, maybe even more so. Indira Gandhi, for example, was well aware of this when they had a long conversation on 22 April 1966. They spent the whole morning discussing the crisis of the moment, which was the subject of his reportage: the food supply in India. In the West, a great deal was being said and written about an issue that was all too prone to vague generalizations. Mrs Gandhi, who had been Prime Minister for three months, was very concerned about Cartier-Bresson's attitude. She was afraid that he might restrict himself to the situation in Kerala, a province in the south-west that was not only very Christian and socially advanced, but was also one of the most densely populated regions and therefore suffered from a chronic problem of food supply. Mrs Gandhi felt this would not be sufficiently representative. Scarcely had he left her than she sent a letter to his hotel urging him not to draw general conclusions merely because of a very localized shortage of rice. She even suggested places for him to visit in order to see at first hand the gravity of the situation: Orissa, Gujarat, Maharashtra, Mysore and Allahabad, her home town. Finally, she added: 'You would give a very bad impression to people abroad if you said that India does not have food supply problems.'

Message received and understood. When he got back to France, Cartier-Bresson wrote the accompanying text to his photos, putting the word 'famine' in inverted commas. He quoted Indira Gandhi's detailed comments, but qualified them by taking up the ideas of the agronomist René Duncan on the need to transform the structures of Indian agriculture so as to tackle the root causes of the problem.

Without having set out to do so, Cartier-Bresson now wielded such influence that his opinions were eagerly awaited. In 1963 the poet Nicolás Guillén, whom he had known 30 years before in the cafés of Montparnasse, welcomed him to Cuba, but it was not so that he could take the fresh sea air. Four years after the fall of Fulgencio Batista's regime, the Americans imposed an economic blockade on the country with a view to bringing down Fidel Castro's revolutionary government. Castro's charisma, and his emphasis on education and health, as well the priority given to agriculture – especially the *Zafra* or sugar-cane harvest, which had taken on a mystique of its own – were not enough to compensate for a one-party dictatorship, a muzzled opposition and an omnipresent bureaucracy.

Diplomatic relations between Havana and Washington had been broken off, and *Life* could not publish any photos accredited to an American. The magazine approached Cartier-Bresson; he immediately contacted his friend Guillén, the 'national poet', who had meanwhile become *persona non grata* in Cuban cultural circles. Guillén found him accommodation in the picturesque Hôtel d'Angleterre rather than the places where foreign dignitaries were normally lodged.

Cartier-Bresson's Cuba was essentially that of the man-in-the-street, the fantastic architecture, the obsession with the lottery, the ubiquitous prostitution – though it was less obtrusive than under the previous regime; guns casually slung over the shoulders of the militia, Russian mechanics explaining how a tractor works, workers rolling their cigars in their own unique manner. But, as might be expected, his was also the Cuba of the two men who exercised the greatest fascination over their people: Fidel Castro himself, 'with the head of a Minotaur and the convictions of a Messiah', in whom he at once detected an element of martyrdom; Ernesto Guevara, known as Che, officially Minister of Industry, but in fact far more than that. In Che Cartier-Bresson saw a true revolutionary, a pragmatist who was not afraid to use force if necessary.

With his friend René Burri, Cartier-Bresson combed the plantations and eventually tracked him down at the Hôtel Riviera. He took several photos of Che making a speech after conferring diplomas on various model workers. Standing at a lectern, he seems as distant as a civil servant behind his desk. Behind him the attention is distracted by revolutionary signs and banners. He might have had more of an air of mystery had he not been smiling, but he seems too much at ease to be fascinating. The photo is good, but no more. At the same time, and under the same conditions, René Burri was also photographing Che, not for *Life* but for *Look*, and not with a 50 mm but with a telephoto lens. He took more photos during an interview with a journalist in Guevara's office. Che leaned back in his armchair, lit his cigar, and offered the journalist a light. In two hours Burri used up eight films, without his subject paying the slightest attention to him.

Burri's Che is better than Cartier-Bresson's because it captures the man's charisma. But neither of them comes anywhere near Alberto Korda's mythical portrait. This is probably because they did not see Guevara in more tragic times, with that haunting, iconic expression. Here, at Cartier-Bresson's expense, is perfect proof of his observations on the state of photographic grace.

So inseparable in everyone's eyes now was the agency from its founding fathers that Magnum was perceived as Cartier-Bresson, and Cartier-Bresson as Magnum. It was unimaginable any other way, 20 years after it had come into the world, and after it had survived so many crises and upheavals. All the same, Cartier-Bresson felt that it was time for him to go. In 1966 he announced that he was leaving, although the agency would continue to handle his rights and his archives – in that respect the umbilical cord remained intact. It was a decision entirely in keeping with his contradictory nature, but it was not made on the spur of the moment. He had been thinking about it for a long time.

If Magnum was a family, it must be borne in mind that family life is not always easy. Cartier-Bresson was the soul of the organization, not its head. He was not made to direct – for that he had neither the taste nor the time. All the same, his tutelary shadow lay over the house, which the others all felt belonged to him rather than to George Rodger, the other surviving member of the founding team. An ironic two-page memorandum dated 26 May 1961 by the photographer Elliott Erwitt entitled 'Why are we at Magnum?' was sent to everyone who worked with the agency, and was pinned up on all the office walls. It said:

> Is it because it's convenient and we are all going to get rich? Is it because we want to see our name beside that of HCB? Is it a hobby? Is it a habit? Is it pure laziness? Is it for the value of our name, like a simple bargaining chip? Is it for the glory of our image? Is it because we can succeed better as a group than as individuals in the jungle of photography? Is it because our passion for the future of the photograph is without self-interest? Is it a trick by the 'historians of our time'? [And so on.]

The litany ended by pointing out the deep splits that had periodically undermined the very foundations of the agency, its structural weakness and its resistance to evolution. But apart from Edward Steichen, to whom a few words of a letter are attributed, the only photographer quoted was Henri Cartier-Bresson. Erwitt had made no secret of the fact that a photo by this illustrious elder had been a revelation which had changed his life, but this did not stop him. The humour was permeated with an anxiety that clearly reflected a malaise common to many members.

A month after this memo had been distributed, another – circulated internally in the American office – proposed that the pursuit of excellence in photojournalism should be extended into the field of 'public drama television'. At the same time, there was more and more focus on the idea that Magnum's quality should be put at the disposal of advertising and industry, two areas which had the means to fulfil their ambitions and could provide the finance in place of the traditional magazines. There were some who saw this as a dangerous route to follow, and discussions were heated. The epithets flew thick and fast – bread and butter, mercenariness, even prostitution were cited. The drift towards commercialism, through which Magnum risked the loss of its soul, was the charge most frequently levelled against the New York office by its counterpart in Paris.

In 1962 Cartier-Bresson issued his own memo with all the fruits of his reflections. With sage maturity he proposed a return to basics in contrast to the current atmosphere, which had become increasingly tainted by commercialism. In other words, even allowing for constraints upon the management, he was urging the other photographers to do everything in their power to resist becoming slaves to the marketplace. After all, Magnum had been created not to reject commissions but to control them. He also talked about a subject that had gradually been lost sight of: the photo reportage.

Still nothing was settled. With little provocation the differences would resurface. Cartier-Bresson's own position was not quite clear-cut, either, since he was soon to publish *L'Homme et la Machine*, a collection of a hundred or so photos, undated, set in such locations as the space centre in Florida, Eton College, a Paris café, the Rolls Royce factory, a sugar refinery in Cuba and a textile factory in China. The captions included quotations from Marshall McLuhan and St Thomas Aquinas, and the preface was by Etiemble, defender of the language against 'franglais', but the marketplace was strongly represented by the client that had commissioned the work: the IBM World Trade Corporation.

It would have been unthinkable that, in a society on the brink of vast changes, an atypical enterprise such as Magnum could be untouched by what was going on. It was in this context of chronic instability that Cartier-Bresson finally decided to step down, without totally distancing himself. In a letter dated 4 July 1966, with a characteristic mixture of humour, sarcasm and acid wit he set out his reasons and his concerns:

Dear Colleagues,

Having for many years been in profound disagreement with the direction that Magnum was taking, and in my capacity as one of the two surviving founders, I asked you to be so kind as to grant me the status of 'contributor', hoping that by keeping my distance I might cause a cathartic shock in the organization. You replied that I should wait till I am 60 years old to become a contributor – but I do not know when I shall reach that age, or what you mean by 60 years.

In the meantime, I have observed that with a certain number of my associates the gap continues to grow between the spirit of the Magnum that we created and that of the present. I have profound respect for the personal reasons and contingencies that motivate them, but I do not wish our past to serve as a cover for a photographic spirit that is not the one which governed the great achievements of Magnum.

I am therefore obliged to ask you to create two associations, which will put an end to the current ambiguity and the unhealthy situation from which we are all suffering: a small, traditional group, in the initial spirit, devoted to living photography, editorial and industrial reportage, and also souvenir photographs; on the other side, an organization devoted to fussier photography, more inventive, glorious and weighty – the name of Magnum being reserved for the first group, and a name like 'Mignum' or 'Mignon' [...] for the other, with ties of friendship linking the two branches.

This would allow us to respect one another, with photographers co-opting others, and I can even think of a case where in my view two photographers could – if they wished – belong to both groups, in a proportion to be determined. Our lawyers and administrative services and accountants will ensure that the little group does not devour the big one – or vice versa.

Should it be that this system – which in my opinion would preserve the spirit of the founders and of a certain number of photographers – cannot be accepted, I would find myself under the extremely painful obligation of having purely and simply, immediately and mellifluously to resign, with all my greetings, congratulations and condolences.

Yours,

Henri Cartier-Bresson

PS: I should like to express all my admiration for the dedication of the people who work in our offices and for the self-sacrifice of all the photographer presidents, vice-presidents etc., past and present.

PPS: I might add that some people have taken it upon themselves – without evil intent, I'm sure – to miss out the word 'photos' from our company name 'Magnum Photos'. This lapse seems to me very significant. Nevertheless, since I remain a photographer, I am ready in a civic capacity to talk a little about photography and other 'cultural' matters. And at this juncture I shall go and see what's happening in the street.

And so he did, for that was what he had always done – going and seeing. The great onlooker had perhaps had enough of workaday photojournalism, but not of landscapes, and above all not of portraits. Landscapes were never urgent, because they were there for good, so he could leave them to Edward Weston or Paul Strand, comfortable in the knowledge that they would still be there when he got back. But human beings were not there for good, and it was the ephemeral that had to have absolute priority.

Cartier-Bresson was far from being tired of photography, but the basis of his disaffection was clear and irrevocable. Gradually he distanced himself from what had once been his pride and glory. It was precisely at the moment when the threat of television had begun to loom large. The illustrated press had to face up to the fact that its golden age was past, and technical advances now gave every Tom, Dick and Harry the illusion that he was a photographer.

In *L'Express*, the journalist Daniel Heymann described him as a man of 60, disenchanted and disillusioned, unhappy, as anyone would be if they thought they were no longer needed; someone who no longer believed in photography at a time when everyone was beginning to believe in it; a sceptic who was convinced that too much travelling had killed travel, and that the invasion of newspapers by colour had turned reality into a lie. Another journalist, David L. Shirey of *Newsweek*, who met him early that summer, said that he was preoccupied by the idea that a photographer could be cut off from reality, getting more and more obsessed with his own anonymity, and that he had agreed to do a television interview only on condition that he could have his back to the camera. Above all, Shirey drew a picture of a man separated from his wife, rarely answering the telephone, and spending all his spare time painting. This was isolation turning into desolation.

Between the lines of these two articles the spectre of depression is discernible. Cartier-Bresson was shattered by his break-up with Ratna. After 30 years together he still loved her, but what he saw as her domineering attitude created such unremitting tension between them that he had made up his mind years ago that they would have to separate.

Cartier-Bresson said himself that he never underwent psychoanalysis. But at this turning-point in his life, when his mind was clouded and his mood dark, he received fascinating reassurance from his friend Masud Khan, whom he had got to know when doing the piece on his wife Svetlana Beriosova. Khan, with disarming and provocative charm, simply said to him: 'Perhaps you are mad, but you are not ill!'

In 1967 Henri Cartier-Bresson took another step towards sainthood. For the second time, the Louvre exhibited 200 of his photographs, some of them enlarged to a format of nearly 200 cm (6.5 ft). Although the selection mixed pictures from the previous retrospective with more recent work, the choice revealed a much subtler self-portrait of the photographer – that of a man who seemed to reconcile a vast number of contrasts, combining sagacity with concern. This was a quiet man with an unquiet vision, a compulsive portraitist who was attracted more and more to the solitude of the individual, whose refined irony never spilled over into the anecdotal or the picturesque.

For any doubters who still put words before image, and others still fighting a rearguard action, this exhibition demonstrated once and for all that photographic reportage, or photojournalism, constituted an art in itself. It opened on the brink of all kinds of intellectual upheavals, but it came just after the appearance of *Un art moyen*, a publication investigating the social uses of photography, commissioned from the sociologist Pierre Bourdieu by Kodak-Pathé. It was dedicated to the great right-wing sociologist Raymond Aron, and one of the photographers most frequently quoted was Henri Cartier-Bresson.

A year later, he launched himself into another major project, which may have been a consequence of the Louvre exhibition: France in all its states, purely France, but the whole of France. The idea came from Albert Blanchard, literary director of *Sélection du Reader's Digest*, and he had no doubt that Cartier-Bresson was the right person to do the photographs. But who was the right person for the text? The perfect candidate presented himself quite spontaneously. From time to time Cartier-Bresson did some work for *Vogue* under the direction of Edmonde Charles-Roux, and they often met at L'Oenothèque, a restaurant on the rue de Lille, where she used to dine once a week with Aragon, his wife Elsa Triolet, and the writer and critic François Nourissier, who was very close to the couple. It seemed to have been written in the stars that Cartier-Bresson and this writer, the author of *Une histoire française*, a novel awarded the *grand prix* of the Académie française, should team up to tackle a project that was so completely and utterly French.

Initially they decided to work in tandem. It was Nourissier who came up with the title *Vive la France*, and it was he who suggested to Cartier-Bresson that it would be worth going to certain well-known social haunts or occasions such as the Jockey Club and the ball at the Polytechnique à l'Opéra. Subsequently, each would send the other off in a particular direction so that they could work on their own side of the project. The photographer had the writer's text, the writer had the photographer's pictures, but this in no way affected the independence of their respective visions. They did not try to illustrate each other's work, because each aimed to provide a counterpoint to the other, but there was no danger of a clash either, as they were in total agreement on the basic approach: to look at the country with an ironic eye on its traditions.

Cartier-Bresson did his exploring between April 1968 and December 1969 (though this did not stop him from making a few trips abroad as well). He came back with people, places, atmospheres, emotions, all mingled together in a kind of ethnological inventory. This was the France of the Citroen DS and the Crédit agricole, the café de la Gare and Monoprix, Cézanne's Mont Ste-Victoire in Aix-en-Provence, the Deux Magots in Saint-Germain-des-Prés, the cathedral square in Bourges, a new estate in Grenoble, a street corner in Uzès, the grape harvest in Beaujolais, the presidential election campaign, the anniversary of the Normandy landings at Sainte-Mère-Eglise, the brasserie Lipp, a rugby match at the stadium in Toulouse, horse owners at the Prix de l'Arc de Triomphe, a Club Méditérranée village in Corsica, the place de l'Horloge during the Avignon Festival and countless other places and events.

People still talked about his famous 'luck', but whether by chance or not the fact is that Cartier-Bresson cast his eye over France at yet another decisive moment, just when it decided to give itself a good shaking. This all happened on the eve of May 1968.

At the beginning of March he had the chance to show which side he was on by signing a petition in support of Henri Langlois after the Minister of Culture, André Malraux, had decided to sack him. Cartier-Bresson's sympathy could not have been only because the head of la Cinémathèque had saved *Partie de cam-*

pagne during the Occupation. Right from the start he had been on Langlois's side. But although he was at the centre of the great upheaval experienced by millions of Frenchmen (not to mention photographers), he was not carried away by the intense atmosphere. That he supported the student revolt was quite clear, but this is not necessarily apparent in his photos. He was delighted by the irreverence, irony and imaginativeness of the slogans – his eye lit on a banner concocted by the students from the Beaux-Arts that read: 'For posters sincerity is preferable to technique'.

Paris was in turmoil, and Cartier-Bresson was in the thick of it, with the stone-throwers on the barricades in boulevard Saint-Michel, on the Champs-Elysées with the supporters of General de Gaulle, at the Trocadéro during the demonstrations by the bourgeoisie, in the occupied Sorbonne, in the rue de Lyon amid the debris after the fighting, at the faculty in Nanterre, where the students were urged to turn their wishes into reality, at the Gare d'Austerlitz during a sit-in, and at the Charléty stadium with the statesman Mendès France.

Only at the very beginning did he allow himself to be swept along by the frenzied atmosphere. It was difficult to resist covering the demonstrations for what they were. But then his natural control reasserted itself and the reporter reverted to the Zen archer, standing on the fringes and looking to capture not the event but the emotions reflecting the event. More than ever he was the photographer of attitudes. If a single photo could encapsulate the spirit of this upheaval, it would certainly be the one in which an elderly, middle-class gentleman is making a disapproving face as he reads a slogan painted on a fence: 'Feel free to enjoy yourself'. Once he had spotted this inscription, Cartier-Bresson hung around waiting for the right person to convey the full force of the message. After five or six passers-by, he found the icon of May 1968. Here the old and new worlds came face to face, challenging each other, though without a real shock of any kind. The contrast between generations said it all with an economy of means that made words unnecessary.

The turmoil of spring 1968 forms only a small part of the project. The liberal Cartier-Bresson and the Gaullist-Pompidou supporter Nourissier had their own notions of France, which did not necessarily coincide and which certainly ranged far beyond this single explosive blip in French history. But while the writer could sit at his desk and work in splendid isolation the photographer had to go outside, for his workplace was the streets of France. He wanted to see French people living in every condition. He would have liked to cross the country by motorbike, but in the end, as it was so vast a subject, when he wasn't doing his customary long-distance, all-seeing walks he used a car. Dominique Paul-Boncour, a sub-editor for *Sélection*, was his chauffeur and punchbag. The principal difficulty with this project, however, was not technical. He had to wipe clean his vision and his memory before setting forth. When you try to discover your own country, in which you were born and have lived for over half a century, the hardest thing of all is to preserve your freshness of mind, so that you are open at all times to being surprised by what you think you already know.

Cartier-Bresson's photographs were fascinating, Nourissier's text was dazzling, and the combination should have been a winner. But the result was one vast, disastrous platitude, anything but a work of art. The design, layout, printing, even the paper were not of good enough quality, and what should have been a classic proved to be very ordinary indeed. The self-same photographs, when exhibited all over the world by Robert Delpire, were superb, and one can just imagine how the book might have turned out if he had been the brains behind it.

In the course of its pages the constraints imposed by the original commission are apparent. The various aphorisms used as captions weigh heavily on the scenes captured by the pictures, some of which were cropped – a process which Cartier-Bresson had always vehemently objected to. Of the 250 photographs, 15 were in colour – again, something that he detested, for such things dated all too quickly.

Vive la France was published in 1970, the year of the retrospective *En France* held at the Grand Palais in Paris. This was a landmark, after which he was a national institution. While the careers of other photographers rightly or wrongly referred to as 'humanist' – observers from his own generation, such as Robert Doisneau, Willy Ronis and Edouard Boubat – underwent an eclipse, his star continued to shine. It was the rise and rise of Henri Cartier-Bresson, and whether he was its meticulous architect or its detached observer, whether he accepted it passively and reluctantly or treated it with complete indifference, his fame was beyond all doubt.

America, to which he owed so much, allowed him to indulge his passion for the documentary. The CBS network commissioned two from him, each 25 minutes long. There were ten days of filming, with a small crew, one of whom – a certain assistant producer named Christine Ockrent – was almost carried away by a wave. *Impressions of California*, the first, was not his favourite. He felt out of tune with the subject, a world that was too superficial and gimmicky for his taste. 'If there was an earthquake,' he said, 'California would detach itself and drift – and then what?'

He much preferred the second, *Southern Exposures*, which depicts a world that spoke to him and touched him, for it shows racism and segregation as he saw it in Fayette, Mississippi. This was reflected less in the talk than in the faces, eyes, hands and the constant look of distress. As a documentary-maker he still observed the world in the same way as the photographer, in word and in spirit. He was not responsible for the camerawork, but his cameraman, Jean Boffety for *Impressions of California*, filmed under his direction. These documentaries, however, are not a mere sequence of photographs. Once the filming was over, the producers for *Southern Exposures* thought they could isolate individual pictures and make photographic proofs out of them, which they could then call unpublished works by Henri Cartier-Bresson. One attempt was enough to show how wrong they were, for the pictures simply didn't work in isolation.

Cartier-Bresson's publications, books and exhibitions were dazzling proof that if, to France, he was the photographer of the world, to the world he was the supreme French photographer. In both contexts he was unique. And it was precisely at this point that he chose to disappear. At the official age of retirement, having reached the very pinnacle of his art in a profession that knows no retirement age, he decided to take a new look at himself. He abandoned photography, and went back to his first passion: drawing. It was not a revolutionary step, nor a metamorphosis, but a return to his beginnings, something that might lead him to a new life.

8 TOWARDS A NEW LIFE
1970–2004

From the beginning to the end of his life's adventure, Cartier-Bresson never changed. From a very early age he had a world vision that he stuck to, and that was the deepest secret of his huge accomplishment. A single vision does not imply narrowness of mind, but means following a path all the way through to its end – because what we find there tells us what we were looking for.

Although he was now in his sixties, Cartier-Bresson had still not achieved peace of mind – the combination of wisdom, harmony and equilibrium that equates to a personal 'golden section'. But by returning to drawing, he took one more step on the long journey to this inaccessible ideal. More than ever before, he could take his time, and he did not have to expend his life on earning his living.

When he announced that he was giving up photography he was closing off that section of his life, almost as if it were in brackets. He had, as it were, allowed himself to be distracted by it into moving far away from the form of expression that he truly favoured. Photography, after all, was not real life but simply a metaphor for life. It was never the be-all and end-all for him, which was clear from his earlier renunciations of it – in the Ivory Coast in 1932, in New York in 1935, in the Stalag during the 1940s. Whether it was painting or drawing, art was his world, his motivating passion, and he had never left it. This was pure vision, and he lived and fed on it. It was not work, but something that he did all the time. He was an artist in the sense that, to quote his friend Claude Roy, art is the shortest route from one human being to another, but he had little time for the nineteenth-century concept of the self-promoting artist – he preferred that of the self-effacing artisan.

The die was now cast, and Henri Cartier-Bresson went home.

At the same time as he gave up photography, he moved house, withdrew from Magnum, finally (in 1967) divorced Ratna, from whom he had been separated for many years, and remarried. The clairvoyant of his youth, whose predictions had all come true, had told him that during the last part of his long life he would leave his wife for a much younger woman, and they would be very happy together. In 1970 he married a photographer 30 years younger than himself. It was almost as if he was handing over to her.

Martine Franck is the daughter of Louis Franck, who was not only a banker and collector but a great art-lover, as his own father – a friend of the painter James Ensor – had been. The Franck family, members of the bourgeoisie of Antwerp, are descended from the Francken brothers, pupils of Rubens. Martine was brought up in an artistic environment, and not surprisingly studied the history of art, writing her thesis on the influence of cubism on sculpture. Her career as a photographer started with reportages in India, China and Japan, which she did with the stage director Ariane Mnouchkine. She worked with other photographers in the Paris offices of *Life* before going freelance. When she opted to share her life with Cartier-Bresson she almost gave up photography, as she found it too difficult to reconcile the work with her new situation. For a while she turned to documentary films and video, but in due course she returned to photography with the Viva agency and, from 1980 onwards, with Magnum.

With Martine and their daughter Mélanie by his side, Cartier-Bresson at last began to find peace. This did not, however, stop him from speaking his mind. In conversation with friends and colleagues, the more he enthused about drawing the more he tended to denigrate photography, and this inevitably caused confusion. For a very logical mind, which likes clear classifications, his far-reaching decision was disconcerting, and those who thought they might be attending the last rites of Cartier-Bresson no longer knew whether they were dealing with the greatest Leica artist or a Quattrocento photographer. He himself was desperate to escape the tyranny of fame – to him the most detestable form of power – and he wanted to meet the challenge head-on by questioning his own decision, thus putting himself at risk. But he was not sure which was the more dangerous choice: to go on with photography, or to go back to drawing.

Cartier-Bresson knew that, to his last day, he would keep a Leica in his pocket. He knew that he would continue to take portraits. And he knew that to abandon the streets would not mean abandoning the landscape and the pleasure he found in revealing its interplay of forms, its qualities of light and its internal rhythms. His photographs were successful because he had put more into them than he imagined, and what had kept him going was the prospect of more and more.

Many of his colleagues were irritated. The breach became permanent. His taste for provocation, his trenchant and often hurtful words, his impulsive and sometimes clumsy nature did not help to heal the wounds. Some people who thought they knew him were distressed by what they felt was a betrayal. When they talked among themselves the name of Cartier-Bresson, which used to be mentioned with the admiration appropriate to a living legend, became tinged with treason. He was accused of cheapening the profession, and, when asked who were the master photographers, of belittling his colleagues by talking only of the master painters. Cartier-Bresson – who never ceased to pay homage to André Kertész and Walker Evans – replied with a mere shrug of the shoulders. Till the end of his days he would remain a hunter at heart, but his life did not depend on what he caught in photos. On the walls of his home were drawings, engravings, paintings – but hardly a single photograph.

The logic behind this was straightforward enough, but not many people were in tune with his thinking. His criteria were so different from the rest of the world's that he may have given an impression of arrogant superiority; but the line of thought was simple and direct. In the beginning was the vision. The technical means used to convey this vision were of little consequence, for what mattered was the quality with which beings and objects were captured. Cartier-Bresson began with drawing, continued with painting, went on to photography and documentary films, and then went back to drawing. There was no break in this line; it was simply a full circle. Nor did these successive activities indicate an ephemeral passion, for they all expressed precisely the same single-minded pursuit of the vision with which he had begun. Pencils, brushes or cameras were nothing but tools – different means to the same end. The soul that governed the vision remained unchanged.

Nevertheless, because he felt he had to, Cartier-Bresson did explain, and he justified the course that he had taken. He never shut himself away, but went on participating in the life of his time, even though his legend preceded him wherever he went. To listen to him, one got the impression that he could not go any further, that he was waiting for the day when he would no longer have the energy to cover the ground. He had had enough of walking the streets, and the change that he had made arose from inner necessity. He had found himself in a cul-de-sac, and did not want to remain trapped there. He needed to change his instrument, as the world was now dancing to a different tune, but he had any-way exhausted his art: he had taken it to the heights, and it had exhausted him in turn. He had fathomed all its mysteries. In similar circumstances, painters such as de Staël and Mark Rothko had made the great leap. He himself pre-ferred to go back to his first passion – because he wasn't a virtuoso, he could escape from the grind of repetition and from the dread of boredom and depres-sion. When he said that in 50 years of practising photography he had not made any progress, he was telling the simple truth: right from the start he had been good. He had gone through half a century seizing the ungraspable without changing his style, and that in itself was reason enough to turn a new page.

Whenever he reached a crossroads, Cartier-Bresson felt the need of sound advice. After the Liberation, when he launched himself into reportage, he would heed Capa's words of wisdom advising him to change tack and renounce his surrealistic tendencies. Now it was Tériade, his artistic mentor, who came to his aid – a man for whom he had so much respect that he never dared say *tu* to him, even though their age difference was only 11 years. A photograph, acutely penetrating for all the softness of the lighting, taken by Martine Franck in 1974, shows them side by side at a table in the great publisher's dining-room. Cartier-Bresson is in the background on the left, facing the camera, wearing a tie – unusually for him – and looking shy and awkward, his eyes lowered like a well-behaved child presenting his work to the teacher and uncertain what grade he is going to get. Tériade is in the foreground, seen in right profile, with heavy eye-lids and somewhat morose expression, suggesting the Last Judgment as he pores professorially over some drawings held between his hands.

'You have done all that you could do in photography,' was his conclusion. 'You have said all that you had to say, and you have nothing more to prove. You would not be able to go as far, and then you would stumble, repeat yourself and become fossilized. You should go back to painting and drawing.'

At least that was what the pupil remembered, or wanted to remember, of the message. And yet the advice seemed untypical of Tériade, who hated any-thing that might smack of diversification – a dislike that had even prevented him from collaborating on books with Jean Cocteau. But Cartier-Bresson became a regular visitor, if only because he needed reassurance about the qual-ity of his drawings. Whenever he dedicated a photo to Tériade, it was always in unequivocal terms of affection, admiration and gratitude.

Doubts did, however, continue to assail him, but other well-known friends encouraged him to pursue this new path. From Beverly Hills, California, Jean Renoir wrote to him on 1 July 1975:

> I know that the pictures you have sent me represent the last stage before physical authenticity: you even manage to give an idea of the sound of voices, but I do not regret the fact that you have given up photography. You have made these visual means say everything they are capable of saying. You have reminded us of what is essential within the human being. But at your age you can throw yourself into the study of a new mode of conversation. All my good wishes go with you on this bold adventure.

It is worth pointing out that, ten years earlier, Renoir himself had sat down to write a novel, though not without wondering whether writing really was his true vocation.

A year later, in August 1981, a postcard came from a New York admirer – the artist Saul Steinberg: 'I often look at your drawings in the catalogue of the Museum of Modern Art. It seems that photography has just been callisthenics, an illusion, an alibi for the real thing.'

But it was André Lhote, the old master from his youth, who, when looking at the photos shortly before his death, hit the nail on the head: 'It all stems from your formation as a painter.'

Initially, when he had taken his great step, Cartier-Bresson concentrated on painting gouaches. He thought the results were less bad than the attempts he had made ten years earlier, but he felt that his work was too small-scale and finicky. His reaction was much the same as Hergé's at the same time, and they were not alone. Strangely enough, various creative artists were convinced that they had the eye of a painter, with which they were ennobling other forms of visual expression. But for many of them, neither photography nor the comic strip had yet achieved the cachet of being raised to the ranks of the visual arts, and so these masters were not considered to be artists. The essayist Jean-François Revel, who had known Cartier-Bresson for many years, described this view as follows:

> Henri Cartier-Bresson used a method even more radical than ratiocination to annihilate his colleagues: he declared that photography was not an art. Every time I asked him for his opinion on photographers other than himself, he replied that he could not have an opinion because photography did not exist. In such a void there could be no first place and, consequently, no risk of anybody challenging him. Having dealt with this absolute void, he established

himself within it, both conscious and certain of being its only occupant. And so it was a threat to his imperial solitude and a dangerous irritant for him if you maintained that – with all due respect – photography was an art.

Drawing was what Cartier-Bresson wanted to do, and he did it with utter devotion. It was not a choice by default, for it gave him the chance to remain within the realm of black and white, which in itself was a form of abstraction. When he did turn again to painting he used tempera, a much faster technique than oil (which required a studio and specialized materials – both contrary to his nomadic instincts). For drawing he needed only a sketchpad and a hard pencil, graphite, black chalk or a pen.

He drew not from memory but from observation, following a theme, using models or imitating the works of the great graphic artists. He focused upon neither the centre nor the edges, preferring to reduce and intermingle the different lines and shapes. It was only the form, not the light, that mattered to his painter's eye, which still saw the world in black and white.

His main fault as an artist was obvious: he worked too fast. He was a bundle of nerves in action. He wanted to create the whole layout in one go, but what was the trump card for the photographer became a handicap to the draughtsman, and so he had to learn to slow down without dimming the inspirational fire of his instincts.

The great thinkers on the art of drawing – who were not necessarily the great doers – never left his side. He was constantly mulling over their teachings, whether in the form of a book, a page, or a single sentence. There was Goethe, who argued that he had never seen what he had never drawn. (Zola said the same about photography.) For Goethe, the only way to understand a picture was to copy it. And there was Paul Valéry, who regarded drawing as an obsessive temptation. Above all, there was Bonnard, for whom drawing was emotion, whereas colour was mere reason. The contrast, even if debatable, perfectly fitted Cartier-Bresson's approach, for he never ceased to reproach his contemporaries for too much intellectualizing – they were guilty of identifying instead of seeing and penetrating, of using the brain to the exclusion of the heart. Finally, there was Alberto Giacometti. Cartier-Bresson photocopied an early text of Giacometti's on the unity of body and soul as a means of attaining absolute truth and beauty, and sent it to all the members of Magnum 'to raise the level of discussion, if possible'.

On another plane, more intimately human because it was more down-to-earth, he acknowledged the influence of four artists in particular: the Austrian

Georg Eisler, for whom he had unswerving admiration; the Englishman Raymond Mason, whose drawings fascinated him; Avigdor Arikha; and Sam Szafran. He went to the museum with them to listen to the silent masterpieces, or to wander among the works of Nicolas de Staël, taking in their depths and variations of light – when he wasn't thinking of standing on his head before the canvases of Georg Baselitz in the forlorn hope of grasping their inner truths.

The first time they met, Cartier-Bresson was looking over Arikha's shoulder while he was sketching the musicians in an orchestra. As they went from one exhibition to another their friendship ripened, fuelled by their shared passion. But although the painter happily considered the photographer to be an artist because of his eye and his sensitivity, he could not extend that recognition to Cartier-Bresson's art. From the outset he tried to persuade him to give it up: 'You have made your name in photography, so why do you come and pester us with your drawings?' he said, in as discouraging a tone as possible. Painter and draughtsman, critic and art historian, the Israeli Arikha, a close friend of Samuel Beckett, was too knowledgeable to compromise. He was one of those who could see at most in Cartier-Bresson's drawings the drafts of work that might be to come. But he was the only one who dared say so to Henri's face, and their long friendship flourished in spite of – perhaps because of – his honesty.

With Szafran it was the opposite. Szafran forced him to practise like a musician, going over his work again and again, becoming more disciplined, more thorough. His conversation was sparkling, but devoid of the small talk so beloved of the English. There were to be no generalizations in his comments – only short, sharp observations, pithy and to the point. When Cartier-Bresson showed him his work, he would never say if he liked it or not, but would simply indicate that this line or that didn't fit. Criticism is not necessarily destructive, and self-criticism does not come amiss. When he looked at his own work, Cartier-Bresson found his drawings lively and spontaneous, but they lacked the finished, confident touch of the professional. Along with Tériade, Szafran was the one who did most to encourage Cartier-Bresson to change his tools and to draw without inhibition.

There were other faithful friends, including some famous names from the world of art, who supported him by writing forewords to his exhibition catalogues. Among the writers, curators, critics and art historians were Jean Clair, Yves Bonnefoy, James Lord, Jean Leymarie and Ernst Gombrich. In 1978 Gombrich began his foreword to a catalogue by calling Cartier-Bresson an artist, and went on to place the best works of this 'veritable humanist' in the line of

Vermeer, Le Nain and Velazquez. But he was talking about the photos and not the drawings. He did not even know that Cartier-Bresson drew, for the artist did not exhibit his drawings until 1975, at the Carlton Gallery in New York.

Others generally praised the intensity and vitality, the curiosity and the sincerity of work that was very much influenced by Bonnard and Giacometti. Like them, he tended to seize on the central core of a landscape or a face, but he would somehow get there almost by default. What is exuberant in their pictures becomes too deliberate in his, with the structural lines too deep, the forms too marked; one can sense the scaffolding, the hard work, the effort – all completely absent from the photographs. The quest for lightness weighs heavily, and the pencil moves accordingly. It is striking that Cartier-Bresson the draughtsman quite readily discussed technique (the swift movement of pencil over paper and so on), whereas such talk was anathema to Cartier-Bresson the photographer.

There are some things that cannot be done nonchalantly, as Poussin said. At those times when Cartier-Bresson was prepared to share his solitude and to put pride aside, he would confess – if we can believe certain commentators – that it was troubling to dwell on qualities that would have shown up better had they not already been noticed in another sphere. In the work of Cartier-Bresson, grace was granted in only one sphere, and it was not that of drawing.

From his reading, his visits to exhibitions, his conversations with painter friends and above all his lifelong habit of going to the Louvre he derived his own philosophy of art. It drew its values from his own logic – the thinking of a man who was said to be more of an artist than a photographer, and who, at one point in his life, had found it best to express his artistry by way of the photograph. The following passage sums up the spirit that pervades *The Decisive Moment*:

> Photography for me is the spontaneous impulse of a perpetually visual attention, which seizes the moment and its eternity. Drawing, however, by its graphology, elaborates on what our consciousness has seized from this moment. The photograph is an immediate action; the drawing a meditation.

Every time he compiled a list of the comparative virtues of photography and drawing, the impression was that he was troubled by a bad conscience. And yet he never stopped listing the parallels. He always linked photography to the Zen archer's bow and drawing to the glove of the masseur. As if to convince himself, he would say: 'One does a painting, whereas one takes a photo.' You can draw anything, but photography is restricted to reality. You can look at a drawing or a painting for hours, but unless it has been touched by grace a photograph will normally stand no more than a few minutes' scrutiny. A photographer is entirely responsible for the shot, but not always for what is in it. A draughtsman or painter is responsible for everything, because he is in charge of what he creates and what it becomes. Drawing forced Cartier-Bresson to master himself, whereas photography provoked him into frenetic activity. Drawing made him control his instincts and channel his energy; taking photos, he could give them free rein. It could be said, though, that there is a natural progression from concentration (photography) to meditation (drawing).

If truth be told, Cartier-Bresson was never closer to the great painters than when he was a photographer. The comparison is scarcely paradoxical when we remember his sincere and oft-repeated gratitude for his artistic training. His portrait photography, which is anything but flattering, owes most to the great Renaissance painters in the modelling of the face, to Renoir and Seurat for the fullness, to Cranach for the value of the lines, to Cézanne for his priorities in the fervent quest for the sublime, and again for a quote gleaned from a conversation with Joachim Gasquet: 'If I think while I'm painting, everything falls apart!'

From a very early age he had absorbed all the masters' principles of composition so well that a geometrical vision of the world came quite naturally to him. He could console himself with the thought that those photographers who criticized him for this were the same breed as those who attacked Juan Gris for being a grammarian. Each was said to have been excessively rigorous, whereas to critics the rules existed only to correct emotion.

Cartier-Bresson had long since given up wondering whether the golden section was an illusion or a mathematical reality, for all his work was in fact an intuitive illustration of it, thanks to the miracle of an ingenuous eye that focused on it, as his friend the art historian Jean Leymarie put it. Certainly his success derived from order based on chaos, a disciplined mental architecture arising from a profound disorder within. It became a natural reflex with him, when he was shown a print, to observe it from all angles, like a painter trying to see if all the elements fitted together, for the masses and proportions were of more importance than the tale that was being told. This habit was emphatically not an affectation. Just as for Mallarmé poetry was made not of ideas but of words, the photo for Cartier-Bresson was made not of stories but of lines.

There is no shortage of examples among the photographs which have become icons in their own right, and which offer a striking parallel with the masterpieces of western art. It was not that he ever set out to copy them, but his mind simply made these extraordinary connections, which certainly owed more to his visual training than to the correspondences so dear to the surrealists. It is impossible to have such long, close contact with masterpieces without being in some way unconsciously influenced by them. The parallels can be found in all periods of art. How can you avoid thinking of Piero della Francesca's *Flagellation* when you see Cartier-Bresson's spectators on the lawn during the interval at Glyndebourne (1953)? They seem to have been posed deliberately by the photographer, and they have a grace that would do credit to the most inspired choreographer and to all the masters of perspective. Cardinal Pacelli's visit to Montmartre (1938), Nehru announcing the death of Gandhi (1948), the moving scene of the sailor's family at the Bougival lock (1955), all evoke fifteenth-century Italian masterpieces, with their Pietà faces, echoes of the Madonna and Child or neophytes baptized by St Peter. Cartier-Bresson was their Masaccio, and the film in his camera unfolded a whole fresco. But these parallels were not confined to pre-Quattrocento works. We have already mentioned the Curies, whose pose is so similar to that of Van Eyck's Arnolfini couple. The correspondences cover all the great phases of art, because he had internalized them all. The duck lost in the midst of the perfect sculpture formed by the lights of the Isle-sur-la-Sorgue shining on the undergrowth (1988) seems to have wandered out of one of Monet's *Waterlilies*. The château Biron in the Dordogne (1968), with the building in the background majestically dominating the plain while in the foreground a labourer bends over his plough, might almost have been taken from a miniature in the fourteenth-century book of hours *Les Très Riches Heures du duc de Berry*, by the Franco-Flemish Limbourg brothers.

Cartier-Bresson was one of the truly great artists because he remained true to himself and never set out to imitate anyone. In this regard, there was no finer tribute than that from the art historian Ernst Gombrich. As far back as 1972, when he was director of the Warburg Institute in London, Gombrich chose *Aquila degli Abruzzi* (1952) as a unique 'photographer's photo' to illustrate a new edition of his classic *The Story of Art*. In the chapter in which he discusses the rivalry between photography and painting, and mentions that 'photographic' is a derogatory term among critics, he points out that the situation has changed over the years, that photographers like Cartier-Bresson are just as respected as any living painter, and that the composition of this Italian picture loses nothing by comparison with that of many far more elaborate paintings. In 1995, in his essay on shadows and their representation in Western art, Gombrich did it again. He published only one photograph among dozens of reproductions of paintings: *Ahmedabad, India* (1967) by Henri Cartier-Bresson shows a man stretched out in the shadow of a finely wrought minaret – an image which Gombrich considered to be exceptionally moving, and which he saw as the perfect illustration of an object out of shot.

With his paintings and drawings, Cartier-Bresson was one among thousands; but with his photographs he was unique. Some of his work shares a common trait with the finest art in that it makes visible the invisible. Out of reality emerges a subliminal truth that reveals itself quite naturally to the naked eye. It is a feature of his photographs, but not of his drawings.

There would be no problem if he had done these purely for his own pleasure – just for the sake of drawing, for himself and for his friends. But they hesitated to hurt him, and the indulgence and sycophancy that followed from this seemed to block all criticism, with one or two notable exceptions. It was hard for him to progress when he was stifled with all this approval. For such a mind, a critical challenge would have been far more beneficial than universal respect. After all, he who exhibits reveals himself.

From the moment he began to show his work in the most prestigious galleries, such as Claude Bernard's in Paris, and museums in Paris, New York, Rome, Montreal, Athens and Tokyo, he acquired a certain view of himself and of his talent – even though he never sought it, and it was others who actively approached him. It was Tériade, for instance, who advised him to sell his work, as the best way to be taken seriously. He played the game their way, but on the other hand no one is compelled to give away his secrets, or to elevate a private passion to the level of the fine arts, or to participate in the rituals of official recognition, especially when he has already achieved fame in another sphere. His status gave him all the more freedom to refuse their advances, and to avoid the ever-nagging question: was it the drawings that they wanted to exhibit, or merely the name of the greatest living photographer? Cartier-Bresson was no fool. He knew very well that some curators were trading on the name, just as some wine experts cite the label. Officially he was recognized, but he was never really accepted. The doubts remained, but he could always console himself that French society had become so specialized that no one was allowed to move from one pigeonhole to another.

Live and look, that was all that ever interested him. He was aware that when he lost his sense of curiosity his life would be over. Looking means winning the battle against habit, banishing the spectre of routine, always expecting to be surprised, and obeying one's instincts. Look, but do not identify – that was his constant refrain. If he had dared, he would even have written false captions for his photos, so that only the eyes would observe, never the intellect. But they would have been true enough to make it impossible to tell how true they were.

Cartier-Bresson always hated talking about photography, but never were his views more eagerly sought than when he had abandoned the profession. He felt like a divorcee being constantly pestered for information about his ex-wife. He loved to take his shots, but he had no interest in commenting on shots, the theory of shots, schools of shots, shotology…. Would anyone turn their backs on a writer who refused to talk about literature? His friend Balthus summed it all up when he refused to talk about painting because, he argued, such talk would be redundant, since painting was already a language.

Cartier-Bresson did not wish to be his own commentator, his own archivist, his own curator, but at the same time he did wish to control what was said about him. The fact that he could not do so made him feel that he was no longer master of his own destiny, and he found that the more he distanced himself from photography, the more it came after him. He shunned interviewers who tried to put official pronouncements into his mouth – galling for someone who so loved to contradict himself. He once read a definition that greatly appealed to him in Michel Leiris's *A cor et à cri* ('Hunting with the Hounds'), for it summed up his own horror of the interview: it was 'an interrogation without physical abuse… a deceitful reconstruction (fiction that does not admit to being fiction) and at the same time a hybrid'.

Inevitably, though, he was forced into conversations, and inevitably these bordered on interviews, and inevitably the same questions arose again and again. As Braque once remarked, proofs exhaust the truth. Cartier-Bresson never stopped not answering. Why are there so many moving children and sleeping adults in your pictures? Why is the hole a recurrent theme in your work? Why did you go over the pedestrian crossing in front of Giacometti if it was not in anticipation of his attitude in the rain? Why, why, why? And every 'why' drove him further away. It was pointless for him to repeat that the secret of a truly incandescent image lay in the relationship between forms, for back would come the same old questions, as if he had not said a word. It was no use even appealing to common sense: 'Would you ask the father of a pretty girl how or why he had made her? Of course you wouldn't!'

It was useless. From one article after another, the public, for whom he had become a living legend, continued to learn from his own lips the thoughts of the author of that mythical text, *The Decisive Moment*.

So how did he manage to take all those photographs?

He would go for a walk, furtively take his shot, and walk on as if nothing had happened. By being furtive and by walking on, he probably avoided all sorts of trouble. He was the invisible dancer pirouetting around a totally unsuspecting partner. He was also the fencer who took his stance, hit the target, and was out of there all in one movement. It is astonishing that a man who was a bundle of nerves could always keep his cool in even the most fraught of circumstances.

A photographer is a pickpocket. He inserts himself into the action, takes what he wants, and withdraws without ever being involved with the people he has robbed. But to do this, he must be discretion personified if he is not to cause offence. That was Cartier-Bresson. He would even approach a still life on tiptoe, and in the course of time the hunter became the will-o'-the-wisp.

More than one of his friends fell victim. They would be walking side by side along the street, the friend might glance at a pretty girl passing by, and a moment later, when he looked round again, he would realize that Cartier-Bresson had seized the instant to record something special; still seeming to keep him company, the dancer would have executed his solo, seen without being noticed, and fallen back into step and into the conversation as if there had been no interruption. He did not have a sixth sense – just a third eye. He had a capacity to merge with people and objects, and an intuition that penetrated nature; he saw human misery where others saw nothing; and he caught the world napping.

The camera, the only machine that can stop time, is simply an optical extension of the eye, but it is the eye and not the camera that watches out for the chance encounter. It is the eye that translates reality into form, with felicity or with no talent at all depending on whose eye it is. That is a matter of training, experience, personality and above all instinct. Instinct does not permit premeditation or the calculation of composition. It is subconsciously governed by an artistic culture that, in Cartier-Bresson's case, was vast. He swiftly reached a creative peak, with results that are universally known, because there was a perfect synthesis between perception and the 'decisive moment', based on a lifelong knowledge of what constituted an integrated image. His friend the poet Yves Bonnefoy once provided an enlightening insight into the alchemy of the creative process:

When after a year, the Emperor of China receives the great painter who has promised him for that day the most beautiful crab in the world, but who since making his promise has done nothing but wander along the shore without brush or ink, with no hesitation at all the painter dashes off on the sheet that has been given to him the shape – vibrating and precise but as if open to the breeze – which is the crab as it has never before been represented, body and soul. Why does the crab painter proceed in this manner, and with such wondrous success? It is because, by filling himself through all these months with the smell of the kelp and the sound of the waves, the cries of the birds in flight, the leaping foam, the diagonal ripples in the sand, he has become so intimately familiar with all the lives on the seashore that he no longer needs to observe them from the outside, to imitate their appearance piece by piece, but he can bring them to life with the black of his ink as if from the very bosom of nature; only on condition, however, that he never with a single hesitation in his movements allows thought to trap him once more in the network of ideas, of observations, of knowledge – for knowledge can hold on to nothing that is not already dead.

Like the Chinese painter, Cartier-Bresson the photographer had the genius not to construct but to know that he must not deconstruct. He filled himself with an atmosphere and absorbed the spirit of place as Georges Simenon did. Exceptional photographs such as his are like memorable poetry, in which words meet each other for the first time to create a new and miraculous harmony.

There is little point in speculating about the role of chance in all this, though much has been said about Cartier-Bresson's luck. Let us say that fortune was kind to a man who never ceased to marvel at the coincidences punctuating his life, and, strangely, they brought a degree of order into the chaos of his world. But fortune smiles on those who are willing and able to embrace it. It is equally pointless to ask whether, for the 1932 picture in which a man jumps over a puddle (*Derrière la gare Saint-Lazare, pont de l'Europe*), he did indeed hide for 24 hours in the hope that a scene he had glimpsed would repeat itself. All of his works urge sharpness of vision and plead against taking things for granted. His capacity for concentration was not a gift but the result of self-discipline, and he believed less in talent than in hard work. He was dismissive of jacks-of-all-trades who are masters of none. If pressed to explain the more enigmatic of his pictures, he would go to the very top, pulling out a letter written in 1944 by Einstein to Max Born which reveals that the great physicist felt so close to all forms of life that he attached virtually no importance to the question of where the individual began and ended. But if someone persisted in asking him to explain the unexplainable, he would quote Francis Bacon: 'If you can say it, why bother to paint it?'

When he spotted a likely subject in the street, Cartier-Bresson would proceed like an Inuit sculptor confronted with a block of stone. The sculptor will spend days walking round it, and only when he can actually feel the polar bear that inhabits it will he begin to sculpt the bear. The only difference between the Inuit sculptor and Cartier-Bresson is that the latter condensed the whole process into the few seconds before he took his shot. He had a unique instinct for instantaneous composition, the autonomous image in which the strictness of the form harmonizes with the resonance of the content. Light only interested him when he could use it to enhance the geometry. He felt that a portrait was successful when he captured not an expression or a pose, but an inner silence – something like the gap between the instant and eternity. Sometimes his photographic vision could take on unexpected forms, and when it went beyond the traditional borders of visual language it entered the realms of the unknown. Then technique and even art became irrelevant, for his vision emanated mystery, resisting analysis, requiring no special pleading, but simply imposing itself. There is nothing quite so delightful as that which defies critical discourse, for then the intellect must surrender to a superior force. Indeed, one of the properties of most masterpieces is that they make us feel things in ways that transcend what we can feel for ourselves.

Photography has certain things in common with the sexual act. If the climax comes with the 'shot', the voluptuousness comes with the caresses. Cartier-Bresson put film in his camera only to communicate with his subject, his partner in the shot, but the Zen archer in him could gain the same satisfaction even without the film. One day he visited Cecil Beaton, whom he had not seen for some years. Suddenly, while they were talking, Beaton asked permission to take a portrait of him. Cartier-Bresson refused but, in return, asked permission to do the same.

'Ah no,' replied Beaton, 'there's no reason why I should let you do what you refuse to do for me! Tit for tat.'

'Too bad,' said Cartier-Bresson. 'But allow me to tell you that at all events I have an advantage over you. In my eyes and head I still have all the moments when I could have taken a shot of you.'

Sir Cecil did not know that in his memory Cartier-Bresson still stored even the photographs that he never took when he was a prisoner of war. Nor did he know that the Frenchman possessed a strange object given to him by the artist

Saul Steinberg: a block of wood fitted with a hinge in place of a viewfinder and a large nut for a lens. Taking 'photographs' with that became a kind of absolute, for only the gesture mattered, and the tension leading up to the climax. There were, of course, no results. James Joyce captured the essence of such an experience in the last line of the last page of *Ulysses*: '...and his heart was going like mad and yes I said yes I will Yes.'

Of all the classical myths, that of Antaeus is the one with which Cartier-Bresson most closely identified himself. According to the Greeks, this giant – the son of Poseidon and Gaea – received new strength from his mother every time he touched the earth, and so Hercules lifted him up in the air and squeezed him to death. Cartier-Bresson also needed to stay in contact with the concrete reality of tiny fragments and minor incidents from which can emerge truths of far greater import. At the heart of events, he saw himself as a kind of Stendhalian hero at Waterloo, and indeed his poetry of the real owed far more to the *Chartreuse de Parme* than to any other photographer, for nowhere did he see life more clearly than in the little details lost among chaos. Reality is in the fragments, and his creed was reality, the whole of reality, and nothing but reality. Among the snippets that he noted down during his reading was one from his friend Francis Bacon, for whom the contemplation of things as they are, without error and without confusion, without substitution or pretence, was far nobler in itself than the sum total of all the greatest inventions.

Following his essay about the decisive moment (1952), Cartier-Bresson's poetic art changed very little, though he certainly refined it. In 1968, when Robert Delpire published his *Flagrants Délits* ('Caught Red-Handed'), Cartier-Bresson gave him a few manuscript pages intended as a preface. It was typical of him that he should once more stake out his photographic territory just when he was planning to give it all up. The gist of his comments was that he saw the photograph as a magical, but not premeditated, combination of such disparate qualities as enthusiasm, concentration, respect for the subject, intuition, knowledge, freshness of impression, mental discipline, sensitivity and economy of means. These were not unusual in isolation, but when they all came together in one man's vision they were exceptional. In this piece of writing there were also some passages well worth quoting for their clarity – characteristic of his style – and for their educational value and firmness of thinking:

> Photography is an immediate operation performed by the senses and the mind; it is the world translated into visual terms, simultaneously a ceaseless

quest and an interrogation. It is, at one and the same moment, the awareness of a fact in a fraction of a second and the strict organization of visually perceived forms expressing and signifying this fact. The main thing is to be on an equal footing with the reality that we are dividing up in the viewfinder. The camera is in some ways a sketchbook drawn in time and space, and it is also an admirable instrument that seizes life just as it presents itself.

With hindsight, what kind of photographer was he? To those who insist on classifying photographers as either image-makers or image-takers, he offered a third category: the photographer who is taken by the image. But truth to tell, he was unclassifiable, because he created his own genre, part head, part eye, part heart, all lined up and on a level. Everyone has his own agenda. Lartigue spent his days being grateful for life, and was happy. Kertész was swift to complain, and melancholy. The former was very French, the latter very *émigré*. Cartier-Bresson, the cosmopolitan Norman, was both, and remained ever himself.

As an observer, he followed Baudelaire, a prince moving everywhere incognito. As a participant in the dramas of history, he gazed tentatively into the soul, for he did not record events so much as moments, latching on to traces instead of solid proof. As an analyst, he had a way of seizing on coincidence to demonstrate that the roots of the image are in the unconscious. As a witness, unlike so many others, he fought shy of giving testimony. As an acrobat, he skilfully avoided the traps set for those with eyes to see, and took each metaphor as it came. As an animal, Cartier-Bresson was a predator, for he had the charismatic power and the will to destroy in order to defend his territory – but no more than that, for his prey never became his victim. As a poet, he was a discoverer, not an inventor, for reality is dangerous. The outstanding poet René Char summed up the difference: 'He who invents, unlike the man who discovers, adds to things and brings to creatures nothing but masks, insertions, a pulp of iron.'

Despite the black and white, and the details and attitudes typical of the different periods, there is nothing dated about the photographs – nothing, at any rate, that prevents past and present merging in them. Cartier-Bresson rightly maintained that some of his photographs remained current because they were not taken in a rear-view mirror. In other words, they are timeless; they detach themselves from their temporal context, they give permanence to the fleetingness of humanity. There is no other means of expression that can claim to fix the transient precisely as it was.

What about technique? In his eyes, it didn't matter, or at least he didn't want to talk about it. He preferred to talk about style: not about humanism, social fantasy or poetic realism, with which interpreters have tried to categorize him, nor about the grammar of the image, the geometry of the vision, but about the spiritual movement which encompasses all these. And he would talk about his Leica, his third eye, his instinct for a shot, his taste for the sharp image, his art of living.

It is the soul that makes all the difference. And so he was against the concept of photographic schools: you don't teach walking, looking, seeing, and you can't teach instinct or discipline. There are some photographs of landscapes that are disarming in their sober simplicity, and you might think that they could have been taken by anybody, but look closer and you will see that they all contain a detail that takes them on to a higher plane, into the zone of the timeless. It may be the solitary bent figure of a man seen in the left-hand corner between two trees in the gardens of the Palais-Royal, taken from the terrace of the Ministry of Culture (1960). It may be the carcass of a car stark against the Arizona desert, while in the background a train races full steam ahead as if to show the railway taking its revenge (1947). It may be the three perfectly symmetrical couples on three stands in the Tuileries (1955). There are countless examples of the touches that made Cartier-Bresson inimitable.

For portraits, he usually went to the home of his subject, though not without first familiarizing himself with the subject's works. The sitting itself would last for about 20 minutes – the length of a courtesy call. He did not shoot like a machine-gun, and would not use more than a single film. He gave no directions, chatted only to distract the subject's attention from the fact that he or she was being looked at, tried to fade into the background but was ready to sting like an insect. What he waited for was the unusual, especially that moment of inner silence. With Paul Léautaud (1952) it proved virtually impossible, because Léautaud, a cat-loving recluse, never stopped talking. On the other hand, with Ezra Pound (1971), who had taken refuge in a Venetian palace, there was nothing but silence. Cartier-Bresson spent an hour and a half kneeling in front of him without opening his mouth, while the poet, hallucinating, also said nothing but went on rubbing his hands and blinking. Neither of them found this situation embarrassing. The subject had to be respected, whatever his attitude, and Cartier-Bresson treated them all alike, for to do otherwise would have been unseemly.

Only once did he accept a particular private commission. This was in Paris in 1951, and came from the Duke and Duchess of Windsor. The moment he entered their house on the rue de la Faisanderie, he knew that he was in for a hard time. Both of them were as uptight as could be. They posed very formally, and were not prepared to do otherwise. He was on the point of giving up, particularly since the Duke's small talk was excruciating: 'What do you think of my tie?'

But at that moment the butler burst in and involuntarily dispelled the frostiness in a scene of pure comedy. 'Your Highness, please forgive me,' he said with Olympian dignity, 'but we've just been informed that there's a fire in the lift, and it would be a good thing to get it under control without delay.'

The result is for all to see: the Windsors sitting on the edge of their chairs, caught in an admirable triangular composition, both with a touching half-smile of complicity.

When it came to the technical side, Cartier-Bresson left it to the experts. His confidence in Pictorial Service and particularly in his friend Pierre Gassmann was total. These people knew that he didn't like contrasted or soft prints, and the older he grew the more purity he wanted. Nothing was more important to him than respect for the various shades of grey. His luminous *Ile de la Cité* (1952), a beautiful palette covering every nuance of grey, is a model of its kind. There is no more sculptured weather than the light grey, thinly clouded sky. Other photographers may have mocked his obsession with grey, but that was up to them. Perhaps one day people will speak of CBG (Cartier-Bresson Grey) in the same tones as they speak of IKB (International Klein Blue). He delved with fascination into Delacroix's *Journal*, in which he said that great art consisted of making colour with greys.

Colour photographs, however, were indigestible, the negation of all his visual values. He never liked them even when he took them – in very small quantities, admittedly, and under the heading of experimental – throughout his stay in the Far East, before the commercialization of Ektachrome in 1959. In his eyes colour was the exclusive sphere of painting, and he said so explicitly as a postscript to the captions for his photos of Shanghai and Nanking:

> It must be clear that I keep the Plaubel for colour photos for covers, static subjects or something important, but I consider it to be practically impossible to do good colours (I mean from a painter's perspective) for action pictures (news etc.) with any camera other than a 35 mm. Some reportages are possible in colour (good colours as one conceives of them in all serious painting and not in postcards).

If he did occasionally consent to use colour, it was not in the spirit of compromise but was a concession, necessary perhaps to fulfil a commission from an editor, as he did for *Vive la France* and for *Paris-Match*, and indeed during his stay in China. In 1954 he did the cover for the magazine *Camera* with a colour photo of the Seine – the only one that he ever thought good, even though he regarded it as meaningless because it is purely aesthetic. According to his logic, it is not possible to say that colour photographs are natural, for all they offer is a toned-down version of reality, fit only for salesmen and the press. Asked in 1958 for his views on colour, after he had had ten years of practice, he maintained that for him it was purely a means of documentation, certainly not a means of expression. Faced with colour, he was always the painter and never the photographer. Faced with a choice between colour and other values, as all artists are when confronted by nature, he gave priority to the most dynamic and mobile elements – even if that meant conceding, along with the great philosopher Walter Benjamin, that the nature which spoke to the camera differed from that confronting the eye. This was the case when colour was in its technical infancy, and it remained so ever after. The fact is that Cartier-Bresson could not ever remember feeling any emotion when looking at a colour photo. His 1985 postscript to *The Decisive Moment* should be taken not as a correction, but merely as a clarification:

> Colour in photography is based on an elementary prism, and for the moment it cannot be otherwise, as no one has yet discovered the chemical processes that would allow the immensely complex decomposition and recomposition of colour (in pastel, for example, there are 375 different shades of green!). For me colour is a very important means of conveying information, but it is very limited at the level of reproduction, which remains chemical, not transcendental and intuitive, as it is in painting. In contrast to black, which covers the most complex range, colour offers only a totally fragmentary range.

Even the most sophisticated chemistry changed nothing. Despite technical progress in the field of colour, the evocative power of black and white remained unmatched in his eyes.

Cartier-Bresson considered contact sheets – preliminary prints, in the format of the negative, of all photographs taken with the same roll of film – as the equivalent of a writer's manuscript or diary, or the artist's sketchbook. There was no judge more lucid or more ruthless than he, for after all, one mistake can kill a myth. It is understandable therefore that he never wanted to show them, even though he had little to fear from doing so. Pierre de Fenoyl, who was the archivist at Magnum in the late 1960s, said that the truly original thing about Cartier-Bresson's contact sheets was that all the photographs on them were good. But, for him, a single failure was enough to taint all the others.

Archives, like cemeteries, are the true repositories of time. There is no more intimate reflection of the enduring pleasure of photography, even although Cartier-Bresson himself did not like this word. When Vera Feyder devoted to him a programme called *Le bon plaisir* ('The Good Pleasure') on *France-Culture*, he immediately disputed the title, which he adjudged too superficial and sybaritic. Pleasure, he argued, was like tickling, whereas joy was an explosion and a surprise.

Anyone contemplating this vast collection of unpublished material must wonder not so much how many photos he took in his lifetime as how many miles he must have walked in order to take them. Yet his curiosity never flagged, neither did his capacity for astonishment. The contact sheets, the secret garden of his private life, were at the same time studio, kitchen and bedroom. Here you can see the daily labours of the photographer, with all his errors, corrections, deletions, hesitations. But suddenly, framed in thick red, you come across the photograph, the only one worthy of being seen, to the exclusion of all those before and after it. It is up to the author to edit his work, and only he can pick out the diamond from the rest. In 1958 there was a discussion as to whether certain magazines should be allowed to edit the contact prints submitted by the members of Magnum. Cartier-Bresson immediately fulminated against such a vile proposal. When he was told that, if it came to the crunch, he would not be affected because he was regarded as a special case, his fury redoubled. In a letter to Michel Chevalier, the director of Magnum-Paris, a man whom he greatly respected, he explained his point of view. He considered this letter so important that he asked for it to be added to his will:

> There are no double standards in Magnum, and it is all the more dangerous to send the contact prints of other Magnum photographers to be edited by the magazines since they will not have the same right of appeal if they disagree with the choice, assuming they even have time to do so before the magazine is put to bed. The contact sheets are a fascinating interior monologue, but they are full of dross – dross which is inevitable, for we do not pick off petals in our living-room. This interior monologue is not something that one shouts at the top of one's voice before an examining magistrate; after all,

when one speaks, one chooses one's own words. What I have just said applies to all photographers; when you tell me that one cannot make exceptions for other photographers, it means that one must resign oneself to allowing the interior monologue to be moulded by other hands.... All this in the name of 'speed and celerity'! It's exactly as if you were giving a racing car to a taxi driver, while telling yourself: it'll move fast because he's used to being in a hurry.

In principle, a good photograph should tell us nothing about the work of the person who has taken it – it hides the scaffolding. Only the contact sheet will take us behind the scenes and show us the different approaches and uncertainties. It offers the most authentic insight into thought in action. Cartier-Bresson often used the image of the nail and the plank of wood to describe it: you begin by giving the nail a few light taps with the hammer to position it, and then you give it one or two far heavier blows to drive it into the wood. The contact sheet of the true photographer reveals exactly how he manoeuvres into position before delivering the hammer blow. Ara Güler, Magnum's man in Istanbul, recalls seeing Cartier-Bresson furiously hurl a whole packet of contact sheets to the ground when he realized that the films of different subjects had been mixed up. The dedicated photographer will always prefer to look at his contact sheets rather than view his work in books or magazines, because it is only there that he will find his own private truths. They are like the psychoanalyst's couch.

Cropping: to Henri Cartier-Bresson it was a forbidden word, a forbidden action, interfering with reality and betraying the subject. For complete safety he even insisted on leaving the thin black line around the photo as proof, if needed, that the negative had been left intact. There was nothing vain about this, although it is sometimes regarded as his true signature, for it arose out of ethical rather than aesthetic considerations. For him, a photograph was just like a drawing or painting – a composition that obeys its own laws – and if that was how the eye saw it at the time, nothing should be changed after the event. The frame of the photo and the frame of the viewfinder are one, and the decisive moment is not to be shaped in the darkroom. You cannot improve on intuition, and so if things are not in the right place from the start, with that miraculous congruence between time and geometry, the photograph is no good. It became such an obsession with Cartier-Bresson that even when he wanted photocopies of a text, he insisted that the white margin be cut off all round.

The photos that he allowed to be cropped are rare in the extreme: *Derrière la gare Saint-Lazare, pont de l'Europe* (1932) was one, because he took it from a hiding-place behind a fence that obstructed part of the image on the left-hand side; another was *Le Cardinal Pacelli à Montmartre* (1938), which he had to shoot blind from the midst of a crowd, with the camera (9 x 9 plates) held at arm's length above their heads. However, while he forbade cropping, he did allow retouching in special circumstances. A number of his old negatives were damaged or worn, and it was essential to restore them. When necessary, he also allowed the experts at Pictorial Service to clean up prints from more recent negatives, such as *L'Ile de la Cité*, which had been ruined by a fingerprint.

When it came to directing a scene, Cartier-Bresson practised the very opposite of what he had always done, said and loved in the world of photography. He would have preferred to give it up altogether rather than be forced to manipulate reality, as Eugene Smith did in Japan when he photographed a mother holding her child paralysed by the effects of pollution in the village of Minamata. And when the nasty business of the *Baiser de l'Hôtel de Ville* ruined the last phase of Robert Doisneau's life by casting suspicion on the authenticity of the rest of his work (as it turned out, the lovers were in fact actors paid by the photographer), Cartier-Bresson refused to join the chorus of disapproval. His reticence was partly out of friendship, partly out of dignity, although of course he risked nothing by keeping quiet.

In any case, he himself certainly 'organized' the occasional photograph, even if this was as rare as permission to crop. The few instances include *Santa Clara* (1934), when he asked Nacho, his Mexican friend, to sit down, his trousers half open, his hands curiously crossed over his naked chest, beside boxes of shoes, two of which appear to be women's, the heels deliberately arranged to form a heart. The following year in Paris, in completely different circumstances and for a photograph that was never published, he suggested to another of his friends, the American poet Charles Henry Ford, that he should button up his flies again while leaving a public urinal on the side of which, in the foreground, was a poster advertising Kréma sweets and showing an enormous tongue pointing in precisely the right direction. But that was all. Cartier-Bresson would have been mortified at the thought of some investigator poring over his contact sheets in the hope of finding the tiniest hint of a scene being staged. His picture *Rue Mouffard* (1954), of a little boy proudly carrying bottles of wine under each arm, which was as famous and as typically French as

Doisneau's *Le Baiser de l'Hôtel de Ville*, certainly ran no such risk. After one of his female colleagues traced the child nearly half a century later, Cartier-Bresson took him two bottles of vintage wine for his birthday. Only then did he learn that, when the boy's parents saw this famous photo and realized that he was doing his neighbours' shopping for a bit of pocket money, he had received the most fearful telling-off.

The tools for the job were one or two Leicas M4 or 3G, their chrome covered with black tape, usually fitted with a 50 mm Elmar, the lens that doesn't cheat because it allows the photographer to view the world at eye-level. The Cartier-Bresson distance was, of course, never too near or too far. In his bag, although they were rarely used, were a 90 mm lens to capture the foreground of landscapes, and a wide-angle 35 mm lens. He generally avoided using the former because it distanced him too much from the subject, and the latter because it could jeopardize the balance between forms. They both reminded him of old-fashioned ear trumpets. The crucial piece of apparatus, however, was the viewfinder, for that was the framework within which everything took place. As for film, he generally used Kodak-Tri-X 400 ASA; his speed was 1/125th. When it came to measuring light and distance, he relied on instinct. From 1932 he was faithful to the Leica, and he often used to go to Wetzlar and Salms to see the Leica factories. He actually knew the Leitz family.

If the camera lens was the extension of his eye, the body was part of his hand. The Leica could have been invented just for him. There is nothing less aggressive or more polite than the Rolleiflex, which makes the photographer bow his head and even his body before the subject, obliging him to enact an almost Japanese-style ritual of courtesies. But it would have taken much more to get him to accept the monotony of the square 6 x 6 format and to give up the beautifully proportioned 24 x 36, which was perfectly suited to the directness of his vision, practicable and flexible, and with its 36 exposures just right to keep him going through the heat of the action.

The flash, to him, was an act of barbarism that was strictly forbidden – the executioner's axe that cut off all human feeling. Using a flash was the equivalent of firing a gun in the middle of a symphony concert. It did further violence when even the simplest snap was already in itself an aggressive intrusion. If authenticity was a prime virtue of photography, then the lighting had to be natural. And so, by definition, all artificial lighting was unphotographic. He was unbending on this subject, though he put his views in less radical and rather more poetic terms: 'The flash destroys the secret network of relations that naturally exist between the attentive photographer and his subject. You do not thrash the water before you start fishing.' The flash not only displayed a lack of good manners but was pretentious, for it sought to dazzle rather than to illuminate.

Cartier-Bresson the photographer was a man apart. He defied classification. He was the unstoppable passer-by – no sooner had he arrived than he was gone. Nevertheless, in the half-century when he was active, he wrote enough essays and gave enough interviews to shed at least some light on some of the darker areas. But the man himself remained unreadable – the anonymous celebrity who preferred to keep himself to himself.

Despite all the photographs of him in action, there were very few actual portraits: he who takes the image steals the soul. He always avoided photographers – not, of course, his friends, but intruders, and one can view this as misplaced vanity, bad character, or simply an expression of his own contradictory nature. There were many public occasions on which he deliberately covered his face when confronted by a camera, and sometimes he even pursued the nuisance, yelling and threatening him with his pocket knife. As for television appearances, they could be counted on the fingers of one hand. He hated anything that deprived him of his status as the invisible man, without which he could never have been the photographer he was.

Fame is vulgar in the extreme, while recognition has to be avoided with as much grace as possible. Fame is a scandal, but recognition is a catastrophe. Fame does confer power, but recognition disempowers. To be or not to be – the best of all is neither. Only his kaleidoscopic view of the world could give some idea of the multiplicity of his character. If anyone were to have made a portrait of him, it was understandable that a photographer would not have been his preference.

Physically, too, Cartier-Bresson was something of an enigma. Rosy complexion, blue eyes, sparse hair, sensuous mouth, angelic smile; his demeanour suggested purism, puritanism, moralism. Presumably he had an iron constitution, since he survived a number of serious illnesses contracted in various latitudes. In later years he had eye surgery twice, and two heart operations. The onset of old age slowed him down only a little and failed to change his boyish appearance. At a lunch in 1951, when he was 43 years old, he sat next to Paul Léautaud, who subsequently described him in his *Journal littéraire* as 'a young man from the family of the thread manufacturers' – which gives a good idea of who and what mattered in Fontenay-aux-Roses.

Cartier-Bresson had a natural elegance, old-fashioned, self-effacing, with a kind of tweedy Britishness. In conversation this came out in his small talk and his tendency towards understatement. His clothes seemed somehow to float around the body. He never wore a tie unless required to, as at the Reform Club where he stayed whenever he went to London – he was for a long time one of its very few French members, thanks to his friend Georg Eisler, the Austrian painter. He liked the patina of age, and hated ostentation and the *nouveaux riches*. He turned his back on virtuosos and on manufacturers, finding nothing more contrived and unnatural than people who act without being driven by their inner needs. For him life counted, nothing but life. That might have been the title of the memoirs he never wrote.

In moral terms he was even more of a mystery, for he was not one man but many. What was consistent in him was a restlessness of mind and body, and if he never tired he certainly tired others. He was never still, never quiet. He was constantly fleeing: from the religion of his ancestors, from the studies he had planned, from his father's factory, from the family home, from the prisoner-of-war camp, from the traps and trappings of fame, and from photography.

His character was a mass of contradictions. He did not like others to do unto him as he did unto them. He was regarded as a 'Protestant Jesuit' by a friend in Balanchine's ballet company. He was controlling to the point of bending geometry to his will to bring order into the world's chaos. He was always doing something other than what he seemed to be doing. He was scrupulously unstable. He would have liked to start his life again from scratch, to do something totally different and yet still be master of himself: a taxi driver, perhaps, but not a chauffeur. He had no time for those who had no real experience of life. Bad-tempered from birth, he was rebellious and moody by nature, tense, always alert, as if convinced that nothing would ever happen unless it was awaited with unwavering attention. Perhaps that was the secret pressure that always drove him, the source of his anger, his emotion, his insults, his generosity. It was amazing that this constant pressure did not get him into more trouble than it did. One day in 1949 he was in Shanghai, jammed up tight against the other passengers in a tram, when suddenly he felt the strap of his Leica being cut. By the time he had managed to turn round it was too late. He was furious, but had to contain himself until they reached the next stop. He alighted first, made all the passengers get off, and proceeded to search them one by one. There could be no question of his doing without his camera, especially during the blockade. But he did not find it. He got back into the now empty tram and searched it from end to end. The Leica was lying on the running-board where the thief had abandoned it. Everyone had a good look at it, and left amid gales of laughter. In another place and at another time he would have done exactly the same, but he might have been lynched.

He would say what he thought, without caring if someone was hurt. He was not rude, but he could be curt, even tactless. When a photographer showed him his work, Cartier-Bresson was capable of destroying him in a few words. Robert Doisneau remarked that he was perhaps a good judge but a bad diplomat. Indeed, bearing in mind his prestige and his personal charisma, his dealings with others could sometimes be murderous, and the victim needed a very strong character to survive – shades of Gertrude Stein's treatment of him years before?

There was something English about his pragmatism, although it was difficult to say precisely where it lay – was he a man who believed in reality, or a man who thought reality had to be shaken up before it could be absorbed? It bothered him that he could not be everywhere at once. He didn't want to miss anything going on in the world around him. Always it was his eye that took the decisions, while the man behind the eye just hunted for decisive moments and movements. He never stopped wondering whether life was or was not a photograph.

Socially he was unpredictable – delightfully urbane or utterly odious. Generally, if some unfortunate had been the butt of his anger, his cynicism or his sheer perversity, he would soon turn on the charm in order to repair the damage. After all, a man who could harmonize humanism with geometry couldn't be all bad.

He loved to surprise. He had a talent for making fun of the absurdities of our age that everyone else was resigned to. One day in 1996, shortly after seeing Marc Riboud's exhibition of photos of China, he arrived at lunch with Robert Delpire on all fours. This was his way of showing how ridiculous it was to put the captions so low that people were obliged to bend down to read them.

He was fanatical in the cause of freedom, but within a fixed framework he wanted rules and limits. He could never forgive Aragon, despite the latter's affectionate dedication on his copy of *Blanche ou l'Oubli* (1967). He voted communist until the Soviets crushed the Hungarian uprising in 1956, but it was a communism equivalent to Christianity without God. From then on he voted for the ecologists, whom he saw as the only politicians interested in the future of the planet. It seemed to him disgraceful not to vote, considering how many people died for the right to do so. Some saw him as élitist, others as populist, but if he had not progressed from his youthful attitudes he would have been against universal suffrage, for fear of mob rule. However, such attitudes were swept away by his experiences in the war. He had no real sense of politics or of history, but that didn't matter since he had something far rarer – a sense of the long-lastingness of things. He never felt under urgent pressure – somewhat paradoxical in a reporter who never had enough time – and he seemed to be able to capture the here and now while keeping his distance. Facts never interested him as much as their effects, and he left the outer shell to others while he sucked out the juice. Positivists and behaviourists bored him, and even looking at his own photos – let alone commenting on them – raised barely a flicker of interest. The only joy was in the capture, in winning his personal battle against time. The frantic pace of his life was a eulogy for stillness.

When he said that he had not taken any photographs for 30 years, he was telling the truth: in his language this meant that he had not done any photographic reportages.

He called himself a libertarian or an anarchist, depending on whether he needed to think or to act. He took up the cause of a detainee after reading a letter from him in *Le Monde libertaire*, one of his bedside newspapers along with *Le Monde* and *Le Monde diplomatique*. He was impressed, and wrote to Serge-Philippe Dignon, who had come to France from the Ivory Coast at the age of twelve. A regular correspondence developed. Dignon considered himself a sort of social ectoplasm in his nightmarish battle against the government, for he found himself in an absurdly Kafkaesque situation: he had been expelled from France, but had been given permission to remain under supervision in Hauts-de-Seine because he was HIV-positive; however, in order to get treatment, he needed to go to Paris, and that would have been illegal; he had no papers, and since the only way he could earn a living was through crime, he was asking to be returned to prison to prevent him from having to do this. Cartier-Bresson went so far as to write to the Minister of Culture and the President of the Republic in his efforts to help the man.

He did not believe in God or the Devil, but only in Chance, another way of describing the moment of grace. He found an illuminating explanation of this in Arthur Koestler's *The Roots of Coincidence* (1972), which suggested that the study of 'confluent events' should be elevated to a university discipline. With an argument situated on the borderline between quantum physics and parapsychology, Koestler claimed that phenomena of extrasensory perception (telepathy, premonitions, clairvoyance and so on) seemed less absurd when considered in the light of modern physics and its hitherto unthinkable propositions.

This was all very stimulating, though it scarcely explained why, one morning in February 1979 when going through his papers, Cartier-Bresson unintentionally tore up an envelope which he thought was empty, when in fact it contained a deeply upsetting letter from Jean Renoir, and why that very evening he learned that his friend had died. This sort of thing was not exceptional in his life, and was frequently a source of delight. In 1987, Jorge Luis Borges rang him up: he had been awarded a major cultural prize financed by a rich Sicilian, and had the right to choose his successor; he had chosen Cartier-Bresson. Why? 'Because I am blind and I want to express my gratitude to you for your vision.' The offer could hardly be refused. And so Cartier-Bresson, intrigued, made his way to the Grand Hotel in Palermo where the official ceremony was to take place. It was only when he put down his suitcases in the hotel room that he realized this was where his parents had conceived him during their honeymoon.

His taste was classical: he needed that kind of order to counter the vulgarity of the world outside. He was appalled by modern society's love of litigation. He hated the growing proprietorial ethos, which allows all sorts of abuses of a person's right to his own pictures and threatens the very existence of photojournalism. He urged his colleagues to stand firm or they would soon become nothing but conceptual photographers. In most of these cases, he believed, honour played no part, for behind all these developments was the glitter of money, the grasping hand of profit.

In affairs of the heart, he was a seductive romantic. He was married for the second time for well over 30 years, but he was not one to parade his emotions. His life was punctuated by many deep and intense relationships with women, and he was always very conscious of his gratitude to them. He did not see women as mere conversation-makers – it is the female sex that gives a sparkle to any social gathering, and he judged women, even more than men, by their vision.

There was a certain ingenuousness about Cartier-Bresson. His enthusiasm and air of astonishment were totally genuine, and if at times they seemed almost childlike, it was because in some respects he never grew up. His chronic impatience was another manifestation of this. He was always on the move; he sometimes talked nonsense; he was insatiably curious.

His puritanical streak explains why he rarely took photographs of nudes. When he did, they were headless, so that they could not be identified. *Nu, Italie* (1933), his most famous nude, in fact revealed the voluptuous curves of Léonor Fini, with whom he and Mandiargues had bathed naked during their first wanderings round Europe. Much later, the draughtsman allowed himself to be taken over by the photographer when he snapped his two models, minus their heads, stretched out on a sofa in *Pause entre deux poses* (1983). But his most sensual photos are not of nudes at all. The most erotic of them is *Martine's Legs* (1968), showing the gorgeous legs of his wife. Again she is headless, like his nudes, although in fact she is fully clothed; he has caught her reading, but the pose is so sexy that it would persuade even illiterates to take up reading. His most pornographic photo was *Brie, mai* (1968), a magnificently bare landscape in the heart of France, where a line of leafy trees forms a tunnel shaped exactly like a vagina sheathed in its tufts of hair.

For him the equivalent of Citizen Kane's 'Rosebud' was the countless knives of all kinds and origins scattered around his home. They constituted a real collection, the most important pieces of which were perhaps those that looked most innocent. These included the all-purpose knife that he always kept in his pocket for anything from peeling an apple to making running repairs. The Opinel pocket knife was not an affectation. His father had one, and his grandfather before him, and he himself had had one from childhood. When you have been a boy scout, your Opinel is for life. To attempts to find out the reason for this obsession with knives he would simply reply: 'Have you ever tried to peel an apple with a Leica?'

Something else that he always kept close by was his collection of little books on painting: *Les Maîtres* ('The Masters'), by Georges Besson, published by Braun. He had nearly all of the series, from Bonington to Watteau, via Ingres and La Tour.

He hated opera, because he could not understand how people could look and listen at the same time: to him you had to choose. Once Carmel Snow of *Harper's Bazaar* took him to the Vienna Opera. He sat in a corner so that he could listen without looking. Perhaps his attitude was influenced by his happy memories of the Marx Brothers' film *A Night at the Opera*, but it certainly had nothing to do with Hergé's famous diva Castafiore in *The Adventures of Tintin*, since he never read a comic book in his life.

He did not read many contemporary authors either, even those who were his friends. That would be time spent not reading or rereading the greats who were indispensable to him: Proust, Chateaubriand, Dostoyevsky, Saint-Simon, Conrad. He saw no reason to be ashamed of the gaps in his reading. But he did make exceptions – Paul Virilio, for example, whose theories fascinated him, even if they were somewhat complicated. He was particularly interested in the brilliant connections that Virilio found between the appearance of the virtual and the invention of perspective. Not long ago he realized just how old he had become when he read a biography of Proust, and saw that he himself had actually known or met many of the people that had inhabited this long-lost world.

He never went out without a cheap edition in his pocket. Often it was Lafargue's *Le Droit à la paresse*, which had enchanted him for decades, but there were others too, chosen at random. On the day of his heart operation, he mischievously asked the surgeon to look in his pocket and see what he was reading. It was *Mon coeur mis à nu* ('My Heart Laid Bare') by Baudelaire. The surgeon was not amused, and thought his illustrious patient was pretty childish.

He was astonished to find that he was the model for a character in Bruce Chatwin's *In Patagonia*, for Chatwin considered himself to be the writer of the 'decisive moment'.

He thought the English were just like everyone else, except for their modesty. Of all the people that he photographed in all the streets all over the world, only English people, on seeing him point his camera, would duck down and apologize, thinking that he was trying to photograph someone behind them.

He was eternally grateful to America for giving him his chance in the 1930s by mounting his first exhibition, and for continuing to support his work after the war. It was an American, Dominique de Ménil, who in the 1970s was the first to buy a selection of his photos – some 400 – to form a collection for her museum foundation.

He was scrupulous in keeping up his correspondence, which was both a pain and a pleasure, and he also carried on long-distance conversations by fax – a *fax-à-fax* if it couldn't be a *tête-à-tête*.

He never stopped photographing faces and landscapes, but towards the end virtually gave up commissioned portraits. He photographed people for pleasure – and more often than not they were his friends.

He had no idea how many negatives he took, and he didn't want to know. An estimate might be 15,000 times 36 exposures, but it is as unimportant as calculating how many words an author has written.

In his last years he did not travel far – only to England, Italy, Switzerland or Spain. He loved the world, but not worldly matters. He would go to openings but only with much fuss. He gave the impression that he was only there so as to make clear to everybody that he would rather be somewhere else. After all, photography is an activity that demands inconspicuousness, and so exhibiting a photographer at such ceremonies is a bit like asking a fish to jump into a frying pan. When he went to private views the first thing he did was to check out the emergency exit – a useful means of escaping all the people who wanted to congratulate him. On the other hand, he was not monastic or single-minded enough to shut himself off from the world. He knew a lot of celebrities all his life, and was a proud man who feigned humility, partly in self-defence.

He did not interfere in exhibitions dedicated to his work, but asked only for the privilege of going to see them alone for an hour before the opening. Then he would perhaps suggest, if necessary, that a photo might be moved. In this respect, exhibitions to him were a little like books – he preferred to trust experts in the field such as Robert Delpire and Maurice Coriat. He left it to them to show his work, deciding on positions, sequences and combinations. But his was the final choice of picture.

He shunned honours, but did not refuse awards. It is the duty of a libertarian to snub the powers-that-be when they claim to recognize you, but it is only polite to accept a prize if it comes from an association. Between the two are the honorary doctorates, of which he could have made quite a collection had he not dampened the ardour of the universities: 'What do you think I'm a professor of? The little finger?'

Those in high office who more than once thought that such a celebrity should be wearing their badges of vanity used to get short shrift: 'Have a look in your files! You don't offer the *Légion d'honneur* to an anarchist!' A passage in his Baudelaire breviary would have helped them to avoid such clumsy approaches:

> He who asks for the cross seems to say: if they do not decorate me for doing my duty, I shan't do it again. If a man has merit, what is the point of decorating him? If he has none, one can decorate him because that will give him prestige. To agree to be decorated is to recognize that the State or the Prince has the right to judge you, to distinguish you etc.

Cartier-Bresson gave the great and the good no such recognition, no matter what shade of government was in power. His V-sign to the *Légion d'honneur* was not a V for victory. It cannot be said that it was easier for him to refuse because his work was a tacit acceptance; that would be to ignore the fact that such an 'honour' would have been an obscene denial of everything he had always stood for. There was only one official medal that he wore with pride: that of the escaped prisoner. Nevertheless, he felt badly about having criticized his friend Max Ernst when the latter did accept the honour. As a foreigner, he was in a different category. The Académie française, which in its time has suffered many an attack from many a different quarter, never took a worse battering than from *l'Académicien français arrivant à Notre-Dame* (1953), a Cartier-Bresson photograph showing a member all decked out in his plumed finery getting out of a taxi, much to the amusement of the passers-by. There could be no more subversive critique than this ethnological vision. In 1983, when Jean Mistler, the permanent secretary, wrote to tell him that his candidacy had been registered for the seat of the Duke of Lévis-Mirepoix, he replied, 'I don't know what joker has been using my *nom de plume...*'.

He regarded the Academy as a penitentiary for the supervision of linguistic deviants. Its inflexible attitude was to him all the more remarkable for its ability to ignore those who say no – although perhaps that is understandable too, as non-events usually occur in silence.

Cartier-Bresson was his own censor. He would put his camera back in his pocket while others would still be taking shot after shot. He could spot love, death, violence – but if he refrained, that was a private matter. So too was his generosity. If that had become public knowledge, it might have been misunderstood, but he kept quiet about it, even if others didn't, always. In 1981 political prisoners from Poland's Solidarity movement received 20,000 francs, the value of the national prize awarded him for his life's work in photography. And a few years ago a charity found itself $40,000 richer when a British collector paid Christie's that sum for a Leica bearing his signature, on the occasion of his 90th birthday.

To find himself beatified, universally admired, unopposed – all this was very bad for a man who was constantly afraid of being bogged down in his own verities, a quicksand that is all the more dangerous because it lulls with a false sense of security. He wanted to have the strength and the courage to challenge and change his own rules and values.

There were others too who hoped for a healthy corrective in the face of his massive prestige. In summer 1999, *Le Figaro* carried an interview by the photographer Lucien Clergue, who described how Cartier-Bresson had put a spoke in the wheel of his famous series *Rencontres photo d'Arles*, writing to the

Ministry of Culture, for instance, and arguing against the project for a school of photography separate from a museum of fine arts. Clergue was stung into commenting: 'One can go on and on about Henri's attitude, which has had a negative effect on many aspects of the evolution of photography.'

And yet he constantly campaigned – in his own way, which was not necessarily the same as other people's – for photography, for the freedom of the press, for reporting without restrictions. And it is true to say that indirectly and in various ways he inspired as many careers as he discouraged. His obsession with geometry certainly paralysed a number of young reporters who wanted to be Cartier-Bressons before they had learned to be themselves. His formal perfectionism became a commonplace, as happens to all modern classics, and so it was inevitable that what had begun as revolutionary became establishment, and equally inevitable that a new generation should dare to challenge the tyranny of form. A powerful argument was put by Robert Frank's Les Américains (1958) – a brilliant book that made a big impact – in favour of all moments as opposed to the single decisive moment. But it was not enough to liberate two generations of photographers from the influence of Cartier-Bresson. In 1974, he gave an impassioned interview to Yves Bourde for Le Monde, which aroused intense controversy. His straight talking was certainly not that of someone on a pedestal, but his iconoclastic ideas lay behind his official renunciation of photography, and that was what upset people. The two pages of reactions to this interview attacked his élitism, his irresponsibility and his arrogance. The most provocative thing of all was the title of the interview: 'Let no one enter here but geometricians'. After such an injunction, how could any ordinary mortal dare to enter the sacred realm of photography without risk of excommunication? It was no use Cartier-Bresson explaining that he was not the pope, not even a holy father, least of all a master – it made no difference. Later he regretted having mentioned so many names, but he did not retract any of his basic ideas.

He could be very hard on his colleagues. A few months before triggering shock waves with this interview, Cartier-Bresson had already caused a rumpus at the annual meeting of Magnum by sending each member an unequivocal letter: he no longer considered the agency that he had co-founded to be a cooperative, but 'a commercial establishment with aesthetic pretensions'. This was not to everyone's liking, but Cartier-Bresson was never a man to mince his words.

Generally, press photographers are unstinting in their admiration for their masters, their predecessors and their peers, recognizing their debt to others, even their own contemporaries. Cartier-Bresson knew and acknowledged them all, even though strangely enough he only portrayed one of the truly great photographers that practised between the wars – Alfred Stieglitz. His most frequent 'partner in crime' to the very end was Doisneau. They used to doff their hats and greet each other as 'Monsieur Henri' and 'Monsieur Robert', like a couple of businessmen.

Cartier-Bresson would always judge a photo by its ability to stimulate him and to make him want to emulate it. André Kertész was one of those who provided his poetic inspiration; others were his wife Martine Franck and his friend Josef Koudelka, who called himself a 'collector of photos' rather than a photographer. What they all had in common was that they did not set things up or stage their scenes, and they were not slaves of fashion or of advertising. Such things only interested him on a sociological level, for there is nothing subversive there.

When he looked back over the century that he had lived through, he would single out as the great turning-point in contemporary history one phenomenon, along with the development of information technology, which revolutionized communications, and television, which killed curiosity. This was not a war or a revolution, as might be expected, but the birth of the consumer society between the late 1950s and the early 1960s. For him, this was the real end of the nineteenth century. When he came back from the Far East, he could scarcely recognize Europe. It had lost all its visual joy, unlike India which fairly bloomed with it. From that time onwards, western society seemed to him constantly to be on the verge of suicide, ruined by sterile egocentricity and technological neuroses. He had no desire whatsoever to wallow in what he regarded as 'all this twenty-first-century crap'. The change was as important as the discovery of quantum mechanics, except that the consumer society made him sick, and he felt globalization was a new form of slavery. His practical protest against all this came in the form of his instruction to Magnum, forbidding them to give any advertising company the reproduction rights to his photos.

Where does the money come from? Cartier-Bresson never stopped asking his childhood question. In spite of the importance of his archives and Magnum's wide distribution of them, latterly he lived mainly on the sale of his prints to collectors – not his vintage works, but modern signed prints especially made to order for collectors. He simply put his signature on the prints – an act he considered as immoral as speculating on the stock market, because it wasn't work. 'This is the shameless way I earn my crust,' he would confess. The fact that half of it went to the taxman meant only a 50 per cent reduction in the shame. Helen Wright, his New York agent and a friend of many years' standing, was the key player in a trade that was particularly successful in the United States. Of all the great press photographers, Cartier-Bresson was one of the most sought-after, and of all his photographs, *Rue Mouffard* was the most popular. It was his best-seller, although at least 30 others were and remain constantly in demand.

The arrival of Disneyland Paris in Marne-la-Vallée, near the village of Chanteloup where he was born, caused him nightmares. It was the horror of horrors – commercialized happiness. Such an obscenity may not be the end of the world, but it was the end of his world. It was here that as a child he used to go beetroot-gathering with his father.

He was never at ease with the big spectacular, or with commentary, noting that reporters were becoming fewer and fewer while there were more and more columnists. For him, the highest form of intelligence was disinterested, in the sense of selfless, and he could never issue enough warnings to his fellow photographers against the perversity of the consumer society, which in the name of economic imperatives continues insidiously and ceaselessly to separate us from all that is human. He was outraged to read an article in 1998 in which a critic wrote: 'Today, with digital photography, one can do Cartier-Bressons without Cartier-Bresson.'

As his life drew to a close he felt less and less like a photographer in a rampantly technological world that has triumphed over vision: the more the cameras, the fewer the photographers, and too many images kill the image. He regarded the notion of the picture as something literary. Drawing is the thing itself; photos are merely instantaneous drawings made with an instrument.

He refused to appear on television except one-to-one, and then strictly on the condition that it should be a proper conversation. He did allow himself to be talked into taking part in a *Marche du siècle* ('March of the Century') programme on Buddhism, but the very idea made him feel sick, and then he really did fall ill – an allergic reaction that required hospitalization – and so he was spared the ordeal.

The little things of life caused him much amusement. While he was not latterly mistaken for Raymond Cartier, people often thought he was the proprietor of Cartier the jewellers. In 1978 he found it hilarious when, arriving late for a retrospective of his own photographic work at the Hayward Gallery in London, he was stopped by the doorman: 'Sorry, sir, but cameras are not allowed inside.' Cartier-Bresson duly deposited his Leica in the cloakroom.

He gained much pleasure too from his trips to the country, in the Alpes de Haute Provence, where everybody knew him. There were very few village weddings, baptisms and communions to which he was not invited, and more often than not he took the photographs. Proud of their quality, he gave the prints to the families.

He used words in his own way, often from another age. An anaesthetist was an *endormeur* ('putter-to-sleep', or bore), and television was never referred to as anything but 'the instrument'. Some terms had terrible connotations for him. He could never hear the word 'drug' without thinking of his friend Christian Bérard, an opium addict, and his tragic cry through the door of his hotel room: 'Never, Henri! Never try drugs, not even out of curiosity. It's terrible...'.

He would have liked to be free of nostalgia, and tended to look back less on his own life than on other people's. That did not, however, mean that he was never stirred emotionally. When he watched 'Une Soirée Renoir' on television in 1994, after seeing *La Règle du jeu* and listening to a long interview with the great director, he was surprised to hear himself applauding at the end. He was trying to stop himself from weeping.

He did not like people trying to delve into his memories, but if you shook him gently they would come tumbling out. Like the writer Jacques Perret, he felt that reminiscences, for all their richness, were 'story-telling by yours truly'. You needed to talk about other things if you wanted to get to the people and things he knew. The roundabout approach was best. This man had walked the streets of Paris, and each place had its own associations. When he went to the ticket office at the Louvre he thought of the German soldier, face covered in blood, slumped at his feet beside his motorcycle, shot by a Liberation sniper. Passing the brasserie Lipp on the boulevard Saint-Germain, he would recall the hot summer nights spent there. But a single word or picture would be enough to bring back the ghosts of his fellow prisoners of war, and then he felt a lump in the throat, and everything else – his fame, his Leica, his exhibitions – would fade away.

He could shut out hope and despair, the past and the present, for nothing mattered to him except the actual moment. There were days when fame, or what Prévert called 'funds collected for the cult of the personality', was such a burden that he longed to be able to walk through walls rather than be invisible. A photographer who is recognized can no longer be a photographer.

His faith in mankind remained intact, while his rejection of society was absolute. That was what he wanted to be the lasting vision behind all his photographs, and nothing made him more optimistic than the thought of continuity through art.

He admired the Picasso of the early years through to the 1920s, and regarded him not as a great painter but as a wonderful draughtsman blessed with a kind of genius. He sent an angry letter to Claude Picasso, criticizing him for having sold his father's name for a make of car and his picture to an advertising agency. True to his reputation, he also attacked his friend René Burri and the Magnum agency for their part in this disgraceful episode.

He was passionately interested in the development of modern painting, and admired Max Ernst, Balthus, Kokoschka, Truphémus, Avigdor Arikha, Sam Szafran, Georg Eisler, Fairfield Porter, Francis Bacon, Biala, Lucian Freud, Richard Lindner, Bram Van Velde, Louis Pons, Saul Steinberg, Willy Varlin, Willem de Kooning, Calder, Nicolas de Staël and many others. He could not, however, raise any enthusiasm for conceptual art. He liked Marcel Duchamp for his intelligence, his elusiveness, his art, his sophistication, his humour and self-mockery, but he could never forgive him for fathering so many illegitimate children. And he would never forget Doisneau's comment one day when Cartier-Bresson had forgotten to reload his camera: 'Careful, Henri, you'll be making conceptual art!'

It was more natural for him to see references to painting than to anything else, no matter what the field. When he came upon the agency of the architect Louis Kahn in Philadelphia, it made him think of the studio of one of the Renaissance masters. He regarded Bach as the greatest of all composers, and praised the exactitude of his composition and the grace of his geometry. Bach's music to him was all that was best in prose and poetry; above all, it was so beautifully drawn.

He never stopped going to the Louvre, and would wander wherever his feet took him. He would sit on his shooting stick, which customs officers always took for a swordstick, stopping in front of Chardin's *The Rayfish* or Le Nain's *The Cart*, and copying them in his sketchbook. The Louvre was his favourite memory lane, for it was there that he learned about photography. He was fascinated by romanesque art; along with the Quattrocento it was the twelfth century that he liked best, for its sobriety.

He campaigned against I. M. Pei's pyramid in the Napoleon court of the Louvre, in spite of its beauty. He felt that it was out of place there, and wrote to President Mitterrand to say so. He thought that the introduction of such a structure would ruin the perfect proportions and balance of the square courtyard, a marvel in itself, and could not understand why people should insist on filling a space that did not need to be filled. The only kind thing he had to say about the pyramid was that at least it hid the ugly Second Empire façade of the Palais.

He criticized the Grand Louvre for its *nouveau riche* element, could not stand the growing didacticism of museums in general, and accused some curators of being more concerned with art history than with vision. Following on from this he wrote a preface to *Paris mystifié, la grande illusion du Grand Louvre* which ended in typical fashion: 'Excess is fascinating for a moment, but in the long term it becomes unbearable. Only moderation never unveils its secret.'

That was in 1984. Four years later he returned to the attack, denouncing the lack of 'voluptuousness' and of harmony with the environment, and complaining that the single, subterranean entrance to the Louvre symbolized the centralization of cultural power. He suggested that the pyramid, which was always an invitation to meditate on death, should be moved to the cemetery at Père-Lachaise.

At the end of his life he lived right by the Louvre, at the top of a house in the rue de Rivoli, enjoying an exceptional view over the gardens of the Tuileries. Designed by Le Nôtre, sumptuously combining the spirit of refinement with the spirit of geometry, the gardens are classical and rigorous but never dull – typical French qualities, and typical Cartier-Bresson, for this was very much his world. Victor Choquet, the great early collector and promoter of Impressionism, used to live on the fourth floor of the house, and it was from that window that Monet painted four views of the Tuileries in 1876. A century later, from exactly the same viewpoint but just one storey higher, Cartier-Bresson photographed the railings, trees and *boules*-players, all ranged in impeccable parallels. He rarely went out, and rarely wanted to. At the risk of being thought eccentric, he tried to have the newel-post on the staircase listed for conservation, for it was a knob that had been caressed by the hands of Monet, Pissarro and Cézanne as they climbed the stairs to see Choquet.

He enjoyed taking photographs or, especially, drawing, on his balcony – gardens, people, sky, birds. Kertész did the same for many years on Washington Square in New York. After all, a photographer at his window is not just a man staring out of a window.

He was a wanderer but with roots. Max Leibowicz deduced this from the astrological details of Henri Cartier-Bresson, born 22 August 1908 at 3 pm under the sign of Leo: solar balance coupled with lunar disturbance. The bohemian was stabilized by the practising photographer, while allowing him to blossom. He was a Frenchman marked by foreign influences, and loved nothing more than being a Frenchman abroad. Actor and spectator, he was a fusion of opposites: opening access to the world and closing access to himself, bearing witness and withdrawing, engaging and disengaging. His obsession with geometry tied in with his need to provide a strict framework for his sensitivity, which could then reveal itself. It was something with which to structure reality and at the same time to enrich it by stripping it bare.

He claimed that such concepts as sin and guilt meant nothing at all to him. They made him shun Judeo-Christianity; the notion of a chosen people appalled him. He was convinced that the great monotheistic religions are responsible for our decline, for they have made the terrible mistake of separating body and mind, imprisoning man in a dualism that separates him from nature. He had no doubt at all that the spiritual future of mankind was to be found in the Orient, and from the 1970s he found the path. He did not need to be converted: there was a rebellious, Buddhist streak in him already, and he disciplined himself to follow the instructions of a Master. It annoyed him when people talked about spirituality, because there is no God in Buddhism and so he refused to regard it as a religion. He saw it more as a science of the mind, an ideal way of living for a man so filled with paradoxes. To him it was the only way to transmute emotions internally, to reconcile action and thought, movement and reflection – everything happens internally. 'It is a method that consists in mastering the mind so that one can yield to harmony and, through compassion, then offer it to others,' he said.

Until the very end he would go on looking, drawing and taking photographs. One of the last, taken on the eve of the new century, was a self-portrait. The first self-portrait, taken in Italy in 1933, showed his naked foot right in the centre of the picture. The second showed his shadow cast on a field, with the twisted shadows of poplar trees. He dreamed of dying in action, like Martin Munkacsi, leaping up during a football match in New York in 1963 with his Leica in his hand. And so he always kept his in his pocket, wrapped in a handkerchief, just in case.

Some of his photographs are unforgettable, haunting us until they take on a reality of their own. Anyone looking at the Ile de la Cité from a certain angle will no longer see it as the physical Ile de la Cité but as a Cartier-Bresson photograph. Without him, our vision of the world would be a great deal poorer. He simply changed the way we look at it.

He hated birthdays. He felt that we die every night, and are born every morning. Dying is simply a matter of entering the darkroom for good. Or changing costumes, as the Dalai Lama once said.

'En rit Ca-Bré' was not afraid of death, though that did not mean he was not afraid of pain. He avoided pain, as he had done throughout his life of flight, from 1908 onwards. But he awaited with equanimity the day when he would perform his last pirouette, in the manner of KG845, prisoner of war, and would make his final escape.

EPILOGUE: THE EYE CLOSES ON THE CENTURY

The day came when we heard: 'Henri Cartier-Bresson is dead and buried.' No one greeted the news with disbelief, as we usually do when great people depart. Such caution was unnecessary; his manner of disappearing from our field of vision was entirely consistent with his manner in general. This man, let us remember, since the age of 20 had had the privilege of knowing both the time and the circumstances of his end. How many people can pride themselves on knowing so far in advance the details of their death, assuming we can believe that Pierre Colle's mother did indeed tell him his future as read in the cards? Not one of her other predictions was ever wrong.

Rightly called 'the eye of the century', Cartier-Bresson turned his gaze for one last time upon the world. Then, curtain. More than just tired, he had had enough. He did go gentle into that good night. We could well believe that he let himself die: 'To die – to sleep,/No more; and by a sleep to say we end/The heartache and the thousand natural shocks/That flesh is heir to: 'tis a consummation/Devoutly to be wish'd. To die, to sleep;/To sleep, perchance to dream...'.[1]

A few days later he would have celebrated his 96th birthday. He died on 3 August 2004 at his house in the Luberon, and was buried in Montjustin, his chosen village in Haute Provence, in the presence of about ten people: his family, friends such as the painter Sam Szafran, Josef Koudelka, Elena Cardenas Malagodi, Agnès Sire, and close acquaintances such as Marie-Thérèse Dumas, with whom he had worked for 12 years. Robert Delpire led the tribute, followed by his brother-in-law Eric Franck, and the violinist Anastasia Khitruk played Bach. The news flashed round the world. Martine, his wife, received some 1,000 letters and made it a point of honour to reply to all of them. The inhabitants of Montjustin planted an olive tree at the foot of his tomb and the photographers of Magnum offered an olive tree that was subsequently planted at the head of the tombstone. To judge from the press's response, it was as though a head of state had died. In his own way, that's what he was; even if his empire extended over many generations, he exercised his power without authority but with a natural sovereignty.

Le Monde devoted its main headline to him as well as four pages of his own sayings and writings. Among the reactions was one from Richard Avedon that was especially noteworthy for its brevity and clarity: 'He was the Tolstoy of photography. With profound humanity, he was the witness of the twentieth century.'[2]

The whole of the front page of *Libération* was devoted to him. Beside his portrait, a kind of 'handsome young man with Leica' taken in 1935 by George Hoyningen-Huene, the caption proclaimed: '*Cartier-Bresson L'instant décisif*': the instant of his death. On that day, as well as nine pages covering his life and work, all the pages of this newspaper were illustrated by his photos, no matter what the subject. It was an honour even rarer than for those artists whose work is rich, diverse and timeless enough to adapt itself to all realities.[3]

The other French newspapers fell in behind them. The two great national dailies gave the overture to the great concert of praise that followed his departure. It was the same throughout the rest of Europe and in the United States, but it was even more pronounced in Britain, where he was extraordinarily famous, on a par with the greatest painters, as was borne out over the years by the number of exhibitions devoted to his work. It will be recalled that Cartier-Bresson was the only photographer to figure – at length and with much admiration – in Ernst Gombrich's *The Story of Art*.[4]

'Technique enabled Cartier-Bresson to find pose and balance; a chaotic content disclosed the grace of form. He may well have been the greatest photographer of all,' wrote Peter Conrad. In the same issue of the *Observer*, his friend the writer John Berger celebrated the artist.[5] It took an event of this magnitude for *The Times* to publish a large-format photograph, daringly just below its front-page headline, of Spanish transvestites – a photograph which, of course, bore the stamp HCB, 'the photographer who transformed the black-and-white image into a fully fledged art form'. Rarely in the inside pages of *The Times*, even for a figure described there as 'legendary', are so many photographs to be seen on such a scale as on the obituaries page that day.[6]

In turn the *Sunday Telegraph* chose to publish an extract from *Anglo-English Attitudes*, in which Geoff Dyer drew a pen-portrait of Cartier-Bresson.[7]

The Daily Telegraph gave a lengthy account of the life of this 'photographer who created the language of photojournalism and elevated the medium to the level of art',[8] while the *Guardian* preferred to describe him as 'the photographer who turned a hobby into an art form'.[9] The account of his life published in the *Independent* was one of the most detailed and comprehensive.[10] Never before had readers had the chance to see so many close-up portraits of the man who always refused to let himself be photographed.

In Perpignan at the end of August 2004, when the 16th 'Visa Pour l'Image' festival opened, this international forum for photojournalism could scarcely do other than pay homage to Cartier-Bresson. Interviewed by Michel Guerrin, who devoted a whole page of *Le Monde* to their testimonies, the greatest photographers of the different generations acknowledged their debt to him.

WILLY RONIS: 'After the war, he succeeded in balancing a freedom of view with perfection of composition. He composed in the street in the same way as the seventeenth-century Flemish artists painted ordinary people in bistros. Capturing things on the spot, compass in eye, marking the photographic boundary with a black border, that was him. He was not a leader (he was too independent and anarchistic), but he brought respect for the profession. He, together with André Kertész, was the eye of the twentieth century.'

ABBAS: 'The influence of Cartier-Bresson is intact as a lesson on life, moral discipline, independence of view, and ceaseless indignation. His comments on composition remain valid. HCB was involved and yet always kept a critical distance. HCB, along with Capa, contributed to the photographer's being regarded as a journalist who conveys his vision and signs his images, and not just as an illustrator.'

NOËL QUIDU: 'He was the boss. He taught me one thing: one has or one hasn't the right moment; there is no point in just struggling on. He had the ability to seize the intense moment. And without a motor. Through him, a photographer can show what interests him.'

OLIVIER CORET: 'He ennobled the profession. HCB transformed the profession into an ethic of life.'

RAYMOND DEPARDON: 'He was the modern photographer *par excellence*, because he was recognized both as an artist and as a journalist. That is unique. He wanted his photographs to be multiplied, not rarities. To be seen as much in newspapers as in museums. That was fundamental. And he invented a way of working and functioning. He imposed a vision and a status on photographers. Henri taught us the lesson of staying free. And that is how he succeeded in giving energy to his pictures. He favoured the street as a space where society reveals itself. He also imposed the single lens, the 50 mm. The future will show that Henri was more political than people have said. HCB knew how to keep his distance while still adopting the position of the photographer. He has left us this heritage.'[11]

A creator in the twilight of his life could not dream of finer expressions of admiration than these demonstrations of gratitude.

A few days later, on 7 September, the Henri Cartier-Bresson Foundation in Paris mounted an exhibition of exceptional quality: 'Documentary and anti-graphic photographs'. Prepared long in advance, this retrospective set out to reconstruct both the letter and the spirit of the famous exhibition of 1935 at the Julien Levy Gallery in New York, where the youthful talents of Manuel Alvarez Bravo, Henri Cartier-Bresson and Walker Evans had burst upon the scene. It was no less of a sensation. Its repeat 70 years later scored a notable and lasting success both public and critical, in spite of the restricted capacity of the venue, with no space to step back, and the unspectacular quantity of snapshots.

So what was the secret of this unlikely success? It was that *je ne sais quoi*, that indefinable something which has changed everything since the beginnings of art, a supplement of the spirit, as people have called it who don't want to overstate the fact that a collection of works at a certain time and place has been touched by grace.

Shortly after that, Cartier-Bresson was brought back to life at a memorial soirée organized for his friends. In order for them to be able to pay their own tributes, his widow Martine Franck, with the Henri Cartier-Bresson Foundation and Magnum Photos, invited them to share his memory with words and music. It was Tuesday 19 October, in the magical surroundings of the Théâtre du Soleil at the Cartoucherie de Vincennes. The evening was formally under the lofty patronage of Jacques Chirac, President of the Republic, but there was nothing official about it, despite the presence in the front row of the Minister of Culture. An HCB photograph figured on the front of the invitation, with the caption 'Yin and Yang of a Japanese stream, 1966': a programme in itself.

Three musicians from three different continents began the evening: Sharmila Roy sang and played the *tampura*, John Boswell was on percussion, and Haroun Tebul played the *ney* and the *oud*. They set the tone for the whole event. After a showing of *Flagrants délits*, his 1967 film about HCB's work, his friend Robert Delpire spoke the first words of homage. They were followed by those of Agnès de Gouvion-Saint-Cyr, inspector-general of photography at the Ministry of Culture, Peter Galassi, head curator of photography at MoMA, the biographer Célia Bertin, who was a close friend for many years, Ferdinando Scianna, a photographer from Magnum, myself, and finally Anne Cartier-Bresson who is curator and restorer of photography for the City of Paris. There were endless memories and stories, moments of emotion, laughs and smiles. Of all the speeches, it was that of Peter Galassi which, through its elegance, perceptiveness, intelligence and humour, made the most vivid impression.

Music had opened the evening, and music brought it to an end. The enchanting sounds of the Far East were echoed by those of the West. The pianist Hortense Cartier-Bresson and the 'cellist Dominique de Williencourt played suites, partitas, improvisations and sonatas by Bach, Beethoven and Bartók. The serene and ineffable beauty expressed in these harmonies transformed the reunion of friends into a single family gathered round the delights of an Indian meal.

It's sometimes said that a friend is like a Swiss bank account: you don't need to see him every day; you just need to know he's there. Since 3 August it had been rather difficult for his friends to see Henri, but on 19 October they were all convinced that he was there.

When they left the Théâtre du Soleil to disappear into the night, each of them still had ringing in his ears Henri's words, his own special phrasing, a touch snobbish and precious, basically so very *vieille France*; and his rhythms, his elocution, perfectly in tune with his flashes of temper, of indignation but also of enthusiasm – not to mention the most essential of all, his silences. His silences had quality, in complete harmony with the infinite discretion of his Leica at the moment of shooting. All of us went away from that evening buoyed up with lightness, our gaze still focused on his photographs, our souls gently melancholic. All of us had in our pockets a little square of paper given to us as we went out. It was a sort of flexible visiting card and on it, apart from the dates of his birth and death, were lines written in his unmistakable hand – a script beautifully drawn though often irritated by punctuation and accents:

'Time runs and flows and only our death succeeds in catching up with it. Photography is a blade which, in eternity, impales the dazzling moment. Henri Cartier-Bresson'.

As 2004 drew to a close, those who had learned to look at the world afresh thanks to his unforgettable photographs felt that suddenly life had become less enjoyable since the successive departures of Helmut Newton, Henri Cartier-Bresson and Richard Avedon. It was time for the year to end.

When the eye of Henri, or Cartier, or HCB closed for ever on his century, we all knew that only then had the new century begun.

1. Shakespeare, *Hamlet*, III, 1 (58–70)

2. *Le Monde*, 6 August 2004

3. *Libération*, 5 August 2004

4. Ernst Gombrich, *The Story of Art*, 14th edn, Phaidon, 1972

5. Peter Conrad, 'Light and magic', in the *Observer*, 8 August 2004

6. Adam Sage, 'Henri Cartier-Bresson, a life in black and white', in *The Times*, 5 August 2004

7. The *Sunday Telegraph*, 8 August 2004

8. The *Daily Telegraph*, 5 August 2004

9. The *Guardian*, 5 August 2004

10. Val Williams, 'Henri Cartier-Bresson', in the *Independent*, 5 August 2004

11. Michel Guerrin, 'Visa pour l'image rend hommage à Cartier-Bresson', in *Le Monde*, 29–30 August 2004, p.15

BIBLIOGRAPHY

This biography is principally based on five years of conversations that I held with Henri Cartier-Bresson in person, at his home or at mine, by telephone, by letter, by postcard and by fax. This continuous exchange about his life, his work, his tastes and his ideas was the rarest of privileges for me, a biographer who was also a friend. Cartier-Bresson allowed me to delve deep into his archive of personal material: thousands of letters, telegrams and notes of all kinds that had been accumulated since his youth. This rich corpus, through which I rifled freely without making an inventory, shows through on every page. The same is true of the captions for his tens of thousands of photographs, captions he wrote himself, which he allowed me to consult at Magnum. Because all this material was of course previously unpublished, I did not feel it necessary to 'source' every piece of information precisely, pleading for the trust of my readers, after ten previous biographies in which I used the same method more or less successfully.

However, for some specific points, there were books, interviews and articles, mostly written by specialists, which I found extremely useful. These notes give credit where it is due. I need hardly add that the greatest debt is to the HCB Personal Archives now housed at the Henri Cartier-Bresson Foundation and the Magnum Archives.

CHAPTER 2
Michel Guerrin, 'La jouissance de l'œil' (interview with HCB), in Le Monde, 21 November 1991
Yves Bourde, 'Nul ne peut entrer ici s'il n'est pas géomètre' (interview with HCB), in Le Monde, 5 September 1974

CHAPTER 3
Peter Galassi, Henri Cartier-Bresson: the Early Work, The Museum of Modern Art, New York, 1987
Letter from Charles Peignot to HCB, 28 June 1934, HCB archives

CHAPTER 4
HCB, 'A memoir of Jean Renoir', HCB archives
Michael Kimmelman, 'With Henri Cartier-Bresson, surrounded by his Peers', in the New York Times, 20 August 1995
Rory Coonan, 'The Man Who Caught the World Unawares', in The Times, 20 September 1984

CHAPTER 5
Letter from HCB to Pierre Braun, 13 May 1944, HCB archives

CHAPTER 6
Claude Cookman, 'Margaret Bourke-White and Henri Cartier-Bresson: Gandhi's Funeral', in History of Photography, vol. 22, no. 2, Summer 1998
Paula Weideger, 'Cartier-Bresson: His Eye, Hand, Lens, Art and Ego', in the Independent, 8 July 1993
HCB, America in Passing, London 1991

CHAPTER 7
Letter from Robert Capa to HCB, 6 December 1951, Magnum archives
Letter from HCB to Marc Riboud, 19 March 1956,
Magnum archives
Letter from HCB to Michel Chevalier, 11 February 1958, Magnum archives
Michel Guerrin, 'La jouissance de l'œil', op. cit.
Letters from Général de Gaulle to HCB, 10 April 1958 and 22 August 1963, HCB archives
Letter from HCB to Beaumont Newhall, 19 September 1960, HCB archives
Letter from Elliott Erwitt to all Magnum members, 'Why are we in Magnum?', 26 May 1951, Magnum archives
Letter from Bill Wilson to Jim Hagerty, 'Magnum in Television', 13 June 1961, Magnum archives
Letter from HCB to Magnum photographers, 4 July 1966, Magnum archives
Letter from Indira Gandhi to HCB, 22 April 1966, HCB archives
Ernst H. Gombrich, 'The Mysterious Achievement of Likeness', in Tête à Tête: Portraits by Henri Cartier-Bresson, London 1998

CHAPTER 8
Dan Hofstadter, 'Stealing a March on the World', in the New Yorker, 23 and 30 October 1989
Jean Leymarie, 'From Photography to Painting: On the Art of Cartier-Bresson', in Bostonia, Spring 1993
William Feaver, 'Still Leaving for the Moment', in the Observer, 20 November 1994
Mark Irving, 'Life through the Master's Lens', in the Sunday Telegraph, 1 February 1998
Frank Whitford, 'A Man of Vision', in the Sunday Times, 1 February 1998
Sam Tata, 'Aku Henri: a Memoir', Montreal, n.d.; HCB archives
Hervé Guibert, 'Les dessins d'H.C.B.', in Le Monde, 4 June 1981
Elisabeth Mahoney, 'An Ever-Developing Reputation',

in the *Scotsman*, 16 March 1998

Postcard from Saul Steinberg to HCB, August 1981, HCB archives

Letter from Willy Ronis to HCB, 18 November 1984, HCB archives

Letter from HCB to Willy Ronis, 22 November 1984, HCB archives

Letter from HCB to Peter Galassi, 24 March 1987, HCB archives

Postcard from Saul Steinberg to HCB, 10 March 1991, HCB archives

Letter from HCB to Thomas Seiler, 30 March 1993, HCB archives

Philippe Dagen, 'HCB raconte sa passion pour le dessin', in *Le Monde*, 11 March 1995

Letter from HCB to Russell Miller, 17 February 1997, HCB archives

In addition to the sources given above for specific points, other bibliographical sources are listed below.

BOOKS

Amo García, Alfonso del, *Catálogo general del cine de la guerra civil*, Cátedra/Filmoteca española, Madrid 1996

Arikha, Avigdor, *On Depiction: selected writings on art, 1965–94*, London 1995

Baldwin, Neil, *Man Ray*, New York 1988

Baudelaire, Charles, *My Heart Laid Bare and other prose writings*, London 1986

Bergan, Ronald, *Jean Renoir, Projections of Paradise*, London 1992

Berger, John, *Photocopies*, London and New York 1996

Bernard, Bruce, *Humanity and Inhumanity: The Photographic Journey of George Rodger*, London 1994

Bertin, Célia, *Jean Renoir: a Life in Pictures*, Baltimore and London 1991

Blanche, Jacques-Emile, *Mes modèles*, Paris 1928, 1984

– *Correspondance avec Maurice Denis*, Geneva 1989

– *Correspondance avec Jean Cocteau*, Paris 1993

Bonnefoy, Yves, *Dessin, couleur et lumière*, Paris 1995

Borhan, Pierre, *André Kertész, la biographie d'une œuvre*, Paris 1994

Boudet, Jacques, *Chronologie universelle d'histoire*, Paris 1997

Bouqueret, Christian, *Des années folles aux années noires*, Paris 1997

Bourdieu, Pierre (ed.), *Un art moyen. Essai sur les usages sociaux de la photographie*, Paris 1965

Bowles, Paul, *Without Stopping: An Autobiography*, London and New York 1972

Braunberger, Pierre, *Cinéma-mémoire*, Paris 1987

Breton, André, *Entretiens 1913–1952*, Paris 1973

– *Signe ascendant* (Poems), Paris 1928, 1999

– *Nadja*, Paris 1964

– *L'Amour fou*, Paris 1937

Breuille, Jean-Philippe (et al.), *Dictionnaire mondiale de la photographie des origines à nos jours*, Paris 1996

Brinnin, John Malcolm, *Sextet: T. S. Eliot and Truman Capote and others*, New York 1981, London 1982

Capote, Truman, *The Dogs Bark*, New York 1973, London 1974

Caracalla, Jean-Paul, *Montparnasse, l'âge d'or*, Paris 1997

Cartier-Bresson, Henri, *The photographs of Henri Cartier-Bresson* (with essays by Lincoln Kirstein and Beaumont Newhall), New York 1947

– *Images à la sauvette/The Decisive Moment*, Paris 1952, New York and London 1952

– *Les Danses à Bali*, Paris 1954

– *The People of Moscow*, London 1955

– *China in Transition*, London 1956

– *The World of Henri Cartier-Bresson*, London 1968

– *Flagrants délits*, Paris 1968

– *Impressions de Turquie* (text by Alain Robbe-Grillet), Paris n.d.

– *Cartier-Bresson's France* (text by François Nourissier), London 1970

– *Man and Machine*, New York 1969, London 1972

– *The Face of Asia*, London 1972

– *A propos de l'URSS*, Paris 1973

– *About Russia*, London 1974

– *Henri Cartier-Bresson photographe* (text by Yves Bonnefoy), Paris 1981

– *Henri Cartier-Bresson* (text by Jean Clair), Paris 1982

– *Photo-Portraits* (text by André Pieyre de Mandiargues), London 1985

– *In India* (foreword by Satyajit Ray, text by Yves Véquaud), London 1987

– *Line by Line: the Drawings of Henri Cartier-Bresson* (introduction by Jean Clair), London 1989

– *Double Regard* (text by Jean Leymarie), Amiens 1994

– *Henri Cartier-Bresson: A propos de Paris* (text by Vera Feyder and André Pieyre de Mandiargues), Boston and London 1994

– *Mexican Notebooks 1934–1964* (text by Carlos Fuentes), London 1995

– *Drawings 1970–1996* (text by James Lord), London 1996

– *L'Imaginaire d'après nature* (preface by Gérard Macé), Paris 1996

– *Henri Cartier-Bresson and the Artless Art* (text by Jean-Pierre Montier), London 1996

– *Dessins* (text by Jean Leymarie), Paris 1997

– *Europeans*, London 1998, Boston 1999

– *Henri Cartier-Bresson, Photographer*, London 1999

– *The Mind's Eye: Writings on Photography and Photographers* (Michael L. Sand, ed.), New York and London 1999

– *Landscape and Townscape* (text by Erik Orsenna), London 2001

– *The Man, the Image and the World: Henri Cartier-*

Bresson, A Retrospective (text by Philippe Arbaizar et al.), London and New York 2003

Chatwin, Bruce, In Patagonia, London 1977

Clarke, Gerald, Truman Capote, London 1988

Clébert, Jean-Paul, Dictionnaire du surréalisme, Paris 1996

Clément, Catherine, Gandhi, ou l'athlète de la liberté, Paris 1989

Cochoy, Nathalie, Ralph Ellison, la musique de l'invisible, Paris 1998

Cookman, Claude, Henri Cartier-Bresson, Diss., University of Indiana 1997

Courtois, Martine, and Morel, Jean-Paul, Elie Faure, biographie, Paris 1989

Crevel, René, Le Clavecin de Diderot, Paris 1932

Crosby, Caresse, The Passionate Years, New York 1953

Danielou, Alain, Le chemin du labyrinthe, Paris 1981, 1993

Dentan, Yves, Souffle du large. Douze rencontres de Mauriac à Malraux, Lausanne 1996

Doisneau, Robert, A l'imparfait de l'objectif, Paris 1989

Douarinou, Alain, Un homme à la caméra, Paris 1989

Dubreil, Stéphane, Henri Cartier-Bresson en Chine, Deux reportages 1949 et 1958, Diss., University of Paris X (Nanterre), Paris 1989

Durand, Yves, La vie quotidienne des prisonniers de guerre dans les stalags, les oflags et les kommandos 1939–1945, Paris 1987

Elton Mayo, Gael, The Mad Mosaic, A Life Story, London and New York 1983

Fini, Leonor, Le Livre de Léonor Fini (design by José Alvarez), Paris 1975

Ford, Hugh, Published in Paris. American and British Writers, Printers and Publishers in Paris 1920–1939, New York and London 1975

Foresta, Merry (et al.), Man Ray 1890–1976, Paris 1989

Foucart, Bruno, Loste, Sébastien, and Schnapper, Antoine, Paris mystifié, la grande illusion du Grand Louvre (foreword by Henri Cartier-Bresson), Paris 1985

Genette, Gérard, Figures IV, Paris 1999

Giacometti, Alberto, Ecrits, Paris 1990

Gombrich, Ernst, The Story of Art, 16th edn, London and New York 1995

Grobel, Lawrence, Conversations with Truman Capote, New York 1986

Guérin, Raymond, Les poulpes, Paris 1953, 1983

Guiette, Robert, La Vie de Max Jacob, Paris 1976

Guillermaz, Jacques, Une vie pour la Chine, Mémoires 1937–1993, Paris 1989

Hamilton, Peter, Robert Doisneau, A Photographer's Life, New York 1995

Herrigel, Eugen, Zen in der Kunst des Bogenschießens, Munich 1951, 1999

Hill, Paul, and Cooper, Thomas, Dialogue with Photography, New York 1979

Hofstadter, Dan, Temperaments: Artists Facing their Work, New York 1992

Horvat, Frank, Entres vues, Paris 1990

Hughes, Langston, I Wonder as I Wander: An Autobiographical Journey, New York 1956

Hyvernaud, Georges, La peau et les os, Paris 1949, 1993

Janouch, Gustav, Conversations with Kafka, London 1971

Jaubert, Alain, Palettes, Paris 1998

Julliard, Jacques, and Winock, Michel (eds.), Dictionnaire des intellectuels français: les personnes, les lieux, les moments, Paris 1996

Kincses, Karoly, Photographs – Made in Hungary, Milan 1998

Koestler, Arthur, The Roots of Coincidence, London 1972

Kyong Hong, Lee, Essai d'esthétique: l'instant dans l'image photographique selon la conception d'Henri Cartier-Bresson, Diss., Lille 1989

Lacouture, Jean, Enquête sur l'auteur, Paris 1989

Lacouture, Jean, Manchester, William, and Ritchin, Fred, In Our Time, The World as seen by Magnum Photographers, New York 1989

– Magnum, 50 ans de photographies, Paris 1989

Langlois, Georges Patrick, and Myrent, Glenn, Henri Langlois, premier citoyen du cinéma, Paris 1986

Lemagny, Jean-Claude, and Rouillé, André (eds.), Histoire de la photographie, Paris 1998

Levy, Julien, Memoir of an Art Gallery, New York 1977

Lhote, André, La peinture, le coeur et l'esprit, Paris 1934, Bordeaux 1986

– Traités du paysage et de la figure, Paris 1958

– Les invariants plastiques, Paris 1967

Maspero, François, and Burri, René, Che Guevara, Paris 1997

Matard-Bonucci, Marie-Anne, and Lynch, Edouard (eds.), La libération des camps et le retour des déportés, Brussels 1995

Maupassant, Guy de, A Day in the Country and other stories, Oxford 1990

McKay, Claude, A Long Way from Home, New York 1937

Miller, Arthur, Timebends: a Life, London 1987

Montier, Jean-Pierre, Henri Cartier-Bresson, Paris 1995

Morris, John Godfrey, Get the Picture: A Personal History of Photojournalism, New York 1998

Nabokov, Nicolas, Cosmopolite, Paris 1976

Negroni, François de, and Moncel, Corinne, Le Suicidologe, dictionnaire des suicidés célèbres, Bordeaux 1997

Nizan, Paul, Aden Arabie, Paris 1960, 1987

Pétillon, Pierre-Yves, Histoire de la littérature américaine, notre demi-siècle 1939–1989, Paris 1992

Renoir, Jean, Ma Vie et mes films/My Life and My Films, Paris and New York 1974

– La Règle du jeu, Paris 1989, 1999/ The Rules of the Game, London 1984

– Partie de campagne, Paris 1995

– *Correspondance 1913–1978*, Paris 1998

Retz, Jean François Paul de Gondi, cardinal de, *Mémoires*, Paris 1998

Revel, Jean-François, *Mémoires: le voleur dans la maison vide*, Paris 1997

Rimbaud, Arthur, *Collected Poems*, Oxford 2001

Roegiers, Patrick, *L'Oeil ouvert: un parcours photographique*, Paris 1998

Roy, Claude, *Nous*, Paris 1972

– *L'Etonnement du voyageur 1987–1989*, Paris 1990

Russell, John, *Matisse – Father and Son*, New York 1999

Savigneau, Josyane, *Carson McCullers, un coeur de jeune fille*, Paris 1995

Schaffner, Ingrid, and Jacobs, Lisa, *Julien Levy: Portrait of an Art Gallery*, Cambridge (MA) 1998

Schifano, Laurence, *Luchino Visconti: Les feux de la passion*, Paris 1987

Schumann, Maurice, *Ma rencontre avec Gandhi*, Paris 1998

Soupault, Philippe, *Profils perdus*, Paris 1963

– *Le Nègre*, Paris 1927

Steiner, Ralph, *A Point of View*, Middletown 1978

Stendhal, *La Chartreuse de Parme*, Paris 1839, 1998/*The Charterhouse of Parma*, London 2002

Tacou, Constantin (ed.), *Breton*, Paris 1998

Tériade, *Hommage à Tériade*, Paris 1973

– *Ecrits sur l'art*, Paris 1996

Terrasse, Antoine, *Bonnard, la couleur agit*, Paris 1999

Waldberg, Patrick, *Le surréalisme, la recherche du point suprême*, Paris 1999

Whelan, Richard, *Robert Capa*, London 1985, Lincoln (NE) 1994

ARTICLES

Albertini, Jean, 'Une aventure politique d'intellectuels, *Ce Soir*', in *La Guerre et la paix. De la guerre du Rif à la guerre d'Espagne 1925–1939*, Reims 1983

Assouline, Pierre, 'Entretien avec Henri Cartier-Bresson', in *Lire*, Paris, July–August 1994

Baker Hall, James, 'The last happy band of brothers', in *Esquire*, New York, n.d.

Bauby, Jean-Dominique, 'Cartier-Bresson: l'oeil du siècle', in *Paris-Match*, Paris, 8 November 1985

Bertin, Célia, 'Un photographe au musée des arts décoratifs', in *Le Figaro littéraire*, Paris, 22 November 1955

Boegner, Philippe, 'Cartier-Bresson: photographier n'est rien, regarder c'est tout!', in *Le Figaro-Magazine*, Paris, 25 November 1989

Boudaille, Georges, 'Les confidences de Cartier-Bresson', in *Les Lettres françaises*, Paris, 3–9 November 1955

Bourde, Yves, 'Une année de reportage, le portrait d'un pays: Vive la France', in *Photo*, no. 38, Paris 1970

– 'Fleurir la statue de Cartier-Bresson ou la dynamiter?', in *Le Monde*, Paris, 17 October 1974

Brenson, Michael, 'Cartier-Bresson, objectif dessin', in *Connaissance des arts*, Paris, August 1981

Calas, André, 'Henri Cartier-Bresson a promené son Leica à travers le monde pour surprendre le secret des obscurs et des grands hommes', in *Samedi-Soir*, Paris, 25 October 1952

Cartier-Bresson, Henri, 'Du bon usage d'un appareil', in *Point de vue: Images du monde*, Paris, 4 December 1952

– 'L'univers noir et blanc d'Henri Cartier-Bresson', in *Photo*, no. 15, Paris 1968

– 'Proust questionnaire', in *Vanity Fair*, New York, May 1988

– 'S'évader', in *Le Monde*, Paris, 30 June 1994

Caujolle, Christian, 'Henri Cartier-Bresson portraitiste', in *Libération*, Paris, 10 December 1983

– 'Des photos derrières les vélos' (interview), in *Libération*, 25/26 August 1984

– 'Leurres de la photographie virtuelle', in *Le Monde diplomatique*, Paris, July 1998

Charles-Roux, Edmonde, 'Une exposition sans bavardages', in *Les Lettres françaises*, Paris, 24 November 1966

Coquet, James de, 'L'Inde sans les anglais', in *Le Figaro*, Paris, 27 December 1947

Coonan, Rory, 'The man who caught the world unawares', in *The Times*, London, 20 September 1984

Dellus, Sylvie, and Dibos, Laurent, 'Cartier-Bresson, le fil de famille', in *Canal*, n.p., February 1999

Dorment, Richard, 'Where journalism meets art', in the *Daily Telegraph*, London, 18 February 1998

Dubreil, Stéphane, 'Henri Cartier-Bresson en Chine', in Delmeulle, Frédéric, et al. (eds.), *Du réel au simulacre. Cinéma, photographie et histoire*, Paris 1993

Dupont, Pépita, 'L'œil du maître', in *Paris-Match*, Paris, 29 February 1996

Eisler, Georg, 'Observations on the drawings of Henri Cartier-Bresson', in *Bostonia*, Boston, Spring 1993

Eltchaninoff, Michel, 'Le jeu se dérègle', in *Synopsis*, no. 2, Paris, Spring 1999

Elton Mayo, Gael, 'The Magnum Photographic Group', in *Apollo*, no. 331, 1989

Étiemble, 'Le couple homme-machine selon Cartier-Bresson', in *Les Nouvelles littéraires*, Paris, 7 August 1972

Fabre, Michel, 'Langston Hughes', in *Encyclopaedia Universalis, dictionnaire des littératures de langue anglaise*, Paris 1997

Fermigier, André, 'Un géomètre du vif', in *Le Nouvel Observateur*, Paris, 14 December 1966

– 'La longue marche de Cartier-Bresson', in *Le Nouvel Observateur*, Paris, 12 October 1970

François, Lucien, 'Le photographe a-t-il tué le document?' in *Combat*, Paris, 2 September 1953

Frizot, Michel, 'Faire face, faire signe. La photographie,

sa part d'histoire', in Ameline, Jean-Paul, and Bellet, Harry (eds.), *Face à l'histoire*, Paris 1996

Gayford, Martin, 'Master of the moment', in the *Spectator*, London, 28 February 1998

Girod de l'Ain, Bertrand, 'Henri Cartier-Bresson', in *Le Monde*, Paris, 9 December 1966

Gombrich, Ernst, essay in *Cartier-Bresson, Henri: His archive of 390 photographs from the Victoria and Albert Museum*, Edinburgh 1978

Guerrin, Michel, 'La belle efficacité du *Vogue*, la beauté géniale de *Harper's Bazaar*', in *Le Monde*, Paris, 3 March 1998

Guibert, Hervé, 'Rencontre avec Henri Cartier-Bresson', in *Le Monde*, Paris, 30 October 1980

– 'Henri Cartier-Bresson de 1927 à 1980', in *Le Monde*, Paris, 2 December 1980

– 'Henri Cartier-Bresson, la patience de l'homme visible', in *Le Monde*, Paris, 24 November 1983

– 'Cartier-Bresson, photoportraits sans guillemets', in *Le Monde*, Paris, 10 October 1985

Hahn, Otto, 'Le fusain du plaisir', in *L'Express*, Paris, 3 June 1981

Halberstadt, Ilona, 'Dialogue with a mute interlocutor', in *Pix*, no. 2, London 1997

Helmi, Kunang, 'Ratna Cartier-Bresson: A Fragmented Portrait', in *Archipel*, no. 54, Paris, October 1997

Heymann, Danièle, 'Cartier-Bresson ne croit plus à la photo', in *L'Express*, Paris, 2 January 1967

d'Hooge, Robert, 'Cartier-Bresson et la photographie mondiale', in *Leica Fotografie*, Frankfurt/Main, March 1967

Iturbe, Mercedes, 'Henri Cartier-Bresson: images et souvenirs de Mexique', unpublished ms

Jobey, Liz, 'A life in pictures', in the *Guardian*, London, 3 January 1998

Khan, Masud, 'In memoriam Masud Khan 1924–1989', in *Nouvelle Revue de Psychanalyse*, no. 40, Paris, Autumn 1989

Kimmelmann, Michael, 'With Henri Cartier-Bresson, surrounded by his peers', in the *New York Times*, New York, 20 August 1995

Kramer, Hilton, 'The classicism of Henri Cartier-Bresson', in the *New York Times*, New York, 7 July 1968

Laude, André, 'Le testament d'Henri Cartier-Bresson', in *Les Nouvelles littéraires*, Paris, 20 March 1980

– 'Un travail de pickpocket', in *Les Nouvelles littéraires*, Paris, 8/14 December 1983

Lejbowicz, Max, 'Astralités d'Henri Cartier-Bresson', in *L'Astrologue*, vol. 4, no. 13, Paris, Spring 1971

Lévêque, Jean-Jacques, 'Henri Cartier-Bresson: ma lutte avec le temps', in *Les Lettres françaises*, Paris, 29 October 1970

Lewis, Howard J., 'The facts of New York', in the *New York Herald Tribune Magazine*, New York, April 1947

Lhote, André, 'Lettre ouverte à J.-E. Blanche', in *Nouvelle Revue Française*, Paris, December 1935

Lindeperg, Sylvie, 'L'Ecran aveugle', in Wieviorka, Annette (ed.), *La Shoah, et témoignages savoirs, œuvres*, Paris 1999

Lindon, Mathieu, 'Cartier-Renoir', in *Libération*, Paris, 21 May 1994

Masclet, Daniel, 'Un reporter ... Henri Cartier-Bresson', in *Photo France*, no. 7, Paris, May 1951

Millot, Lorraine, 'Leica, de l'image fixe à l'action', in *Libération*, Paris, 3 September 1996

Mora, Gilles (ed.), 'Henri Cartier-Bresson', in *Les Cahiers de la Photographie*, Paris 1985

Naggar, Carole, 'Henri Cartier-Bresson, photographe', in *Le Matin de Paris*, Paris, 12 March 1980

– 'Du cœur à l'œil', in *Le Matin de Paris*, Paris, 23 January 1981

Naudet, Jean-Jacques, 'Henri Cartier-Bresson, le photographe invisible', in *Paris-Match*, Paris, March 1997

Norman, Dorothy, 'Stieglitz and Cartier-Bresson', in *Saturday Review*, New York, 22 September 1962

Nourissier, François, 'Henri Cartier-Bresson', in *V.S.D.*, no. 1102, Paris, 8 October 1998

Nuridsany, Michel, 'Cartier-Bresson: un classicisme rayonnant', in *Le Figaro*, Paris, 3 December 1980

– 'L'Artisan qui refuse d'être un artiste', in *Le Figaro*, Paris, 26 July 1994

– 'Lucien Clergue: il faut trouver une autre formule pour le IIIe millénaire', in *Le Figaro*, Paris, 6 July 1999

Ochsé, Madeleine, 'Henri Cartier-Bresson, témoin et poète de notre temps', in *Le Leicaiste*, no. 27, Paris, November 1955

Ollier, Brigitte, 'Quelques lettres pour Henri Cartier-Bresson', in *L'Insensé*, Paris, Spring 1997

Photo, no. 349 (special edition on Cartier-Bresson), Paris, May 1998

Pieyre de Mandiargues, André, 'Le grand révélateur', in *Le Nouvel Observateur*, Paris, 25 February 1983

Popular Photography, 'The first ten years ...', New York, September 1957

Raillard, Edmond, 'Le Mexique de Cartier-Bresson', in *La Quinzaine littéraire*, Paris, 16 April 1984

Riboud, Marc, 'L'instinct de l'instant', in *L'Evénement du jeudi*, Paris, 20–26 August 1998

Riding, Alan, 'Cartier-Bresson: a focus on humor', in *International Herald Tribune*, Neuilly-sur-Seine, 13 May 1994

Rigault, Jean de, 'Un œil qui sait écouter: Henri Cartier-Bresson', in *Combat*, Paris, 18/19 October 1952

Roegiers, Patrick, 'Cartier-Bresson, gentleman-caméléon', in *Le Monde*, Paris, 17 March 1986

Roy, Claude, 'La seconde de vérité', in *Les Lettres françaises*, Paris, 20 November 1952

– 'Ce cher Henri', in *Photo*, no. 86, Paris, November 1974

– 'Le voleur d'étincelles', in *Le Nouvel Observateur*, Paris, 17 March 1986

Rulfo, Juan, 'Le Mexique des années 30 vu par Henri Cartier-Bresson', in *Henri Cartier-Bresson, Carnets de notes sur le Mexique*, Paris 1984

Scianna, Ferdinando, 'La photographie aussi est cosa mentale', in *La Quinzaine littéraire*, Paris, 1 April 1980

Searle, Adrian, 'Memories are made of these', in the *Guardian*, London, 17 February 1998

Shirey, David L., 'Good fisherman', in *Newsweek*, New York, 22 July 1968

Stewart, Barbara, 'John Malcolm Brinnin, poet and biographer, dies at 81', in the *New York Times*, New York 1998 (also anonymous obituary in *The Times*, London, 15 July 1998)

Szymusiak, Dominique, 'Le regard de deux artistes', in Musée Matisse (ed.), *Matisse par Henri Cartier-Bresson*, Le Cateau-Cambrésis 1995

Timmory, François, critique, in *L'Ecran français*, Paris, 30 December 1946

Thrall Soby, James, 'The Muse was not for Hire', in *Saturday Review*, New York, 22 September 1962

Tyler, Christian, 'Exposed: The Camera-shy Photographer', in the *Financial Times*, London, 9 March 1996

Wolinski, Natacha, 'Interview with Sarah Moon', in *Information*, London, 13 July 1994

MISCELLANEOUS

Adler, Laure, and Ede, François, 'Spécial Cartier-Bresson', in *Le Cercle de minuit*, France 2, France, 20 March 1997

Archive, Fonds Brunius, Bibliothèque des Films (BIFI), Paris

Delpire, Robert, Contribution to *Symposium HCB*, London, 23 March 1998

Feyder, Vera, 'Le bon plaisir d'Henri Cartier-Bresson', *France-Culture*, France, 14 September 1991

Fresnault-Deruelle, Pierre, 'L'*Athènes* de Cartier-Bresson (1953), De quelques effets de sens', n.p., n.d.

Moon, Sarah, 'Henri Cartier-Bresson, question-mark', Take Five Productions, London, 1994

Weatley, Patricia, 'Pen, brush and camera', BBC, London, 30 April 1998

ACKNOWLEDGMENTS

My thanks are due above all to the late Henri Cartier-Bresson for allowing me access to him: his memory, his recollections, his conversation, his friends, his letters, his archives; his smiles, indignant outbursts, paradoxes, and that extra dimension of the soul which changed everything. Henri was well aware that I was writing a biography, while all the time not wishing to acknowledge the fact!

Thanks are also due to his widow Martine Franck for having believed in the project, and to Marie-Thérèse Dumas as well as to Marie-Pierre Giffey; all three of them supported and encouraged me for many years, discreetly and effectively as well as with great kindness.

Thanks go to Anthony Rowley for his patient, friendly and constructive criticism; to my agent, François-Marie Samuelson, and the publisher of the original French edition, Olivier Orban, for having been behind me from the beginning in spite of the risks involved in such an adventurous enterprise. Thanks also to everyone at Thames & Hudson, especially Thomas Neurath and Jill Phythian; David Wilson, who did the translation; and Elisabeth Ingles, who edited the English version.

Thanks for their help or their personal recollections go to Célia Bertin, Georgia de Chamberet, Vera Feyder, Kunang Helmi-Picard, Carole Naggar, Bona Pieyre de Mandiargues, Sophie Roy-Boxhorn, Alice Tériade, Helen Wright, Abbas, Avigdor Arikha, Claude Bernard, Jean-Pierre Bertin-Maghit, Christian Bonnet, Claude Cartier-Bresson, Maurice Coriat, Robert Delpire, Laurent Dibos, Michel Drouin, Pierre Gassmann, Claude Gauteur, Philippe Godoy, Laurent Greilsamer, Ara Güler, Jean Leymarie, James Lord, Jean-Louis Marzorati, Raymond Mason, Bernard Morlino, Jean-François Mongibeaux, François Nourissier, Olivier Poivre d'Arvor, Sam Szafran.

Finally, thanks once again to Angela, Meryl and Kate for bringing colour to my life while I was preparing this lengthy black-and-white photograph – thanks to them for existing.